CURING THE
FOUNTAINHEADACHE

Also by Andrew Pressman

Architectural Design Portable Handbook:
A Guide to Excellent Practices

Professional Practice 101:
Business Strategies and Case Studies in Architecture

Architecture 101:
A Guide to the Design Studio

Integrated Space Systems:
Vocabulary for Room Language

Architectural Graphic Standards,
Eleventh Edition (Editor-in-Chief)

CURING THE
FOUNTAINHEADACHE

HOW ARCHITECTS & THEIR CLIENTS COMMUNICATE

Second Edition

Andrew Pressman, FAIA

Sterling Publishing Co., Inc.
New York

This publication is designed to provide accurate and authoritative information in regard to the subject matter covered. It is sold with the understanding that the publisher is not engaged in rendering legal, accounting, or other professional services. If legal advice or other expert assistance is required, the services of a competent professional person should be sought. *From a Declaration of Principles jointly adopted by a Committee of the American Bar Association and a Committee of Publishers.*

Library of Congress Cataloging-in-Publication Data

10 9 8 7 6 5 4 3 2 1

Published by Sterling Publishing Co., Inc.
387 Park Avenue South, New York, NY 10016
© 2006 by Andrew Pressman
A previous version of this title was published
in 1995 by John Wiley & Sons, Inc.
Distributed in Canada by Sterling Publishing
c/o Canadian Manda Group, 165 Dufferin Street
Toronto, Ontario, Canada M6K 3H6
Distributed in the United Kingdom by GMC Distribution Services
Castle Place, 166 High Street, Lewes, East Sussex, England, BN7 1XU
Distributed in Australia by Capricorn Link (Australia) Pty. Ltd.
P.O. Box 704, Windsor, NSW 2756, Australia

Sterling ISBN 13: 978-1-4027-2604-0
        ISBN 10: 1-4027-2604-X

For information about custom editions, special sales, premium and corporate purchases, please contact Sterling Special Sales Department at 800-805-5489 or specialsales@sterlingpub.com.

To Lisa, who is as beautiful inside as out.

In architecture as in love,
we are astonished at what is chosen by others.
—paraphrasing André Maurois

CONTENTS

FOREWORD XII

PREFACE XIX

ACKNOWLEDGMENTS XXI

INTRODUCTION XXIII

CHAPTER 1

DOMESTIC AFFAIRS 1

Conflicts and Closets 2

"All Great Architecture Leaks" 10

The Sauna and the New Jersey Turnpike 17

The New Yawkas 24

Archiphobia! 31

CHAPTER 2

PRIVATE BATTLES IN THE PUBLIC DOMAIN **35**

Fusion of Old and New at the Guggenheim 35

For the Glory of Washington 46

Penn Plaza and the Design Review Board 54

CHAPTER 3

COLLABORATION VERSUS COMPROMISE **59**

Collaboration at St. Matthew's 60

The Closest Kind of Collaboration 66

Contemporary-Traditional in Florida 71

A Collaborative Ideal 78

Working with Specialty Consultants 83

CHAPTER 4

FOREIGN AFFAIRS 89
Emotion and Ethics in Architecture 89
A Project Dies Because a Country Disappears 96
The Hospitable Tunisians 99

CHAPTER 5

IS THE CAMEL A HORSE DESIGNED BY COMMITTEE? 103
The Client of Many Minds 103
Design with Committees 105
Institutions, Clients, and Service 109
Patience Is a Virtue 114

CHAPTER 6

THE POLITICS OF DESIGN: RACE AND GENDER 120
A Black Architect on a Mission 120
Politically Incorrect in Wichita 130
Gender, Marketing, and a Client's Faith 133

CHAPTER 7

ALL ABOUT COMMUNICATION 140
If They Don't Understand You, You Haven't Said Anything 141
Treating Clients as Patients 147
Architects as Great Communicators 151
Legal Pitfalls of Poor Communication 153
The Mercurial Client 155

CHAPTER 8

CORPORATE POLITICS 159
The Power Structure 159
Resolving Profit with Social Responsibility 161
It's All in a Name 173

CHAPTER 9

ALL PROJECTS GREAT AND SMALL **178**

Measure Twice, Cut Once: Architects and Aphorisms—
  Therapy in the Spoken Word 178
Less May Actually Be More: The Politics of the Small Project 184
When Clients Think They're Architects
  and Other Tales of Woe 198
Room without a View 201

CHAPTER 10

THE CLIENT PERSPECTIVE **209**

Sweet Cottage on a Lake 210
The Leap of Faith: What Every Client Should Know
  About Residential Architects 220
Speaking "Client" 226
Clients Behind the Buildings:
  A Conversation with Andrew Wooden 232
From a Client's Point of View 241

INDEX 255

CURING THE FOUNTAINHEADACHE

FOREWORD

FOREWORD TO THE SECOND EDITION

Most every architect has a story to tell about an encounter with a client that went awry. If you are a client looking to hire an architect, it would be wise to ask those whom you are considering to recount the tale and to elaborate on the lessons they took away from it. If they can't tell you what they learned, or worse, they have no such stories to tell, you had best find an architect who can.

The stories that Andy Pressman has collected for *Curing the Fountainheadache* contain many useful lessons for those who are engaged in the sometimes exasperating, sometimes exhilarating, but always interesting give-and-take of architect–client relations. Since the first edition of this book, these kinds of lessons have had their effect on the architectural profession, and in turn, on architectural clients. The big news is that architects have started listening rather intently to their clients (imagine!) and the professional community has responded with a new emphasis on demonstrating the value of design to clients—even recognizing through the *Business Week/Architectural Record* awards program projects that exemplify the very best in value-added design. The American Institute of Architects has also revised its standard contract forms for architectural services in a way that allows architects to package their services in a manner that recognizes the unique nature of every project and every client.

Architectural clients continue to evolve also, as the largest clients are getting ever more sophisticated in the way they procure and manage architectural services. To be sure, there are plenty of first-timers looking for a custom house design or kitchen renovation, and as they venture into the design and construction process, they still rely on their architects for the best professional advice available. Large organization clients, however, treat their architects the way they treat suppliers of other goods and services. Most recently, prevailing management practices have emphasized greater cooperation and partnering among such suppliers, and so it goes with designers and builders. Architects have been more than happy to go along with these longer-term arrangements. After all, architects realize that the lion's share of their fees comes from repeat clients. The days of "design-build-forget," as one much-admired former client of mine once characterized the process, at least when it comes to the largest clients, are disappearing. Architects are more likely than ever to check in on their clients after the fact so that they can supervise the odd refurbishment or renovation, conduct a post-occupancy evaluation, or offer strategic facility planning services, in the hope that they will have a crack at future major commissions.

So, with architects and clients on their best behavior, is there still a need for *Curing the Fountainheadache*? Rest assured there is.

For one thing, architect–client interactions are still fraught with opportunities for misunderstanding. Design conversations consist of both verbal and visual communication—there is a great deal of talking, a great deal of drawing, and there is a great deal of talking about what is drawn. There is an inherent asymmetry in these exchanges, as clients often cannot produce their own graphic images, and frequently they cannot read the architect's two-dimensional drawings. Misunderstandings can and do occur. The funny thing (and one must remember to keep one's sense of humor about this) is that simple misunderstandings can escalate into reactions that approach moral outrage. I recall a design meeting for a hospital project in which one of the physicians nearly flipped when he mistook a dotted line, which actually indicated the structural grid of the building, for a new wall that he thought would have divided his office in half. Smart architects take the time to explain these graphic conventions to their clients.

For another, even when the graphic communication is clear, design conversation can be broadly complicated as people contemplate how to spend their money and organize the physical space around them. Seemingly trivial issues trigger a lot of debate. From my own experience with public housing design, I remember a heated conversation about whether to install ceiling fixtures or switched outlets in bedrooms. The pro–ceiling fixture camp felt a moral obligation to provide light fixtures for poor families so that they would not need to purchase lamps on their own. The switched outlet contingent was concerned with possible vandalism of fixtures and their replacement costs. What began as a discussion of the mundane escalated into a complicated process of interpretative inference about the social purposes of public housing and the fiduciary responsibility of a government agency to the taxpayers. Not only that, these days choices about building material are tangled in a web of ecological correctness and hygiene. Considering resin-impregnated wood flooring for your kitchen? Do you know whether the wood comes from a sustainably harvested forest, or whether the resin that holds it together will off-gas? Design conversation pretty much ensures that you'll think twice about such things, even if you would rather not.

Finally, as this book attests, clients and architects tend to be beholden to separate ideals. Architects represent their clients' interests, yet these interests are typically subsumed by a broader institutional concern for creating good architecture. Conversely, clients may have an interest in acquiring a good building, but this interest is likely subsumed by broader concerns about the utility and financial soundness of the project. The only known antidote for this disjuncture is for architect and client to simultaneously create a joint framework for their actions. You are way ahead of the game if you can agree on a vision of what constitutes good architecture. Consider the following list of potential attributes as a warm-up: experientially rich, beautifully crafted, culturally relevant, environmentally sustainable, socially just, and reasonably adaptable. Feel free to mix, match, and embellish as you see fit.

If you can agree on a definition of good architecture for your project, the next critical question every architect and every client ought to address is: How do you enact the conditions for good architecture (as defined by both sides) to emerge? Unfortunately, this is a question to which researchers of architect–client relations are still searching for more definitive answers. We do know that success depends on more than the design skills of the architect or the poignancy with which the client can articulate his or her needs. The stories told in *Curing the Fountainheadache* advance a number of different strategies: better visualization tools; well-crafted contracts; greater clarity in terms of decision-making authority and reporting relationships; commitment to a common set of ethical, cultural, and financial goals for a project; a good sense of humor; and so on.

These certainly help, but likely the essential ingredient is a genius for organizing for design. Someone involved in the project, be it the architect or client, must cultivate a special feel for choreographing the give-and-take and the creativity and compromise inherent in any project. Comb this volume for examples of organizing genius in projects that are most similar to your own and that match your goals and values. You may find that some of the true geniuses at organizing for design who are celebrated in this book, such as the late Bill Caudill and the late Charles Moore, had a feel for the game that readers of *Curing the Fountainheadache—* architect and client alike—ought to emulate.

Enjoy, and best of luck.

BRIAN SCHERMER, AIA, PhD

FOREWORD TO THE FIRST EDITION

This book is long overdue, and if it reaches its intended audiences it has the potential to build a bridge across the gap that frequently separates architect and client. All too often when this chasm is present, what should be a joyfully creative process bogs down in frustration and failed expectations.

Philadelphia architect Vincent G. Kling, FAIA, one of half a dozen peers[1] who built large, successful, award-winning firms in the 1960s out of a combination of architectural talent and extraordinary skill at communicating with clients, once observed:

> No architect, no matter how good, can do a good building for a bad client. Conversely, no architect, no matter how bad, can do a truly bad building for a good client.

He went on to add: "There is no such thing as an architect alone on a desert island," for without a client there can be no architect. This is the first and fundamental element that clients and architects all too often forget. If anything worthwhile is going to come of an engagement between client and architect, they must see their roles as inseparable.

---

1. For example: William Periera, John Carl Warnecke, Welton Beckett, Victor Gruen, Charles Luckman, and so on.

The legal concept of "agency" gives social standing to the relationship. The architect, as a professional, is different from the vendors, suppliers, contractors, or other businesses that are part of the building process. As a professional, the architect is agent for the client—legally an authorized extension of the client—and obligated to put the client's interest above self-interest.

Thus, when an architect and client first meet to undertake a project they are supposed to become as one. But this happens only when both parties are able to communicate in a manner that this book tries to illustrate: a manner in which the client has full trust that the architect understands and is representing the client's interests above all else, and the architect can trust the client to be dealing from a full and open deck. When this type of relationship occurs, the results are memorable. Making it happen, however, takes some practice. Here are a few illustrations that may point the way.

New Jersey architect Herman Hassinger, FAIA, whose practice is heavily involved with churches, one of the more notoriously difficult clients since it is inevitably represented by a diverse committee, says he begins all his interviews with prospective church clients with this warning:

> You must be aware that, despite whatever your and my best intentions may be, there are three absolute rules of human enterprise:
>
> • Nothing is as simple as you thought it would be.
>
> • Nothing goes as quickly as you thought it would go.
>
> • Nothing ever ends up costing what you expected to spend.

That's true for remodeling the kitchen, your daughter's wedding, and building a church.

He also tells them that if they accept these rules, the results will usually exceed their fondest hopes.

Stuart Furman, a professor of architecture at New York Institute of Technology who maintains a small private practice in Brooklyn, New York, says he breaks the ice with all new clients this way:

> I tell them the process will be like a three-act play: The first act will get us all excited, but there is always a second act when it will

look like it has all fallen apart. At the lowest point everyone may be on the verge of giving up and abandoning the effort. There is always this low point—the client can't agree on changes to the program; the cost has gotten too high; the contractor reads the documents wrong and there is a fight over who will pay; and so on. Only if we forewarn the client can they have the fortitude to see it through to the final curtain—when the result becomes worth all the effort.

This writer's observation is that the single most important place to test and cement the best client–architect relationships is in the development of the program, before any sketches or images are discussed. From the architect's standpoint the ideal program is a statement of functions, and what responses or behaviors should occur around those functions. For example, "the living room needs to seat six for intimate conversation," "the kitchen should have lots of natural light and views of the garden," "the master bedroom needs to be in the quietest part of the house (or closest to the nursery)," and so on. Program statements most often go astray when clients say things like "I want it to look Colonial," or "I don't want it to be brick," and so on. There is a time for discussion of images and materials, but it is best deferred until after the plan has accommodated the program.

A partner of California architect Frank Gehry, one of the most avant-garde architectural image makers, reports that Gehry never shows images or elevations to clients until after the plan is completely presented, understood, and accepted. "If the client is persuaded the building is going to work," said Gehry's partner, "they almost never question what Frank is doing with the exterior design."

One of the most frequent misunderstandings that can sour architect–client communication is over the definition of "architecture" itself. The writer once was asked to advise the building committee of a small city library on how to select an architect for an expansion. The committee included both a builder and an engineer who were offering considerable advice, from their perspectives, about how it could be done most expeditiously and economically. The writer advised:

> The first thing you need to decide is whether you want this addition to be just a building or whether you would like the result to be architecture.

After a little discussion to be sure everyone understood the implications of the difference, the committee retired to executive session and quickly voted, unanimously, that they wanted architecture.

They were a good client, they chose a young but promising architect, and together they produced architecture.

May this book help many others do the same.

WELD COXE

PREFACE

This vivid triumphal image (Figure 1) from the classic film adaptation of Ayn Rand's *The Fountainhead* runs through the imagination of many architects as they struggle to resolve personal ideals with the realities of professional practice. *Curing the Fountainheadache* sets forth many of the potentials and problems of architect–client relations, involving many types of projects and firms working in an era of tight budgets and wary consumers.

The plight of both architects and their clients in today's residential, commercial, and institutional settings is the theme of *Curing the Fountainheadache*. The goal of the book is to serve as a wake-up call both to architects and clients. The message is that much of the difficulty between architects and clients is political, and that projects are unsuccessful when communication fails and the consequent struggles for control are not fully resolved. In other words, it is the quality of the evolving personal relationships between the key parties that is of utmost importance. Personal and professional style may vary greatly, but the one constant in truly successful projects seems to be defined by indelibly etched architect–client relationships.

Curing the Fountainheadache speaks to the array of forces shaping projects and the relationships driven by those forces. The strength of this book is due in large part to the quality and insights of the remarkable group of contributors, many of whom are world-renowned architects. Narratives, interviews, and accompanying visuals describe more than thirty projects representing and defining successful and unsuccessful outcomes. There is broad hilarity and there is bitter disappointment. There are instances in which the client is thrilled, but the architect is barely able to accept his commission. There are cases when the architect is elated and the client is outraged. Finally, there are those special projects in which all manner of colliding values, agendas, expectations, and constraints are somehow resolved and lead to optimal service, good architecture, and satisfaction for all.

Figure 1
A fresh breeze off New York Harbor ruffled through Patricia Neal's hair. She rose higher and higher, riding the makeshift elevator toward the very top of the almost-complete skyscraper. At the top stood Gary Cooper, adding more height and strength to the unfinished building. Shoulder to shoulder with the construction crew, he surveyed his creation and his domain. Photo © 1949 Turner/Time Warner. *The Fountainhead* © Turner Entertainment Company, a Warner Brothers Entertainment Company. All rights reserved.

As a mosaic of people and projects reexamined, *Curing the Fountain-headache* is really a collective memoir—one that I hope will promote interest among those who have even a passing flirtation with architecture as well as among clients of architects, and of course the design professionals themselves. I believe that professional development and public education converge where architects and clients interact to produce excellence in the built environment. This book is intended to promote such interaction through its focus on more effective and gratifying politics between architect and client.

ANDREW PRESSMAN, FAIA
Washington, DC
January 2005

ACKNOWLEDGMENTS

Much appreciation, respect, and gratitude are extended to Julie M. Trelstad, Executive Editor, Acquisitions, at Sterling Publishing Co., Inc.

I would like to acknowledge the contributors who are largely responsible for the depth and high quality of material in *Curing the Fountainheadache* (in alphabetical order): Stanley Allan, Thomas Bakalars, Carol Ross Barney, Marvin Cantor, Claire Conroy, Weld Coxe, Nellie DeBruyn, David Dibner, Duo Dickinson, Jeremiah Eck, Mary Fitch, Robert Greenstreet, Charles Gwathmey, George Hartman, Eugene Kohn, William Lam, Kent Larson, Roger Lewis, William Kirby Lockard, Charles McAfee, Charles Moore, Douglas Oliver, Joseph Provey, Norman Rosenfeld, Brian Schermer, Renate Schweiger, John Seiler, Gary Siebein, Cathy Simon, James Stageberg, Stanley Tigerman, Susan Allen Toth, Jack Travis, and Andrew Wooden.

The following individuals deserve special mention:

- Peter Pressman, MD, for mentorship and essential critical guidance.

- Edward Allen, FAIA, for his continuing support.

- Stuart Ng at Warner Brothers Archives at the School of Cinema—Television at the University of Southern California for his assistance and patience in compiling stills from *The Fountainhead*.

- Eleanor Pressman and Iris Slikerman, as always.

Qualifying Note

All the stories in *Curing the Fountainheadache* are true. However, identifying circumstances for some projects have been changed to maintain client anonymity.

INTRODUCTION

"I don't intend to build in order to have clients. I intend to have clients in order to build."
    —Howard Roark, Architect, hero of Ayn Rand's 1926 novel
The Fountainhead

Howard Roark's attitude toward clients was guaranteed to cause him endless headaches. Most ARCHITECTS understand that they must balance their creative ambitions with the client's need for a building that solves real-life problems, can be built for a reasonable cost, and doesn't leak. Most CLIENTS understand that they must balance their own visions with the architect's ideas, ability, and desire to implement them. Learning to strike these balances, however, can be a painful trial-and-error process that produces its own special brand of headache.

The following stories present and unravel the mystery of the rift between clients and architects, and demonstrate that great architecture virtually never comes off the sketchbooks . . . unless there is a truly collaborative effort. The client–architect relationship might be seen as the single most important element in fostering excellence in the built environment. Succinctly stated, better relationships produce better architecture.

The second edition of *Curing the Fountainheadache* concludes with an all-new chapter on the turbulent affair between clients and their architects—and tips on how to avoid the turbulence—from the *client's* perspective. When clients are involved in the design process from the start, they can be catalysts for creating the highest quality architecture.

Client–architect relationships are fraught with tension; they are intrinsically charged with emotion. Hence the stories, interviews, and essays in *Curing the Fountainheadache* are filled with passion and personal agendas. The architect dreams of creating objects so beautiful that they appear on magazine covers. The client wants his or her dreams translated into their own building. And everyone has nightmares about where the money is going.

Curing the Fountainheadache investigates the complex, sometimes rocky relationship of client and architect through the personal recollections of some of America's best known and award-winning practitioners, academics, and their clients (in addition to those from my own early fledgling practice experiences). Charles Gwathmey, Stanley Tigerman, the late Charles Moore, and many others discuss their methods for establishing effective working relationships with clients, describe the impact of these relationships on the design process, and offer insights and advice on a broad array of issues covering a range of projects from houses to commercial buildings and public facilities. The collective effort provides capsules of wisdom and, I hope, enlivens the text with energy, pragmatism, and idealism. The result is a rich and varied mixture of assertions (that at times appear on the surface to be contradictory), all geared toward infusing a creative spirit within the controversial realm of meaningful design. I have specifically solicited, linked, and interpreted the material—over the last decade—with a single voice and perspective in what I consider a rational conception of communicating with clients and practicing architecture.

Curing the Fountainheadache offers a candid and completely human perspective on the frustrations and joys of the client–architect relationship. It also provides advice that will help both prospective clients and architects turn this potential headache into one of the most rewarding aspects of any building venture.

CHAPTER 1

DOMESTIC AFFAIRS

Clients in the residential domain are generally perceived by architects as the most puzzling. Design input and criticism by clients of proposed schemes often *seem* irrational and contradictory. Decisions may be delayed and, worse, frequently changed even after the project is well into construction. On the other hand, residential clients may justly feel intimidated, as their needs and preferences are ignored by architects. This problem may be amplified since many architects view house design as fertile ground for aesthetic experimentation: pushing the design envelope. Communication may break down, and any feelings of mutual trust and respect—so essential to successful projects—disappear.

Typically, it is the small-size architectural firm that dominates the field in tackling the design of residential additions, renovations, or completely new construction. This small firm is often composed of young architects who are attempting to break out on their own and establish a practice. Profit margins are usually very low, with projects quite time-intensive. However, there is an intrinsic payback: independence, control (within the firm), and pride of authorship—from inception through construction.

Again there is potential for conflict since clients have a tendency to view young practitioners either as inexperienced or uninterested in the more technical aspects of projects. Suzanne Stephens, a noted architectural critic and editor, has said:

> When it comes to the mundane matters of temperature, noise, and the like, there is always the lurking suspicion that the architect is more obsessed with innovative design than the comfort of the building's inhabitants. Frank Lloyd Wright provided a favorite role

model for the profession: When one of his clients complained that a leak in the roof made dinner guests a little soggy in rainy weather, Wright suggested moving the dining room table.

A current trend, driven both by the architect's need to survive fiscally and the client's need to obtain service, has required all parties (architect, client, and constructor) to be more responsible in personal transactions. This somewhat coerced symbiosis has a positive spin: *collaboration*, and likelihood of a satisfying project. Chicago architect Gigi McCabe-Miele believes that active participation and cooperation by the client are necessary prerequisites to every successful residential project: "So much depends on the owner, how much they understand the architect's role and how much they trust you."

CONFLICTS AND CLOSETS

"We can't keep our marriage together unless we have separate closets." After a brief assessment of the impact of her statement, Nancy managed a smile and a pat on the arm for her mate. Larry, unruffled by his wife's blunt comment, continued spooning his Shredded

Wheat. I glanced at my associate, who imperceptibly raised his eyebrows in confirming appreciation of the first clients of my new practice.

Several weeks earlier, the office of Andrew Pressman, Architect, had received a telephone call from Nancy. With a smoothness and tone of authority rivaling those of an anchorwoman, she rapidly summarized her need for "professional services." Wanting very much to hear that Nancy had learned of my firm from the publicity surrounding a design competition win, I inquired about referral source. I was informed matter-of-factly that I was one of "very few" firms listed with the local chapter of the American Institute of Architects that would take on projects budgeted below fifty thousand dollars in construction costs. "Reputation had little to do with my calling, if that's what you're asking."

Nancy continued her telephone monologue with a description of "our global needs." I attempted to interject something about waiting until we could meet face-to-face, but Nancy insisted that it might be more "cost-effective if you would begin prioritizing."

At this point, I felt compelled to learn a bit about my potential client, and since this was the Washington, DC, area, I couldn't resist asking whether Nancy worked for the government. "Yes, I'm an analyst with a subcontractor in Pentagon City." Congratulating myself on such perceptiveness, I figured I had this one typed; whatever it was she wanted would be functional, perhaps minimalist, and modern in style (given the tight budget). Maybe there *wouldn't* be clippings from *Architectural Digest*.

Nancy began to elaborate: "My husband, Larry—a lawyer [for my nosy benefit]—and I are planning a significant expansion of our home in Alexandria. We want kids and a new bedroom suite for us, and you'll probably have to push out one end of the house. Now, my cousin is at Princeton—her second year in the School of Architecture—and she has some wonderful ideas about style we want to incorporate. In fact, you may want to consult with her."

I mustered a rather anemic "Uh-huh." I wanted to know more about the exact location of the site and this seemed like the moment to broach the question. Not surprisingly Nancy had done her homework and was able to recite pertinent facts of the newly enacted regulations that specified constraints on building within the floodplain of the Potomac.

Didactically and with perhaps too much speed, I ventured, "Unique constraints often inspire unique architectural solutions, so this is not necessarily a problem at all. As for style, well, the marriage of any notions about style with the facts of the site is what influences the expression of the addition—so I'm not willing to discuss style by itself just yet."

Silence. Thinking I may have come across sounding too stiff and smug, I waited for Nancy to either hang up or argue with me. Instead she countered with: "Just as long as we can use the antique railings from the old courthouse auction that . . ." The sentence trailed off, allowing me to suggest that we might arrange a meeting at their house to talk with her and Larry personally and actually see the place.

The House

Our visit with Nancy and Larry had a pronounced domestic flavor. We arrived on a rainy Saturday morning and were greeted on the front walkway by two dogs. The scene was one we were later to recognize as prophetic. A sweet-tempered and slightly overweight retriever looked up with one of those sluggish dog smiles accompanied by a slow tail-wag. At the same time, with a loud and strident series of yelps, a tiny terrier flung itself from the shrubs into our path. Dancing over and in front of the sleepy retriever, the creature frustrated our forward progress. After what seemed like an eternity in the otherwise peaceful neighborhood, the side door opened and Larry stumbled out.

Rubbing sleep from his eyes, Larry nearly tripped over the untied lace of a moccasin slipped loosely on one of his large feet. He regained equi-librium and motioned for us to follow him into the kitchen. Before he was able to begin talking, a compact woman with aggressively frizzy hair bounded down the stairs and scolded the three of us. The gist of the outburst was our too-early arrival and, "Oh, I'm Nancy." Following this energetic display, we gathered around the kitchen table and the full story began to emerge. Between bites of multigrain and sesame cereal, Nancy explained that prior to consulting the American Institute of Architects for architectural firm listings, they had obtained proposals from at least two home builders. While apparently sound and slightly under their budget, the schemes appeared boxlike and altogether unrelated to the character of the house, its site, or the neighborhood. With a slightly effortful gesture of deference, Nancy seemed to be affirming my telephone talk. Larry remained half asleep and apparently half interested.

Looking at her huge sport watch, Nancy announced she was late for the 10K Riverfront Shuffle. Moving out the door, she directed her husband to "show them the file."

The file was a vast collection of magazine and newspaper clippings and excerpts of letters from the talented cousin. The range of circumstances, styles, and budgets represented failed to make any sort of impression on the lethargic Larry. When we had finished leafing through Nancy's file, Larry quietly, slowly, and relentlessly maintained that he preferred a "legal motif," built around "found objects" rescued from old municipal buildings.

By lunchtime, Nancy had returned. We told ourselves that at least we knew the worst: We had elicited the entire inventory of Larry and Nancy's contradictory preferences. We had listened well and empathized with both clients without alienating either one. We had tried to bolster their individual and collective self-esteem by acknowledging their taste and their goals. We gave assurance that with just a bit of compromise, we were on the verge of putting together a comprehensive list of functional requirements. The aesthetic aspect would naturally flow from the architectural responses to these requirements, the site conditions, and the neighborhood context. Larry and Nancy seemed appeased if not pleased by this summary.

Field Survey

The clients departed to various corners of the house, and my associate and I began the tedious survey of the existing condition. In the absence of original plans, any structure must be precisely measured and completely photographed. The resulting data are then translated into a set of plans, sections, and elevations from which the architect begins the new design. In the case of Larry and Nancy, we began with our documentation of the interior. I directed my associate to a long, narrow laundry room on one side of the house, while I unsheathed tape measure, knee pads, and camera in the living room at the other end. There is nothing like sketching and dimensioning a room from the bottom up to help one fully experience its contents and character: the layers of dust, petrified animal waste, occasional socks and underwear, bagel remnants (with and without evidence of cream cheese), and a curious assortment of ersatz American Indian artwork. There were prints, wall hangings, and carvings deposited behind and under furniture and appliances. A few of the pieces actually made it to a wall or shelf, though these were in the minority.

Working our way to the second floor was analogous to moving a rock and surprising two insects. Even the sedentary Larry seemed to dart toward the stairs as we approached the bedroom. Nancy was already moving downward in a blur of post-race Birkenstocks. In quiet resumption of our work upstairs, we felt something new. Trepidation, dislike, even revulsion gave way to an eerie sense that we were privileged. Larry and Nancy had entrusted us with the intimate details of their daily lives. There is something sobering about rummaging in a stranger's bedroom. My associate and I cast silently admonishing glances at each other and conducted our work with the implicit understanding that we were, on some level, charged with a sacred trust. Larry and Nancy were really saying: *Here is our life, our confusion, our hopes—now help us to make it right.* We pushed and sorted through the mess and filth with new resolve and affection for our clients.

Wrestling with Design and Presentation

My associate, who holds degrees in psychology, is first a clinician who knows how to spot depression—and rub it in. Over my shoulder I heard him say, "There are no bad clients, only bad architects. Someone famous said that. I think it's probably true."

"Look," I said, "this is an incredibly difficult project; I'm really agonizing about how to give these two what each of them seems to want and meet the objective requirements, too."

Two weeks of intensive brainstorming, model building, and drawing followed. We far exceeded the scope of services outlined in the agreement signed early on by the clients. The project had to and did assume a transcendent importance. We were going to help these people in spite of themselves, and create a work of architecture.

The challenge was to modulate the scale of the relatively huge two-and-a-half-story volume of the addition. The somewhat whimsical architectural response involved a high degree of articulation of the components of the design. This had to be accomplished while gracefully preserving and enhancing the modicum of charm and character of the

FIGURE 1-1

"Before" rendering illustrates the awkward existing back elevation with mechanical equipment shed in the left foreground. Drawing by Andrew Pressman.

original house. And so it was with pride and great expectations that I telephoned Nancy and Larry to set a date for presentation of the preliminary design scheme.

Again it was a Saturday, and a rainy one at that. Protecting blueline prints and a quarter-inch-scale model with hastily assembled plastic bags from the local dry cleaner, I set off toward Alexandria and destiny.

In retrospect, I'm still convinced I made one of my clearest and most persuasive presentations. I am also as certain that Larry and Nancy were happy with what they saw and heard. I would even say they were delighted. Larry displayed some animation and Nancy was disarmingly sweet. With their check and their blessings to proceed with development of construction details, I sped back to the office in an exhilarated state.

On Thursday of the week after the presentation, I received a call from Larry and Nancy. Larry expressed their apologies, but after "sleeping on the design, there were some revisions." Nancy, who had picked up an extension, chimed in with a matter-of-fact recitation of all the changes she'd been thinking about "and really needed." But Larry appeared to be developing a backbone right then and there. He began to assert himself and then fight with his wife. He insisted on the priority of his own list of radical changes in the design. These seemed to align with Nancy's only

FIGURE 1-2

"After" rendering illustrates the proposed back elevation transformed into a new composition, maximizing three-dimensional potential. The addition contains living room and porch with master bedroom suite on the second floor. All new construction was required to be raised about a half level aboveground in response to floodplain regulations. Design and drawing by Andrew Pressman.

in their departure from the substance and the very spirit of the design that they had so warmly embraced just four days earlier: "The valley in the new roof is likely to leak in five to ten years. It looks terrific but I don't want to spend money to maintain it."

My attempts to moderate were ignored as the dispute spiraled and escalated. I managed to end the event by affecting a slightly comic and somehow professorial voice and delivering a stern "I think that's enough, people!" We scheduled a meeting at Larry and Nancy's that Sunday to reevaluate and clarify the situation.

Late Saturday afternoon, the office answering machine played the following message: "Hi, Andrew. This is Larry. Nancy and I see no need to meet tomorrow. We've decided to table all plans for new construction at this point. Thanks for your help. We'll give you a ring when we're ready to hook up again. Bye." When you are a struggling and still-idealistic architect fresh from two hours of bad tennis and you get a message like this one, well, let's just say that some basic existential questions are raised.

FIGURE 1-3

Napkin sketch (left) attempts to capture the best features of the original house: sharply angled gables, proportions, and dollhouse quality. Back elevation (middle) shows how the porch continuously wraps around the façade to unify disparate elements and provide a strong base for the new superstructure. Perspective view of the side yard (right) illustrates how the trellis is extended from the base of the porch and weaves up and down to announce the back entry. This side of the house was built up to the zoning setback line and therefore could not be manipulated in three dimensions. Drawings by Andrew Pressman.

What Should Have Been Different

The preceding story showcases a client who is tough—a product of a rushed and high-pressured lifestyle, and a well-founded but sometimes hypervigilant consumerism. For my part, as a young architect, I was unprepared to assert myself effectively. The two parties in this case were mutually challenging and subtly antagonistic, and collaboration never really occurred.

The client arrived on the scene with a set of needs and preferences and with a propensity to place the architect in a subservient position. The interaction between client and architect became an uncomfortable skirmish for control of the way in which design issues were addressed. From the very outset, the architect's creative power was diluted and generally undermined. My response was ineffectual: first injured, then judgmental, and punctuated with brief, albeit honest, attempts at educating, empathizing, and accommodating. Still striving to provide quality design, I developed and presented a scheme that the client was never predisposed to consider seriously.

A responsible physician could no more be talked into sacrificing expertise simply to give a patient what he wanted than a lawyer would allow a client to formulate his own defense. The responsibility of patients and clients to participate actively is certainly crucial to the success of treatment, litigation, or architectural design, but there is a distinct division of labor that must be preserved if meaningful collaboration and successful outcome are to occur.

The outcome of this particular case might have been different had I gently but directly defined my role along with its intrinsic and necessary authority. Perhaps this could have happened at the client's suggestion of consultation with an otherwise uninvolved family member who happened to be a design student. I might have said: "No, I will not likely consult with a student, but I will pay very close attention to your wants and needs and develop a comprehensive inventory of your requirements. It is then my job to generate a design response to this inventory and other factors. In addition to you and your husband, I may elect to arrange consultations with other engineering professionals with whom I have worked, and whom I know to be fully trained and experienced. So, bear with me—this is how we as architects have learned to provide you with the best possible professional service."

The statement above fundamentally changes the tone of the exchange between architect and client. Regardless of the outcome, which ultimately remains in the hands of the client, the clarifying confrontation returns an appropriate measure of control to the architect. If the client accepts the conditions of the relationship, the architect is then free to perform the service for which he or she was trained.

"ALL GREAT ARCHITECTURE LEAKS." —FRANK GEHRY

Just in the way Theo Petrakis said the word "wood," you knew he was a craftsman. "Of course I can make you a lattice; I make so delicate it's a tracery!" He hugged me, shook his head with a smile, and glanced approvingly at his tattered copy of the plans. This last gesture was for the benefit of my clients, Mark and Vicki, and I was amused. The little man was not only a reliable contractor, but also a salesman who understood that the enigmatic architect had to be affirmed by the person who was actually going to build the project. This was especially true for Mark and Vicki.

The Project

Mark and Vicki came to me through the owner of a local business for whom I had done some space planning and renovation design work. Their children were preteenage, and they all lived in a large "traditional neo-Georgian style" home from which Mark also conducted his suburban orthodontic practice. The affluent neighborhood, on the North Shore of Long Island, New York, was lovely with gracious houses and beautiful old trees that gave the surroundings a tranquility and elegance.

The design problem involved a boxy back room added many years ago that jutted awkwardly into the cleft between the two gently angled wings of the house. Apart from some nice brickwork, its single redeeming aspect was its central location. Standing at the rearmost wall, one could look down a grand entry hall to the front doors some thirty-five feet away. Mark and Vicki hoped to "take full architectural advantage" of this regal entrance to an existing Kleenex box of a room. A glance at a lush garden beyond the box immediately stimulated my image of glass block and trellis as a way of opening up the house to the outside, and maintaining privacy. The clients further envisioned a den, a library, and a "cocktail cove," all communicating casually with the entry hall. It was one of those make it spectacular-but-modest, soaring-yet-intimate tasks that is such a genuinely intriguing as well as challenging problem for the architect.

Since Mark and Vicki were insistent that construction begin as soon as possible, I made their project a priority and within a week had preliminary concepts depicted in sketches: three-dimensional renderings, plans, and cross sections were mounted on large illustration board panels.

Trial by Jury

Filled with the excitement of an accelerated schedule and pending construction, I marched confidently into the initial presentation of my preliminary design. Not only were Mark, Vicki, the kids, and pets in attendance, but there was a stern jury of what appeared to be a room full of neighbors. Apparently I was designing not just for Mark and Vicki, but for their peers, whose approval seemed to matter more than a little.

FIGURE 1-4
Perspective drawing of the existing condition: a backyard afterthought, an empty box interposed between the two wings of the house. A special directive by the clients was not to increase the volume or area for fear of rejection by the town's review board, and of a substantial increase in tax liability. Drawing by Andrew Pressman.

FIGURE 1-5
The back room reinterpreted as an extension of the main entry axis, reinforced by a barrel-vaulted skylight and terminating in a glass block apse. Trellis framing wraps around the new structure, reconciling the awkward array of exterior surfaces and roof lines. Drawing by Andrew Pressman.

I began by describing my idea for a barrel-vaulted skylight extending the length of the grand hallway and terminating in a glass block apse. A delicate layer of trellis on the exterior would wrap the edges of the apse, and the adjacent walls would be shaped to gracefully unite the back room and the house. I continued with my presentation, indicating how the interior was laid out so that all the desired functions could be accommodated. Natural light would play a major role, taking full advantage of ever-changing shadow and leaf patterns from the heavily wooded yard.

I was quite startled by the response. Without so much as expressing an appreciation of the effort or at least acknowledging my first attempt at design, the interrogation began. A gentleman who looked like Jacques Cousteau observed, "With those angles and that long skylight, you're risking all kinds of water coming in, and as we all know, flat roofs eventually leak."

An obviously sophisticated woman asked, "Would you say more about the sources of historical allusion in your work?"

A younger, black-clad creature with a slash of dark red lipstick wondered, "Could you identify any opportunities for infusing your solution with deconstructivist themes?"

Then a large man wearing a down vest asked the inevitable, "What about solar?" and, "I assume this is 'green' and 'sustainable' with no harm to the environment?"

Mark and Vicki presided in silence, apparently evaluating my every inflection during the onslaught of questions and comments, which had little or nothing to do with my design proposal. Every attempt I made to relate the discussion back to the work was lost in waves of tangential and exhibitionistic monologue. At least the gallery was successful at entertaining themselves for the afternoon.

My anticipation of referrals and a backlog of work from worshipful neighbors had all but vanished. Posturing like a harried politician at a press conference, I ignored a question and caught Mark's eye: "So, Mark, what do *you and Vicki* think about the scheme?"

The reply came almost instantly. "If your Mr. Petrakis can build it so it doesn't leak when it rains, then we love it!"

Somehow, I seemed to have cleared some rite of passage. The jury mingled, conversation reached a comfortable buzz, and a uniformed maid emerged from the kitchen to serve beverages and snacks. A little

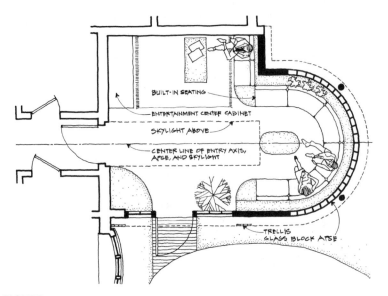

FIGURE 1-6

Floor plan of the remodeled space, with its discrete zones of seating and entertainment electronics. The forms and materials were inspired by a softly curving bay and built-in seating of the existing breakfast nook. Drawing by Andrew Pressman.

FIGURE 1-7

"Napkin" sketch at eye level. The outermost layer of exterior skin (the trellis) is sloped to match the rhythm of nearby roofs, and arched above standard-size window and door units. This creates the illusion of arched glazing without the associated greater cost and detail. Drawing by Andrew Pressman.

unsettled but happy with an approval to continue, I allowed myself to relax in this truly bizarre scene, and enjoy the prospect of the forthcoming construction.

Contractor as Ally

As I developed Mark and Vicki's design, I also cultivated my relationship with the contractor, Theo Petrakis. Though I suspected he really wanted to be Anthony Quinn, Petrakis obviously loved his work, and took pride in his talent and his network of subcontractors. He was also capable of improvising in the field. With old houses full of all manner of quirks just waiting to be uncovered, a builder like Petrakis could help to avoid extra costs to the clients. In light of the limited budget, however, it took a long lunch with promises of magazine coverage to get him to join the team. With all the drama and eye-twinkle of his Mediterranean soul, Theo Petrakis exclaimed, "Yes, I will do it—for you, my good friend!"

Not quite three weeks later, Petrakis dropped by the office at eight thirty in the morning, proclaiming, "I smell coffee! And if I'm wrong, you better put some on!"

Petrakis was actually quite obnoxious, but it was impossible not to like him. Apart from coffee, Petrakis wanted to let me know that he had completed his bid and was on his way to personally submit it to Vicki. Revealing a bit of appealing insecurity, he wondered how many other contractors were following through with bid proposals. I told him that Mark had asked that I send sets of construction documents to two other builders of his choice. As if to reassure himself and me, Petrakis raised his mug and made a toast: "To our victory, fame, and fortune, eh?"

With that, he set his mug down with a jarring crack, turned theatrically, and exited. I savored the moment, grinning and shaking my head. However, the mood was not to last.

The Resolution

Three days later, a letter arrived from Mark. It was typed on his professional letterhead and it stated that he and Vicki had decided not to execute the addition as designed. The reason for this decision was twofold: One involved his assessment that "there is a clear and present danger of the roof leaking." The second reason was the cost of construction which, while not exceeding their budget, "was too out of line." Mark continued to explain: "I determined that the subcontractors were significantly inflating their bids. They would do so upon arriving at my house and taking note of our very high standard of living." This practice of alleged bid inflation was one that Mark insisted he "detected without fail." He concluded his letter by saying, "Our decision is a matter of principle as well as money." The notation at the bottom of the page indicated that a copy of the letter had been sent to Theo Petrakis as well as the other contractors who submitted bids.

What Went Wrong

It seemed as though another visit to Fred's Place, my hangout for regrouping and reevaluating, was in order. Indeed the soothing ambiance of the dining room (which always seemed to be in an off-hour mode) promoted satisfying reflection. I hypothesized that I had allowed Mark and Vicki to get hung up on the construction details—such as the roof issue—and they then lost sight of the big picture, the design solution itself. By presenting the more conceptual aspects of the scheme, it was apparently assumed that I had little control over, or interest in, the more technical aspects. I may well have outsmarted myself. My associate, on the other hand, offered an alternative explanation, one that I found more appealing both intellectually and emotionally, but far less likely. He ventured the possibility that these successful forty-something adults might be having a lot of trouble with aging. The back room project was a concrete symbol of an approaching postparental stage feared by my clients. The room stood for a life stage in which the couple's leisure would be spent entertaining, and alone with each other. I replied, "If you become any more superficially clever, they may accept you into that lovely jury of neighbors who attended my presentation."

At this point, I felt I had to do something different. The business of retreating to lick our wounds and rationalize was becoming unacceptable. I suggested that we drop in on Mark and Vicki, not to attempt a belated defense of our design, but to quietly find out what really happened. Ever since I launched my own practice, I had been solemnly admonished by my mentors to avoid work in the residential domain. Specific reasons were never forthcoming, only a kind of "It's too terrible to tell," in combination with a not-so-vague smirk. I wanted to illuminate this corner of architectural lore, and I would start with Mark and Vicki.

My resolve to drop in translated to an unannounced visit about a month later. I was driven perhaps by pure curiosity. So I found myself behind the wheel of my Honda Civic pulling up to the curb in front of the familiar brick house. After no one answered my ringing and knocking at the front door, I proceeded toward the rear of the house, hoping I would find at least one family member there. I paused at the garage door, which was half open to accommodate several heavy corrugated cardboard boxes of immense proportions. On one side was stenciled FOX VALLEY GAZEBO, MODEL NUMBER 1509A.

I didn't need to go any farther. Mark and Vicki had elected to forgo the building process and to purchase a factory-made structure to be placed in the middle of their backyard. It struck me as quite clear that people who are spending their own money on the place where they live may be reluctant to embrace an architectural intervention, something so often perceived as abstract, expensive, and risky. Maybe there was a certain amount of validity in the mock psychological explanation of what had happened, but I now believe that there are some homeowners who are just not receptive to the process and product of architecture. My failure here may have been in not recognizing this, and encouraging Mark and Vicki toward a more distinctly architectural solution.

THE SAUNA AND THE NEW JERSEY TURNPIKE

"One job superintendent heard he would be working on one of my jobs and he got scared. He started jogging for thirty minutes every day to train in case I attacked somebody. I'll quit architecture when I lose that emotion. You've got to really fight."

—Architect Tadao Ando in an interview with *Progressive Architecture*, June 1993

Meeting the Clients

The deer approached the baseline of the tennis court, pausing only to nibble on one of the potted geraniums that was in front of a small bench. From the breakfast alcove where I sat with Alex and Emily, it seemed incongruous that this scene was unfolding only an hour from New York City.

Alex was an international banker and his wife, Emily, was a mother of three who was also a part-time sculptor. Although located on five beautiful acres, their newly purchased house was too small for the growing family, and did not fully exploit the rural site. During the initial contact with Alex, I learned that the probable architectural scope of

FIGURE 1-8

(top) A view of the new addition, on the right side. It includes a guest suite with private entry above a two-car garage. (bottom) Schematic design sketch illustrates the new addition on the right with the new second floor on the existing house on the left. Photo © Norman McGrath. Design and drawing by Andrew Pressman.

work would involve a renovation to the existing house as well as a significant addition. Upon my meeting with the couple, these expectations were confirmed. I was also struck with how delightful and sophisticated this family was, without any trace of affectation. Alex, Emily, and their children were nice people—*and* they had a subscription to *Architectural Record*!

As time passed and we grew closer, I liked them even more, and I discovered their one flaw. My associate called it "episodic technophilia." Every four or five days during the course of design development, I received a telephone call, usually from Alex, that would go something like this: "We just read about this new automated, voice-activated butler system that can execute hundreds of household tasks with voice command—and there's a modem or something that enables a link with the car phone; I could turn on the sauna or Jacuzzi from the New Jersey Turnpike on my way home from work."

I would patiently listen and respond by acknowledging the seductive luxury features now available with several home automation systems. The image of Woody Allen's movie *Sleeper* merged with my childhood memories of *The Jetsons*. It was hard not to laugh at the enjoyment and fascination with which Alex and Emily pursued microchip technology. And it was sometimes frustrating when this preoccupation excluded discussion about more significant and relevant design issues. But this was a trivial matter in an otherwise ideal architect–client relationship. The architect–contractor relationship, however, was another matter.

Meeting the Contractor

The only time I ever lost my temper occurred at the first meeting with Nick, of Superior Construction Industries. Nick was the general contractor whom Emily and Alex chose to coordinate all the construction work. (I continue to wonder about the nature of Superior's *other* "Industries.") Superior came highly recommended by neighbors who had been very pleased with a new garage Nick had built for them. I entered our meeting looking forward to establishing the kind of team ethic that would neutralize the historically adversarial architect–contractor relationship.

Nick and I sat facing each other at the small table in the breakfast nook. Emily and Alex were visible outside on the court, hitting a tennis ball back and forth. Nick began by presenting me with a wrinkled and smudged business card depicting a disembodied roof on a background

FIGURE 1-9

(right) A goal in designing the guest/garage addition was to relate it to the existing house yet distinguish the functions. Beams unite existing and new roofs and form an entry trellis. (left) The lacy, two-story volume of the guest entry becomes a circulation focus. It contains stairs to the suite, and paths to the garage and adjacent existing studio. Photos © Norman McGrath.

of light green. The telephone number had been crossed out, with a new one penciled in above. Already feeling a bit like the cliché elitist architect, I returned the favor with my immaculate white and gray minimalist card. Stuffing it in his breast pocket, he said, "All right, let's do it."

The Conflict

Nick began to list design changes that he felt were required to meet the budget that he proposed, which had been agreed to by the clients. The result was a completely different project. At first it was his tone more than the substance of what was stated that got to me. Then the wave of anger hit as I became aware that under the guise of meeting the clients' budget, Nick was attempting to cut his costs by bullying me into accepting changes that would motivate me—the quintessential sensitive guy—to dynamite the "tainted" project. When Nick went on to admit that Alex and Emily had not been apprised of his proposed new plans, I accused him of attempting to make unilateral decisions to increase his own margin of profit, to the detriment of design quality. Then the sparks began to fly.

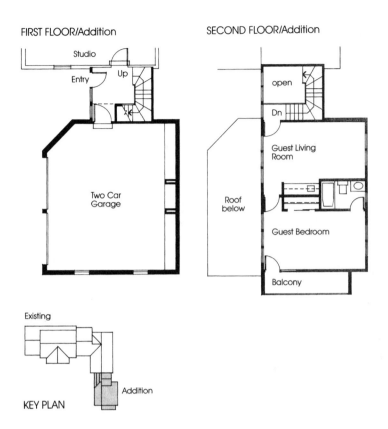

FIRST FLOOR/Addition

Studio

Entry

Up

Two Car
Garage

SECOND FLOOR/Addition

open

Dn

Guest Living
Room

Roof
below

Guest Bedroom

Balcony

Existing

Addition

KEY PLAN

FIGURE 1-10

Floor plans of the new addition. Design and drawings by Andrew Pressman.

Nick stood up, slammed his fist on the table, and screamed, "You obviously have no field experience! Your construction details are just pretty pictures; me and any other builder would go broke fast if we built that kinda crap. My advice to you is learn to work with real life, kid."

I stood up myself and shot back, "You are not the architect. Don't you dare dictate design to me or to my clients. If you promise to do a job for a certain budget, that's your problem! You can't alter the drawings to suit your own purposes after you've agreed to a price. Furthermore, if you had any difficulty or suggestions, why didn't you call me while you were developing your bid?"

Some movement outside drew my attention for a second and I caught an unintended glimpse of the tennis court, and it made me hesitate. A couple of hundred hours of design work may have been saved in that instant. Catching my emotional and physical breath, I knew I had to either make peace fast or risk dragging Alex and Emily into the escalation.

I looked back at Nick, shifted gears, and as softly as I could proposed a meeting of the minds: "Listen, I'm very good. I suspect you're very good. I know we can learn from each other on this project, and that may mean we can produce something special—which could ultimately reward us both far in excess of pleasing Alex and Emily."

Nick interrupted, a faint smile beginning to appear, "Not many of you guys defend their position that way, I respect that. I'll tell you what, let's go through my problems one by one and see if you can help me to bring this baby in with some sane numbers."

I quickly agreed, and in fact we were able to make revisions that did not profoundly alter the spirit of the design, and were more cost-effective. Of course, I shook for three days, but I learned something about the importance of old-fashioned politics in the service of getting the project built. Not that this was any simple or easy matter; Nick was an unwholesome character at best, and this was not going to change. However, he and his crew could be influenced and made more flexible in providing appropriate service.

Ruthless gestures on my part such as arriving during construction armed with fresh doughnuts, bagels, and Danish did much to break down antagonism and resistance. My associate's informal supportive visits with Nick and his lieutenants, usually around quitting time, allowed me to address problems the following morning (we played "good architect, bad architect").

I jokingly predicted a new building industry specialist—a "construction psychologist" who would interpret architect to contractor, and vice versa. I envisioned a *New Yorker* cartoon in which the properly bearded therapist sat between two portable couches with the framework of a partially completed structure in the background; on one couch an over-size bow tie would be visible, on the other a hard hat. "Why are you so angry?" the caption would read. The image was too close for comfort.

Construction

Emily, Alex, and their children remained in good spirits throughout the course of construction. In an undertaking of this scale, disruption of home life is more the rule than the exception. Certain phases of the work seem to produce more distress than others. One of the worst

NEW SECOND FLOOR/Existing

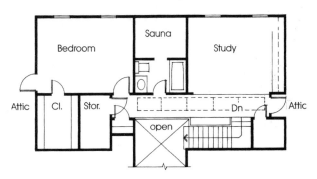

FIGURE 1-11

(top) The project also entailed raising a section of roof on the existing house for a new second-floor master suite. Natural light from new skylights penetrates into the foyer below. Photo © Carl Weese. (above) The new second floor plan of the existing house. Design and drawing by Andrew Pressman.

periods occurs when drywall is installed and finished. White dust is everywhere despite the ubiquitous plastic sheet barriers. Pets become walking time bombs ready to leave a white imprint on a suit or school clothes at the most inopportune moment. And there is always the mud that is tracked in by everyone entering the house. While all this falls into the category of temporary yuppie hardship, the discomfort and inconvenience are nevertheless sufficient to discourage many from embarking on a project.

Why it is that only *some* people are able to initiate and then follow through with large residential additions or renovations remains a tough question. In the case of Alex and Emily, their confident vision of the future seemed to drive their motivation and support their commitment. Equally important was their faith in both the architect and contractor. This promoted everyone's personal investment in the project, which naturally resulted in an extraordinary effort.

THE NEW YAWKAS

The political climate in the state of Maine can be characterized as one that insists upon restraint, tact, and a respect for tradition. Over the course of many pleasure- and business-related visits to the Pine Tree State, I have found the above characterization to be absolutely accurate, with a single exception in the person of Bob Down of Down East Realtors. Bob contends that his people were "Maine-born as far back as the state and longer," but you get the feeling he has as much credibility as Mr. Haney on the old *Green Acres* television show.

I first met Bob on a classic motionless, subzero winter morning with the sun just coming up in a cobalt sky. I pulled into his parking lot between two mounds of crusty snow and came to a stop in front of the office door. Before I unbuckled my seat belt, a large, corduroy-wrapped man swung open the door and bellowed, "C'mon in out' the chill!"

The Deal

Bob ushered me inside and introduced himself as a "simple man who raises sheep and picks a few blueberries, and a' course I do a few land deals as well." (I knew that he did a tremendous commercial real estate business.) Bob said that he had recently been lucky enough to seriously interest a couple from New York in buying a small vacation house. Bob continued: "They're nice folks, and they want to explore the possibility of making some architectural changes. They wanted to know if I personally knew of any architects, so I said, 'Ayuh.'" (He had a talent for affecting the Maine accent that out-of-state tourists have come to expect.)

Bob went on with his story. "So I took the liberty of giving them your name. Now, if I'm able to show a prospective buyer an old fixer-upper, say, and in the same breath name a big-city ahchitect with local ties, well, my Gawd, that helps me make the sale and it keeps you in work. Sound good?"

The apparent package deal Bob was offering to the couple from New York seemed to involve a real and well-defined little project. Without much more detail, I agreed to take on the job. Yet again, I would learn that the absence of a direct relationship with the clients can be disastrous. I should have known as Bob exclaimed, "Well, that's great! Let me take you to breakfast to celebrate." Then, in a conspiratorial aside, he said, "They'll go through money like green corn goes through the new maid!"

The interior of Bob's Saab had just gotten warm as we approached the promised celebratory feast at the Kracked Keel, between Arby's and a drive-in muffler repair garage. During the ten-minute drive from the office, I had learned that the New Yorkers were named Samantha and Murray and that they were both in film production, and were preoccupied with factory outlet shopping. Proximity to L. L. Bean was as important as views of the rolling fields opposite their proposed new home.

As Bob spoke, I felt increasingly comfortable about this particular project, since it was going to be "clean." That is, Bob was acting as my client, and I would supposedly deal only with him. The ideal immersion into the lives of the homeowners would be avoided, but in this case it might be all right—Samantha and Murray did not seem as if they would be a couple in search of architecture.

Bob inadvertently affirmed my initial impressions by talking further about the clients. He had gotten the message that "Las Vegas style" was a recurring theme in their lives. In the case of the house renovation, it translated to a bathroom "the size of Sebago Lake" with a two-person whirlpool set in a marble platform, towel warmers, his-and-hers sinks, a shower with dual heads, a "steam environment," a makeup station, and a hidden, fold-down ironing board. This bathroom was to complement

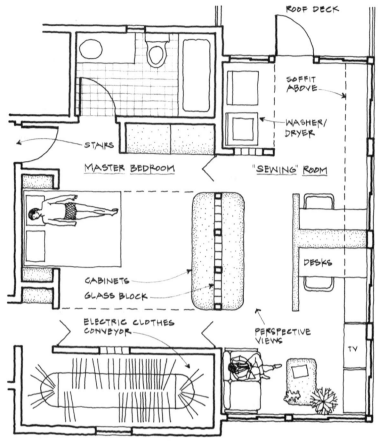

FIGURE 1–12

Floor plan of a proposed new master suite including bedroom, bathroom, home office, and lounge. The requirement for space-efficient storage of the client's large wardrobe is met with a motorized clothes conveyor, similar to that used in the neighborhood dry cleaner. Drawing by Andrew Pressman.

what amounted to a hotel suite that was to be designed within the shell of a farmhouse dating from 1800. Bob concluded with a chuckle and an afterthought, "I forgot to mention, the lady has—I ain't exaggeratin'—a roomful of clothes, and she wants 'em somewhere, somehow in the bedroom."

Returning to a more mainstream and businesslike dialect, Bob opened a briefcase and removed a list of requirements for the renovation that Murray had assembled. The detailed list had been faxed to

Bob's office from Murray's company, Glitz Productions. In addition to the bathroom/hotel suite Bob had described, Murray specified the need to convert an adjacent room to a "rustic and personalized stage set for entertainment."

Instead of a maid or butler, I could envision an assistant director commanding "Action!" as a moose would run across the yard at regular intervals. While this was going on, Samantha and Murray would be reclining in their canvas chairs, sipping something blanc, and awaiting the arrival of guests from the coast.

The Drama

A few weeks after our breakfast at the Keel, I had an opportunity to meet Samantha and Murray. Bob persuaded me to present the design scheme myself; his not-so-subtle tactic was to claim that "If I make the pitch, I might not be up to the sophistication expected by the New Yawkas, there's a chance it might not fly, and I might blow the whole deal." Bob's manipulation was transparent, but he had a point. It was not sophistication I was concerned about, it was "production values."

I arrived at the office of Down East Realtors ahead of time so that I could carefully set up my scale model and drawings. Bob sat at his flea market desk while I positioned myself on the painted picnic table he used as the "conference room."

The office door opened and a short, bald, heavyset man entered, accompanied by a tall, dark-haired woman. Both were dressed in identical parkas that covered tan safari outfits. Their effusive greeting may have surpassed Bob's country welcome.

Following the introductions, Samantha and Murray sat at designated places in front of the picnic table, and I began my presentation.

"Nice prop," Murray interrupted, while grabbing the model, balancing it on his knee, and making it difficult for me to concentrate on the project description. Not even halfway through, Murray broke in again: "We like it—we're going out for a bite—where can you get a good lobster roll around here?"

Then Samantha began to cry. With a thick forearm, Murray hooked his wife at the waist, swept her toward the door, and whispered to us, "We'll see you back here after lunch."

Murray returned to the office alone and fired me. He explained, "It's always very difficult to end a relationship—but we just feel that you were not able to capture Sam's imagination, and Bob, take no offense—maybe we should investigate other options."

Battery Steele

A couple of months later, I received another call from Bob. He wanted a "private consultation, to bounce a few ideas about," for something like two or three hours. This consultation would occur without Samantha and Murray's knowledge, and was designed to help Bob prepare appropriately to ensure the feasibility of his latest state-of-the-art proposal—which involved the conversion of abandoned artillery batteries to luxury housing and studio space. The concept of our couple from New York holed up in an old bunker was somehow right; I took the job.

I met Bob the following week on the ferry wharf at seven in the morning. Bob's idea was actually intriguing: The reuse of hardened coastal fortifications (which had been built for the defense of our key harbors during the early part of World War II) has generated sporadic enthusiasm and some creative efforts. The fortification we were to assess was located on an island only fifteen minutes away via the city ferry.

We boarded the sturdy little vessel a bit after seven thirty. The red and white bows of *Abenaki* sliced through the chop and tossed salty spray to the deck. The surface of the harbor sparkled and the view of the islands was beautiful. The friendly beat of the big diesels below slowed to a steady thrum. The trip was over too quickly; we were approaching the dock at Casco Island. Fresh bread and boxes of groceries were off-loaded along with us, and a group of children rushed by in the opposite direction to board the ferry for the return trip and junior high school in the city.

Map in hand, we made our way to the island's perimeter road. Pretty houses with just-planted gardens dotted the sides of the road. A dog barked, a screen door whacked shut, insects buzzed, and birds sang. Patches of tall grass and tiny yellow and blue wildflowers completed a perfect New England spring day. The road veered left toward the ocean side of the island. Houses were sparse, and a chilly breeze called for windbreakers. The transition in scenery and climate grew increasingly dramatic. Trees and shrubs disappeared, replaced by marsh, rocky beach, and a sheer expanse of the sea.

I felt Bob grab my arm. He pointed inland. I looked and felt a shiver that had nothing to do with the chill. About seventy yards in from the

FIGURE 1-13

(left) "Before" sketch of the room adjacent to the existing bedroom, with a low ceiling of yellowing acoustical tile. (right) "After" sketch showing newly exposed cathedral of roof pitches with new skylights. Drawings by Andrew Pressman.

FIGURE 1-14

View to adjacent room from the bed. Glass block, located between studs in the load-bearing wall, allows natural light to penetrate into the bedroom and visually lengthen the suite. Drawing by Andrew Pressman.

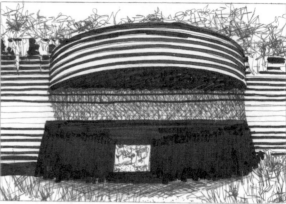

FIGURE 1–15
Field sketches of the World War II bunker (right) and watch tower (left).
Drawings by Andrew Pressman.

road, embedded in a long bluff was a massive and eerie-looking concrete structure. Above a dark, cavernous opening was a thick, cantilevered cap shielding the now empty mounts for the long-gone artillery piece. This was Battery Steele (see Figure 1-15).

I took photographs and made quick sketches as we advanced through the scrub and marsh toward the huge bunker. Bob had briefed me about the installation on the basis of what he had heard through contacts on the city planning board. However, nothing prepared me for the impact of visiting the site. The contrast between the harbor and ocean sides of the island was certainly part of it; but the thing itself produced an unsettling and ominous yet very magnetic feeling.

My consultation report included documentation of a five-hundred-foot-long subterranean tunnel connecting Battery Steele with another emplacement less visible from the road. Storage vaults built on either side of the tunnel constituted a total of twenty thousand square feet of enclosed space. There was some vandalism and graffiti that I speculated might be attempts to humanize the place, but overall, it was in excellent condition. In view of this condition and proximity to utilities and the road, I emphatically recommended adaptive reuse. Even if it would assume the form of an avant-garde studio for Samantha and Murray, there seemed real potential for giving Battery Steele new life.

Successful professional politics can indeed make strange bedfellows. I believe that the overarching lesson here is *not* to rule out even the most obnoxious personalities as clients—they may lead one to the more interesting, important, and ultimately satisfying projects.

ARCHIPHOBIA!

In the following essay, "Archiphobia!," Joseph R. Provey (based in Fairfield, Connecticut) draws on his extensive experience as a journalist, editor, and observer in the world of home improvement. Provey sets the stage for an examination of the often highly political "impasse" between architects and their homeowner clients.

Throughout my fifteen years covering home improvement trends, I've always been fascinated that many homeowners opt for a cautious approach to architecture and design while others are willing to experiment. For the former group, it's okay for a family room to be a big box with windows, as long as it connects to the kitchen. Perhaps there is a half-round window or cathedral ceiling, but that's about as adventuresome as things get. And the budget isn't always the determining factor. Folks with big budgets are just as likely—or rather unlikely—to be experimental as people who remodel on a shoestring budget.

There *are*, of course, lots of reasons for being conservative about making unconventional changes to the space in which we live. For one thing, being different can get expensive. For another, untraditional designs haven't been subjected to the test of time, and they don't always work. Doing things differently can also mean a lot of your time, because client input and involvement are crucial. And, finally, if you let your idiosyncrasies show in a home, what will a prospective buyer say down the road?

It boils down to a general fear or reticence about hiring any sort of design professional. And even if a homeowner works up the courage to engage a professional designer, the results are often unsatisfying. It's almost as if most of us don't believe in the need for designers—and those who do are unsure of how to successfully tap the designer's creative energies. The fault isn't ours alone. Designers can be exceedingly poor marketers of their services and, in some cases, unwittingly breed distrust.

The bottom line is that a professional designer can make a difference—if you pick the right one and take the time to learn how to work with him.

Why Homeowners Don't Hire Architects

Acquaintances like to tell me about their personal building and remodeling projects. At a recent neighborhood potluck, for example, Bill and Elise shared tales about the construction of their summer getaway on the Rhode Island shore. Among the first questions I asked was whether they had used an architect to help them with the project. The answer was, "No. We did the design ourselves." That's the answer I usually get—one that never ceases to surprise me since just about every home improvement magazine or book recommends hiring a design professional.

The homeowners I talk to have lots of reasons for avoiding designers of all stripes, particularly architects. They range from, "My builder can do what I need," and, "They cost too much," to "My wife's a graphic designer and can do it herself." After years of hearing comments like these, I decided to put the question to several architects across the country whose work I admire and whom I knew would be candid with me.

What follows is a list of the basic reasons homeowners give for steering clear of architects, the architects' reactions, and their advice for getting around the impasses.

IMPASSE 1: YOU HAVE TO BE RICH.

Budget is the biggest reason many homeowners avoid architects. But the problem is not necessarily what those architects charge in fees, note several architects. In fact, it often has more to do with the costs homeowners think will be tacked on to their projects as a result of added complexity or expanded scale.

Duo Dickinson, a Connecticut architect [and *Curing the Fountainheadache* contributor—see "Measure Twice, Cut Once" in Chapter 9], suggests there are two brands of political style among architects: those who subordinate the client and those who subordinate themselves. Architects, he explains, are traditionally recognized for the product—not the process—of their design, even though the success of the latter is essential to satisfy most clients.

New York architect Ernie Harris puts it this way: "Will the architect build a monument to himself?" Fears like this, he says, are potent, since homeowners don't have much experience with architects—"and they've all read *The Fountainhead*." He adds that not many people understand how architects work or what they do.

Dickinson comments that architectural schools often imbue students with the idea that design is a magical process that develops more from inspiration than from client need. The houses that are held up as great examples of architecture usually are discussed and studied without much said about the role owners played or should have played.

Dickinson maintains that many architects haven't come to grips with the dilemma of simultaneously serving both the homeowner and the taste "gods" of architecture. It's not uncommon, he says, for a young architect to win a job by appearing sensitive to what the clients want, figuring (consciously or not) he can win them over to his concepts later on.

IMPASSE 2: YOU WON'T BE ABLE TO RESELL YOUR HOUSE IF YOU ACCEPT AN UNUSUAL DESIGN.

It's difficult enough to let yourself be a little different. It's even tougher if you think you'll pay an economic penalty for it. Ernie Harris says there's some justification to this, but what you can get away with depends on where you live.

California architect Heidi Richardson runs into the resale concern often and believes that most residential architects are sensitive to it. She also feels that the fears may be overblown. "After all," she points out, "if you like it, there's bound to be someone else who will, too." Richardson also observes that second-home buyers tend to be less concerned with rules like "it must have three bedrooms and two baths." They tend to be more willing to think of their own needs and desires first.

IMPASSE 3: YOUR BUILDER OBJECTS.

It stands to reason that builders are politically uncomfortable with architects. For centuries, after all, builders performed the design role themselves. They made decisions based on local styles, regional materials, and traditional building techniques. Architects tend to be viewed as extraneous, even after nearly 130 years of trying to forge relationships with homeowners and builders.

Many builders think straightforward jobs don't require an architect—and if you're sure that's what you want, they're right. But keep in mind that builders have an agenda of their own, too. They want to build your house, addition, or dormer as efficiently and with as few surprises as possible. Their profit depends on it. If an architect creates something a little unconventional, the proposition becomes a bit riskier for the builder. Several architects noted that it helps in these cases to find an architect who understands the building process or, as one architect puts it, "knows his way around a two-by-four."

Just as important as finding an architect fluent with residential construction is finding the right builder, notes Harris. Heidi Richardson guides her clients toward builders who have executed demanding designs in the past. She also points out that this type of builder is very likely to appreciate architects. "The architect, while generally thought of as an agent of the homeowner, also can act as a buffer between the builder and an unreasonable or unknowledgeable client," she says. "In fact, some builders won't work without an architect."

IMPASSE 4: BAD COMMUNICATION.

Most architects don't help matters. They haven't marketed themselves to residential clients very well. Consequently, most people think of them as being exclusively for the wealthy. However, many architects who are perfectly qualified to do small-scale residential work don't want to. Narrow profit margins and a huge time and energy commitment are often cited as reasons to avoid the domestic scene.

The Right Reasons for Choosing an Architect

So what can we say in general about finding ways around the typical impasses between architect and client? My advice to prospective clients is, don't fall for the wrong architect! Dickinson says you'll be far better off if you "search for someone who will do a 'we,' not a 'me' building— where the 'we' includes the builder"; in other words, find someone who is politically secure and unselfish. The trick is to make sure that whomever you choose to work with believes meeting clients' needs is the top priority. "Image mustn't terrorize need," says Dickinson, adding, "the *design process* should bridge the void between what the architect knows and what the client knows about himself."

PRIVATE BATTLES IN THE PUBLIC DOMAIN

John Dixon, an editor at *Progressive Architecture*, has almost lyrically stated how architects can sometimes manage the myriad forces tugging at monumental projects: "The strength of architects lies in our ability to synthesize the sometimes contradictory impulses of today's society into responsive spaces and forms."

The following three stories embody the potential that Dixon has expressed. They concern highly visible and important projects *"with design at stake!"* The architects, Charles Gwathmey, Stanley Allan, and George Hartman, persevere against difficult odds to achieve design excellence for their clients and ostensibly for wider society. Scrutiny of their designs by special interest groups and the architects' formulation of a response (without diluting the original intent) are major components of creating great architecture in this realm.

FUSION OF OLD AND NEW AT THE GUGGENHEIM

Preservation and renovation involving all building types are issues that are becoming increasingly important as we approach the next century. Renovation of older buildings is rapidly accounting for the largest percentage of all dollars spent on construction. Moreover, the trend to recycle buildings and preserve those of historic import is consistent with the sustainability message from conservation groups.

The meaning and application of this effort are nowhere better crystallized and exemplified than by the addition, renovation, and restoration effort at the Solomon R. Guggenheim Museum in New York City, by the architectural firm of Gwathmey Siegel & Associates.

Altering the Frank Lloyd Wright masterpiece was a provocative act, and the Guggenheim story yields much insight into the definition and practice of architectural design in this specialized world, as well as insight into relationships among architect, client, government agencies, and public groups.

Charles Gwathmey, one of the partners in charge of the Guggenheim project, is among a small number of world-class talents producing some of the highest-quality architecture today. His firm has received over sixty design awards, including honors from *Progressive Architecture*, *Architectural Record*, and the National AIA. But, more important, he is a decent, forthright, and sensitive guy—the ideal combination of traits for one who must negotiate with distinctive clients and stakeholders, all of whom have their own special interests and agendas.

Gwathmey's point of view may contribute significantly to his effectiveness in reconciling the conflicts between those who often seem to lie on opposing ends of the "change" versus "no change" spectrum. He is disarmingly eloquent about balancing a respectful appreciation of an original building while working to promote adjustments that ensure its continuing relevance and accessibility for a constantly evolving society. The project consists of a new ten-story annex (a limestone-clad rectangular tower)—which adds exhibit space and visually serves as a neutral backdrop to the existing building—and restoration and renovation of the Wright building.

What Gwathmey has to say about the unfolding of the Guggenheim project applies to "everyday" architectural projects in general. That Mr. Gwathmey and his associates were able to persevere and achieve a most successful outcome is acknowledgment that the application of the time-honored principles of history, logic, and creativity truly do result in design excellence.

My conversation with Mr. Gwathmey that follows illustrates the role and influence of the various players in shaping and executing this formidable project.

A Unique Commission

Andrew Pressman (AP): I think it would be fascinating to hear how you successfully completed a project laden with so much controversy and emotion. It seems like an unbelievable achievement to gain approval from all the principal parties. How did you do it?

Charles Gwathmey (CG): You should know that the clients were always supportive. The interesting battle at the Guggenheim involved the preservation and historicist lobby—which in a sense became the counterclient. This situation may be more difficult than a challenging client—especially when they're explicitly the opposition. And I think it's a valuable lesson, not so much because of our perseverance, but because of the strategies we employed—the use of factual research and organized presentation that in a sense balanced and refuted the often emotional and irrational presentations that our counterclients continued to introduce. The six years of hearings and going all the way to the New York Court of Appeals became a lesson in controlling your temper and doing your research and presenting it in a way that was both emphatic and passionate as well as accurate.

AP: Along those lines, how were you able to maintain your cool and resolve in the face of such relentless and vocal criticism?

CG: I admit that when things were the lowest, I would always rationalize by saying, "Well, at least what we were giving back to architects was hopefully documentation of legitimate preservation and extension." A lot of architecture, as we both know, is not realized but is part of the legacy of publication—and the hope always was that it would have some future research value and maybe some future realization. As an academic, I am interested in the *idea* of something as well as the *fact* of something—that's what carries you in these kinds of things.

AP: How were you most persuasive?

CG: We had constant hearings and many interviews with the press, who were predisposed, by the way, to favor the opposition. I think the most crucial series of events was that in the initial presentation, Edgar Kaufmann Jr., who was regarded by the Board of Appeals (the hearing body in New York City—initially the zoning body) as *the* consummate expert on Wright, because of Fallingwater and because of his scholarship on Wright, testified against our initial scheme. He was very effective and was humble in his presentation style and knowledgeable as well, whether you agreed or not—it didn't matter.

When we revised the first scheme, I presented it to Edgar Kaufmann personally before any hearing. He reversed himself and wrote an eloquent letter—because he was sick by then—to the board saying how responsive and sensitive we were to the initial criticism and that the second scheme, which was the one that was ultimately realized, was both sympathetic to and responsible to Wright's original vision, and in fact enhanced the building. This letter, in conjunction with the fact that Donald Trump was Kaufmann's successor as the expert on Guggenheim Museum additions, turned out to be a terrific advantage for us.

AP: You turned Edgar Kaufmann into your biggest and most important ally.

CG: It would have to have taken some overwhelmingly compelling argument to dissuade him. In other words, he was the prime mover in the initial ruling to have us revise our scheme. If he comes out for the second scheme and is still regarded as the expert—that is, changed his

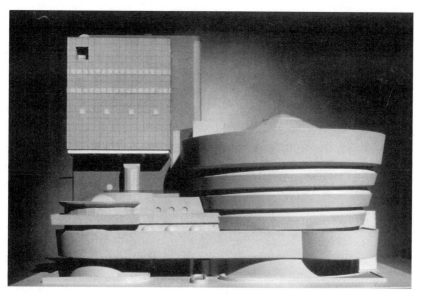

FIGURE 2-1
The first scheme: Model photograph of the proposed addition to the Guggenheim by Gwathmey Siegel & Associates that included space for art storage and conservation as well as increased exhibition area. Photo courtesy of Gwathmey Siegel & Associates.

mind and supported the other scheme—the opposition would require some much stronger argument. They did get William Wesley Peters, who designed the annex, to testify, and he both misrepresented his original annex and he was undoubtedly ailing, perhaps senile. I was polite in reminding him both of his writings and quotations about his addition, all of which contradicted what he said to the board.

AP: So it's at that point where you felt the public audience was on your side for the revised scheme?

CG: I think the public audience—the public legal audience—became swayed. We still had to go through that horrendous time-consuming process: After we got approval from the Board of Appeals, we then had to get approval from the New York City Council, which was a very emotional presentation because they ring the bell after two minutes, and you're supposed to stop talking, and I refused to stop talking. I said, "I've been testifying for four years, I've worked on this project for eight years, and no bell is going to stop what I have to say."

AP: How did they respond?

CG: They let me finish. And it was very convincing. I said, "The opposition has misrepresented, exaggerated, distorted, and it has actually, in fact, presented false conclusions throughout this process. We're at a time now where we have to reevaluate the word and the idea of preservation: What does it mean?" This whole presentation through the legal approval process was six or seven years.

AP: And the criticism was so frankly nasty.

CG: Oh, it was unbelievable. I was vilified. You know, I mean, I'm sort of a sensitive guy—believe it or not—sitting there and listening to people say these things about you—it's not easy when you know that you're honest and you know that you have history on your side.

AP: How did you handle the personal attacks during this process?

CG: You get a little bit thick-skinned; you also wait for the moment—as would a competitive athlete—you wait for the moment to find the weakness. So you have to be patient. And when you see an opening, you have to go in for the score. There's no question, it felt much like that.

AP: What part does charm play—or is it more how you educate people?

CG: I don't think it was my charm. I think that everyone realized that we had a very compelling argument: Frank Lloyd Wright *proposed* an addition and Taliesin West *built* an addition. There was history and precedent on our side that everyone was trying to ignore.

AP: Were you very disappointed about the rejection of the first scheme?

CG: Yes, I was. I was disappointed because I believed in the energy of it and the fact that it was much more contrapuntal as a consummate collage. It would have been controversial and dynamic but still in the spirit of the original building.

AP: But your arguments didn't seem to be quite as compelling or accepted for this first scheme in terms of convincing Edgar Kaufmann.

CG: Two things happened. One was that Michael Graves had simultaneously presented the first scheme for the Whitney and the whole issue was so hot—respecting existing buildings and status quo, and the preservationists were really out there beating the bushes. Paul Goldberger didn't help. The arguments were so irrational.

AP: Do you think you could have gotten the first scheme approved at a later point in time?

CG: I don't think we would have gotten *any* first scheme approved. I think the strategy that we finally understood in hindsight was that no matter what we would have presented first would have met with opposition.

AP: What would you do differently now? Would you have developed a totally outrageous first scheme?

CG: A lot of people thought our first scheme was outrageous. I don't think you can go back. I think the lesson lies in the proof of respectfulness, and understanding the ways in which we reconstituted the original building: The new work has enriched it, it has expanded it, and it still hasn't in any way detracted from it; and it's made it a living extension rather than a static, dying building representing an institution. I think the true test is when architects see it, and architects are not that generous to other architects, as you know, and they are unanimous. I mean that there's a sense about this that's so irrefutable in a way.

AP: That must be very gratifying.

CG: Yes, that's it. I think that, in the end, is where it's at.

AP: What about the strategy: You mentioned that no first scheme would have been approved.

CG: That's in hindsight. I think if we came back now and wanted to make an addition to our building and propose the bay window again, I think it would cause a huge reaction, but I think there would be a lot more sympathy toward it, given the proof of the reality. But I don't think that's going to happen—which is too bad.

AP: How did you adjust or develop your communications—both verbal and visual—to the different groups who were in positions to judge the design?

CG: What we realized was that each time the opposition was able to raise a question of doubt in the view of any board, we had to answer it. So we were always aware of, because of the process, positions that in general were going to be taken. We would establish our presentations to subtly address them (before they were stated by the opposition)—because the applicant goes first and the opposition goes second, and then we have a right to answer.

AP: So you tried to anticipate the specific problem issues?

CG: Yes, there was a certain amount of anticipation and definitely a certain amount of innuendo that we would cast before the opposition—

which would tend to defuse many of their arguments as they were being stated. It was done extremely unemotionally and factually, and we had terrific visual tools. We did terrific drawings, and we had documentation.

AP: It's interesting that with this very logical and informed presentation approach, you ran up against a stone wall with the first scheme. It still strikes me as a bit curious given the way in which you were so successful in getting the second one through.

CG: Well, it's amazing to me that the different perception of the schemes was so violent and so vast. I don't think there's such a big difference, personally. But I think the preconception of what was respectful as opposed to what was contrapuntal was a huge issue. The word "competitive" was used. The perception that our building was *competitive* with the original or *detracting* from it was driven by very emotional responses that were not about the history of intervention and collage, but were simply very conservative and subjective reactions.

AP: Did you have a difficult time at that point when the first scheme was rejected—going back and redesigning—was that a difficult step for you?

CG: That's a good question because I think typically one would, but at that point in time the new director came on board, whose vision of the museum was very different from our original client. He changed the program, which allowed the Frank Lloyd Wright building to be all exhibition-related. We shouldn't try to keep our storage on the site, and we shouldn't try to keep conservation, we should make this building the exhibition center and we should go off site—freed the program—and allowed us to reevaluate the program in a sense to make an uncompromised gallery flow.

AP: So you were essentially given a different project for the second scheme.

CG: Exactly. Which was a very fortuitous occurrence. In this case with the existing specifics and the constraints, we ended up with a more straightforward plan. It is about spatial integration of old and new. The organization responds to the ramp cycles and the interactions between the two buildings, with the idea of moving into the original, then out of it, then back in it again. The most controversial issue,

FIGURE 2-2
View of the expanded and renovated Guggenheim Museum from the northwest. Photo © Jeff Goldberg/Esto, courtesy of Gwathmey Siegel & Associates.

however, may have been the *image* of the addition as perceived from the west—from Fifth Avenue. The building that had become a cultural icon in New York City still is recognizable as such even though the museum has increased exhibition space and offices by over sixty-five thousand square feet.

Our original scheme, despite the fact that it included art storage and conservation, was still more or less about this spatial integration of the new and the old, as well as the renovation of the old. So it got clarified in the revision, and it certainly got refined because you continue working on something.

AP: But the major departure was the imagery.

CG: The major departure was façadal—which is a drag, actually.

AP: Is there anything more you would like to say about this project?

CG: I think the client deserves special mention. The Board of Trustees and the president of the board of the Guggenheim and the director were, despite immense pressure, absolutely committed to the realization of the project as an institution. And they never second-guessed us—which is part of the answer to, "What allowed us to carry on?" We didn't have the battle of the client saying, "We can't go through this anymore—let's retrench, let's reevaluate our whole philosophy." We were bucking the landmark date—that's what the opposition was really trying to do—to delay the process until the building turned thirty (in 1989) and could achieve landmark status [therefore postponing or preventing new construction].

AP: Your client, even though changed, was totally supportive all the way through.

CG: Yes. It had a lot to do with selecting the next director—I wasn't at the interviews but I knew his position coming in was in support of the addition. The other thing I think is true is that if you have an academic basis or a theoretical basis that can be both documented and supported by history and by factual interpretation as opposed to purely subjective, emotional references, then you are going to prevail. I don't think there's any question about that. It's whether you can stand it—that's all. The lesson in the end is that preservation is interpretive and that it doesn't mean simply restoring the status quo. It means there is a possibility for enrichment through interpretation that is both a tribute to the parent building and visionary as well. Visionary in the sense that a new person is coming to an existing condition and seeing something beyond it—which is possible.

AP: Was the change in program driven by, to a large extent, the negative reaction?

CG: No. The vision (which was supported by us 100 percent) was that if we could take the large rotunda and make it a referential space that was in the tradition of a courtyard or cloister, reinterpreted, without requiring it to accommodate *every* temporary exhibition, we would free something that had never been possible before. We weren't obligated to use the large rotunda only for temporary exhibition; it was an available space that could be intervened into creatively. And we had all this other new support gallery space that fed and referenced to it, allowing it to have the ability to, in a sense, free-float. So the whole dynamics of making the Wright building totally public and accessible and about exhibition, and 90 percent of the addition about exhibition—which is what brings the public to the building—I think this was a terrific reevaluation in strategy. This also helped us, by the way, in our later presentations, because what we were offering to the public was a view of Wright that had never been seen before. So culturally, intellectually, preservationally, archeologically—it all supports in my mind the idea of inven-

FIGURE 2-3
New seventh-level ramp and upgraded skylight dome. Photo © Jeff
Goldberg/Esto, courtesy of Gwathmey Siegel & Associates.

tive preservation that extends, enriches, counterpoints, and allows you
to see something both in the frame of history and in the frame of a new
set of perceptual dynamics—which I think is great.

AP: I continue to be struck by how supportive the client was throughout
this process.

CG: I think if they weren't, we never could have kept going. Because the
cost, and the delay, and the threat of coming to the Landmarks
Preservation Commission and not being able to do anything were so
pressing, to give up the opportunity to get something right was, I'm
sure, on their minds.

AP: Were you the only architect considered initially in the selection
process?

CG: We were retained to make a study of the existing conditions and to
evaluate the institution's goals. We learned the collection, thought
about the aspirations of what could be, and also defined a mainte-
nance/renovation program for the existing building, which, by the
way, was in horrible shape. I mean, it wasn't even insulated—did you
know that? It was a Gunite shell. The air-conditioning hadn't really
worked for ten years, there was no humidity control, and all the glass
was single-glazed—no ultraviolet filters. So over the years, systemat-
ically they just kept closing the building down.

AP: Your existing-condition analysis led to further exploration?

CG: Yes, I think an architect had to make a proposal for alternate possibilities. I think they felt very comfortable with us; they felt we were sympathetic to both the institution and to the building. The two-year "getting to know one another," and also having a reasonable reputation, just continued. I don't think there was any question about stopping and interviewing other architects after that happened. I don't want to use the word "lucky," but it was a way of backing into a major commission.

AP: You put yourself in an indispensable position.

CG: Unique!

FOR THE GLORY OF WASHINGTON[2]

Metro received a National AIA Honor Award for architectural design in 1983. The jury for the award stated: "The manner in which many professional disciplines and regional interests were brought together makes it one of the most successful public transportation projects of recent times." And Wolf Von Eckardt, then architecture critic for *The Washington Post*, wrote the following on November 20, 1971:

> [Metro] brings with it a quality of design that is rare in municipal architecture and unheard of in American public transportation since the great railroad stations at the turn of the century . . . suddenly there is noble spaciousness—a Roman vault with coffered ceilings, as in the dome of the Pantheon. . . . This time we really have something. This time the national capital region is setting new standards of excellence for the country and possibly the world to follow.

Occurring in 1966 and 1967 in Washington, this excerpt succinctly tells the story of Harry Weese Associates (the general

---

2. © 1994 Stanley N. Allan. This excerpt taken from *For the Glory of Washington* is under copyright by Stanley N. Allan, FAIA. Stanley Allan, chairman of Harry Weese Associates (HWA), Architects and Planners, based in Chicago, was the project manager for the Washington Metropolitan Area Transit Authority stations (which serve the District of Columbia as well as suburban Maryland and Virginia). HWA was responsible for establishing the architectural concept for all stations and structures, and coordinating the architectural design work with the engineering design team.

architectural consultant), De Leuw Cather (the general engineering consultant), the Commission of Fine Arts, and Washington Metropolitan Area Transit Authority (WMATA)—protagonists with design at stake!

Separate and Equal

Our Washington Metro client's approach to the design for the rapid transit system led to a decision to select separate engineering and architectural consultants, acting as coequals, each reporting directly to the National Capital Transportation Agency (NCTA), yet coordinating their work together. This decision grew as a result of many discussions in Washington during 1954 and 1955 among Darwin Stoltzenbach, John Rannells, Paul Thiry, Nat Owings, Henry Dreyfuss, Fritz Gutheim, Karol Yasko, Charles Horsky, William Walton, and many others.

This was an unprecedented breakthrough. Generally, all previous American public works projects were designed by the engineering professionals with very little if any conscious architectural design input. When Walter McCarter succeeded Darwin Stoltzenbach as the NCTA administrator, he endorsed this idea wholeheartedly. In a collateral action, the Office of Architecture was set on a par with the Office of Engineering.

General Architectural Consultant

Piloted by Chief Architect John Rannells, the NCTA took this approach in their search for an architect, keeping in mind San Francisco's recent architectural setback in the design of their stations for the BART system. Architect Don Emmons had been selected to provide an overall sense of design unity for all of the BART stations. Unfortunately, he was placed under contract to the joint venture of engineers. After a long period of internecine strife, he felt constrained to resign in the face of the engineers' determined opposition to his efforts to give BART stations a cohesive architectural character.

To avoid another architect–engineer standoff, Washington's architect was therefore to be directly under contract to the NCTA, independent of the engineers. It was clear that only by maintaining a certain level of independence could the architectural contribution lead to a higher state-of-the-art. John Rannells clearly understood the nature of his mission: to significantly improve the image of transit facilities, relate

FIGURE 2-4
Plaster model of the protostation vault built for the fourth presentation to the Commission of Fine Arts in October 1967. Photo by Stanley N. Allan.

this system in its setting in our nation's capital, and produce an exemplary system attractive to Washingtonians and visitors—both national and international.

One of our biggest challenges was how to impart our ideas constructively to the general engineering consultant (GEC). They had no way of knowing the extent of what an architectural concept meant. Was it to be merely decorative, devoid of structural implications, especially for underground stations where there was no exterior design requirement, or were the architects going to become involved in the structural design, too? At this point the GEC waited to see what we would produce and waited for us to show the extent of our architectural intentions.

We didn't know until years later, as confided by De Leuw's president, Jim Caywood, that there was, embedded in their contract, a requirement to pursue the design of the stations. And as Jim stated to me, they meant to do just that. So, unknown to us, we had adversarial roles. This fact underlines the dominant regard held by the engineering profession for the scope of their domain on large public works projects. Perhaps one of the GEC's strongest advantages was their assignment to perform all cost estimating for their work as well as ours. In retrospect, I don't think the GEC knew just what to do but wait for us to show our hand. They respected our firm's reputation and by common knowledge knew that Harry Weese was a talented and successful designer, well known in Washington by the cognoscenti, and quite likely prove to be a formidable protagonist.

The big issue the GAC faced, vis-à-vis the GEC, was that both were instructed to develop designs for column-free station train rooms. It was a contest between our vault versus their box.

Thus, the battle was joined between the two consultants, each pursuing the same goal but with different frames of reference and different educational and professional backgrounds. The engineers' experience since World War II mainly centered on designs for the Federal Highway Administration's vast national Interstate Highway Program, not to mention design of dams, bridges, and tunnels. Their transit background derived from extensive railroad design, construction, and operation experience, as well as work for the Chicago Transit Authority and the Toronto Transit Commission. They had little or no experience working with architects who, in this instance, had a clear mandate to establish the ultimate station designs. De Leuw Cather principals—Jim Caywood, Ken Knight, Bob O'Neill, Al Bumanis, and their staff of two hundred engineers—struggled through this difficult design process with us driven by their ingrained instincts as they saw their responsibility to create an economically feasible solution.

Amid all of this design activity, our client commissioned Ammann & Whitney, under the leadership of their president, Ed Cohen, to make a comparative cost analysis of the GEC column-free box structure versus the gravity arch station cross section. Simply stated, their engineering analysis concluded that when there was an overburden load in excess of fourteen feet, the arch was the most economical solution. Since all of the forty-five below-grade stations with the exception of two had an overburden load in excess of fourteen feet, the selection of the arched configuration was further supported by another substantial advantage.

As it turned out, our mandate was taken up by the Commission of Fine Arts (CFA). Working for a client heavily influenced by the advice of their general engineering consultant, we did not underestimate the need to gain approval of our design solution from the CFA.

So it became a joint CFA/Weese objective to balance the forces at work and prevail. The CFA members instinctively realized this unique

FIGURE 2-5
L'Enfant Plaza station of the Washington Metro. WMATA photo by Phil Portlock.

opportunity must not be lost: to select a design concept appropriate for the formal dignified setting in our nation's capital. Ultimately, this off-setting search for a suitable urban design approach was to eclipse the otherwise rational engineering proposals. The engineers had not been invited to these meetings. CFA members, significantly, were interested in talking only to the architect.

Third Presentation

Our presentation to the CFA on Tuesday, September 19, received the third rejection by its members. The meeting lasted more than two hours, during which the CFA members expressed themselves fully, articulating individual reactions to our presentation. At midpoint, Gordon Bunshaft compulsively seized one of our presentation boards and rapidly drew a sketch on its back. The sketch, showing a rough cross section through a protostation train room, replaced the stream of words or rather gave them a form—an idea he had had for some time. At the second presentation, in June, Gordon made an offhand comment that "The stations should be shaped like the inside of a thermos bottle, one station after another."

WASHINGTON METROPOLITAN AREA TRANSIT AUTHORITY

1634 Eye Street, N.W.
Washington, D. C. 20006

October 30, 1967

MEMORANDUM FOR: Chairman and Board of Directors

SUBJECT: Subway Station Design Concept

     1. Attached hereto is a copy of the transcript of the
October meeting of the Commission of Fine Arts at which the design
concept of the subway stations was discussed. It is a particularly
informative transcript of an important meeting, because there are
clear statements (1) of the Commission's unanimous and strong
support of an overall design concept, (2) of their response to the
specific reservation felt by the Directors as to the desirability
of the design concept and (3) of their serious view of their
responsibility to the public in the opinions they state.

     2. The transcript also gives an insight into the friendly
respect felt toward Harry Weese by Commission members who are themselves internationally eminent at the top of their various professions.
Through their attitude toward our consultant, these people have come
to feel themselves consultants to the Authority, rather than critics
or watchdogs, and as such are able to give guidance that would be
the envy of anybody able to assemble, and pay for, such talent.
Parenthetically, the American Institute of Architects is even now
scrapping expensive and thoughtful plans for their national headquarters because of the influence of this Commission. The A.I.A.,
as owner of a national landmark in Washington and as the official
body of American architects upholding aesthetics all around the
country, found their carefully thought-out design unacceptable. As
can be seen in reading the attached accounts, their President and top
people were not able to move the Commission from its position, even
after a joint meeting, and even such an "in-group" as this one is now
revising its plan.

     3. Significantly, however, our position is even less
tenable than that of the A.I.A. should we attempt, not to assert the
worth of one plan over the denial of the Commission, but to deny the
worth of another plan in the face of the Commission's unanimous and
laudatory approval. To deny being bad is no shame, but to deny being
good is a dangerous race to run because to win is to lose after already
having been awarded the medal. We can not defeat nor afford to try
to defeat the Commission on its own aesthetic grounds.

4. San Francisco's troubles have been mentioned often as something to be avoided at all cost, and while they are now mostly financial, there have been expressions by their own Directors that began, at least partly, as aesthetic ones. Their public furor over aesthetics was instigated by a consultant and siezed on by an eager press as a hook on which to hang suspicions, doubts, and innuendo about any person or aspect connected with the system. The idea of this Board turning away a conscientious, gifted, and famous designer who had the enthusiastic endorsement of the most prestigious group of consultants anywhere would surely open the flood gates to public doubts of the system and its direction, and create not just a bigger flap than San Francisco's, but could jeopardize our very existence in much the same way. And the course is a predictable one: a public question of aesthetics raises doubts of the Authority's concern for the public, doubts of their other consultants' work, and especially doubts of the validity of cost estimates. The system becomes a faceless bad guy and is fair game for anyone with a beef or a desire to gain public sympathy for a cause. The public controversy that ensues is not unnoticed by political and financial interests not necessarily directly involved but who nonetheless have an influence on the program. Finally, as the battle rages, the very voices of reason and calm that are needed are not available, through reluctance to join in what is by then a public brawl.

5. As with any question of taste or philosophy or human qualities there can be no right or wrong answer, only opinions, however formed. Just as there can't be a correct answer, nor proof ever demonstrated, the advantage lies with choosing the course that will support a change in direction later on. That course is to adopt the system concept that has been recommended; it need be followed only so long as it produces results that are acceptable. Whenever the consensus is that it produces a dull or drab product, that design can be rejected and the concept abandoned. The reverse is not true, however, because once abandoned the system concept cannot be recovered.

6. I can only recommend as strongly as possible that the course of temporal acceptance of the single design concept be followed, in the knowledge that it will not create a disastrous controversy, it will allow design and construction to proceed on schedule, it will allow economical design and construction costs, and it is a course that, unlike its alternative, can be altered should it be found unsatisfactory. This problem has now been under discussion for six weeks, and its immediate clearance is vital to continued progress.

Encls
as

Jackson Graham

This sketch was not lost on Harry Weese's quick intellect, connecting it with our earlier vaulted station design. He realized the situation was not so far from correction as one might think. It was time to recognize that we now had acquired an additional client—one who would not be rebuffed—whose ideas in effect would eclipse the approach dictated largely by engineering and budgetary considerations. This meeting proved to be the turning point in the balance of power over the nature of the solution. The commission members really interceded to become a design partner with Harry Weese through the sheer power of persuasion.

Jackson Graham's Memorandum

These experiences created an atmosphere that helped shape the client's general manager's [Jackson Graham's] next strategic move. His gift for simplicity and seeing through complex situations was here to give him the ultimate opportunity to make an agreeable recommendation to his board. He wanted no such controversy in the press such as BART had, nor one in front of the American Institute of Architects, much less a confrontation with the CFA. Armed with the imprimatur of the CFA, he was now able to go to his board backed by the CFA as well as WMATA's own architect, Harry Weese, to substantiate his recommendation.

On October 30, eleven days after the CFA approval, Graham submitted a memorandum to the board on the subject of the subway station concept design. The memorandum is reprinted on pages 51 and 52; it is self-explanatory and presents a brilliant case for acceptance.

The First Final Design Contracts

At the executive session of the November 3 meeting of the WMATA Board of Directors, Jackson Graham reviewed the status of the final design contracts to produce the bid documents for the first three stations: Judiciary Square, Gallery Place, and Dupont Circle. The first two had been contracted to Ammann & Whitney, with Kent Cooper as the associated architect, and the third to Kaiser Engineers. These contracts had been put on hold pending the outcome of the decision on the architectural concept. After a discussion of the situation, the board unanimously authorized the general manager to give these firms a notice to proceed, utilizing the general plan drawings prepared by Harry Weese & Associates and De Leuw Cather on the basis of the design concept for the vaulted station train rooms.

PENN PLAZA AND THE DESIGN REVIEW BOARD

Hartman–Cox Architects of Washington, DC, won the prestigious American Institute of Architects firm award in 1988. In more than twenty-five years of practice, they have consistently created buildings that are highly responsive both to surrounding context and to "multiple clients," as George Hartman, FAIA, would say. They are professionals who explicitly strive to provide genuine service to their clients, and aspire to contribute to the larger built environment—with all that the phrase implies.

The story of the design of a mixed-use project for a developer-client and the issue of responding to the criticism of design review boards, written by Mr. Hartman, is an extension of his architecture—concise, to the point, and . . . appropriate.

Penn Plaza

Sometimes, you have to put a lot of faith in your architect. In 1987, a major downtown developer was pulling out all the stops to get approval for a new mixed-use complex just off Pennsylvania Avenue. The block on which the project was located contained a number of historic buildings of various heights and materials, and Hartman–Cox had devoted much effort to design what was hoped to be an appropriate building for the site, with a modest tower to complement the Victorian turrets on the block.

The day of the crucial design review came, and we were scheduled to present late in the afternoon. Unfortunately, that day the review board was subjected to a plethora of towers; every new project seemed to include some overwrought projection. The board's mood was sour when the Hartman–Cox project came before them, and the verdict was disheartening: "The tower doesn't look right; take it off."

The developer was not happy. The logical response was to remove the tower and re-present the project. Upon reflection, though, this seemed the wrong decision. Maybe the review board was reacting less to what we did than to how we did it. We redesigned the tower, increasing its height by a full story and giving it better proportions. Understandably, the developer was anxious; they wanted an approval, not a tower, but they trusted us.

At the next review board meeting, we presented the new, taller tower. A nervous silence followed. Then a few nods were seen on the

FIGURE 2-6

A view of Penn Plaza, the mixed-use complex by the Washington, DC, firm Hartman–Cox Architects. The redesigned tower, a point of contention with a local review board, relates to the tower on the nearby post office and the Washington Monument, reinforces a pivotal corner point in the L'Enfant plan, and also recalls the towers traditionally associated with Washington apartment buildings. Photo by Alex Washburn, AIA, courtesy of Hartman–Cox Architects.

board members' faces. "We like it. The tower looks right. You fixed the problem."

In essence, it proved wise to listen closely to the review board, to read between the lines, and to respond to their concerns rather than their specific suggestions. They identified the problem correctly; we fixed it.

Politics, Feelings, and Details

I wanted to know more about George Hartman's reactions to the review board's criticism, his feelings about redesign, and his relationship to the client. I arranged for an interview.

Hartman responded in predictable fashion: "Don't add too much extraneous junk to this simple little article!"

Hartman's elaboration portrays and further clarifies artful politics in support of design excellence, insight, and experience.

We recognize the existence of multiple clients. The client is *not* the owner of the land, *not* the design review boards, *not* the lender, *not* the tenant, *not* the person in the street, *not* the architectural press—*the client is all of them.* We are comfortable with the notion that just because somebody's hired us and is paying for our services, they are not the client; they're simply part of the client. You have to be a politician to make this point to the person who writes the checks. It's probably no accident that we're practicing in Washington. One needs to deal with a very broad constituency, and we try to show concern and respect for this larger constituency. Urbanism, that is, the preservation and enhancement of the built environment, is one of those things that we feel we need to practice. We don't always succeed in getting this message across to our clients, but we often succeed.

Relative to Penn Plaza: The tower modification *was not* a compromise (although I don't think there's anything inherently wrong with compromise). There were two components to the review board's criticism. One was identification of a problem and the other involved some specific suggestions to address the problem.

The Pennsylvania Avenue Development Corporation Board was *right* about the tower and *wrong* about what they told me to do. It's very easy to see the problem when you've spent some time on these boards—how you solve the problem is another story—there are many ways to skin a cat. We did not compromise the idea of the tower; we fine-tuned it without changing the fundamental character of the original concept.

There's no sense taking the tower off for one agency and having another agency that's already approved it say, "Where the hell is the damn tower? It had a tower when I approved it!" Then you get caught in a battle between two agencies, and anybody can look at the design and see that it's worse as changed. That's an indefensible position.

What's interesting and unique about this is that when you have really good people on review boards such as George White, Carter Brown, or David Childs—when you get three opinions of thoughtful, gifted, talented, perceptive, and highly experienced reviewers—you begin to understand that the stuff that they see wrong is indeed a problem. Now, what to do about it? I can't solve anything instantaneously in my own work, so it's unreasonable to expect that anybody else on a review board can do it. So you take the concern and deal with it, not the specific suggestion. *I've never seen a project that didn't benefit from further study.*

I remember one time, before I was a member of the Commission of Fine Arts, I was bringing in a project for Harvard University—Dumbarton Oaks—here in Washington. As we were presenting (the client was there, of course), I was showing two slide carousels, almost like an art history lesson, so everyone could see what this was about. Carter Brown said, "Left screen: Back up three, please." I knew right then I was in trouble. I backed it up and Carter said, "Have you noticed how the existing building intersects previous additions? Why doesn't your work relate in the same way?"

I paused for a minute and looked at it and said, "There's no sense in your watching me think—I didn't see that, and if it's all the same to you, I'll see you next month." When I came back a month later, Carter said, "That looks much better now; are you comfortable with this?"

I said, "Absolutely. I just didn't see it." The client was horrified, but it went right through, bingo, this time. And it *was* better.

When you have a consensus of the review board, then you almost always know you have a problem to deal with. You can sometimes have a member say something and someone else will disagree—you don't have to deal with it. On the other hand, note who is making the comment and if it is justified—you might end up with a better building.

The Role of Education

The important thing about our relationship with clients is that I spend as much of my time on *education* as I do on anything else—on my education and the education of our employees, consultants, clients, and public. When I talk about design, I'm talking about the relationship of buildings to their surroundings, to their users, to other buildings, and, of course, by extension, of buildings to their parts and parts to the buildings. Education is a wonderful thing because it's irreversible.

How do you effectively educate? *You spend a lot of time with people and you look at a lot of buildings with them.* Sometimes when we attempt to educate clients, and have explained an issue several times, they say, "Hartman, that's bullshit!" Maybe it is. And we have to rethink it.

Our clients tend to be supportive but also demanding and exacting. They will certainly come to us and say, "Okay, the job is high, I told you it was supposed to be thirty-five million dollars and it's thirty-seven— we've got to get two million dollars out of it. Fix it." Then there's the famous Mike Prentice line, "Hartman, how good is this estimate?"

"It's a good estimate—it's really close."

"How close?"

"I'm sure it's within ten percent—I promise you it is."

"Hartman, do you know what ten percent of fifty million dollars is?"

The estimate then got a lot closer. We have good developer clients and, by and large, they're repeat clients: Prentice Properties, Trammel Crow, Prudential, and Boston Properties. They hire us for appropriate jobs. One of the things that smart clients do is match up the architects with the jobs. One of the things that smart architects do is match up the developers to the job. We don't take every job that is offered, even in these terrible times. We try to do work that is consistent with our practice and interest. We also don't work for clients who don't know what they're doing. We want a client that will pay a fair fee, has a fair budget, and a realistic time schedule. Most successful, smart people are educable; however, not all of their employees are, I've found out.

The lesson of this article is a very useful one. It's important to separate *what* is being done from *how* it is being done [Lou Kahn]. Remember Kahn saying he'd rather be doing the right thing badly than the wrong thing well. Of course, what you've got to do is the right thing well.

CHAPTER 3

COLLABORATION VERSUS COMPROMISE

Architects and clients working together—collaborating—to create a great design is clearly a superior alternative to sacrificing part of what each party wants or believes. There is a fine line between diluting powerful ideas—compromising—and developing beautiful designs to be most responsive to particular circumstances, requirements, and preferences. The skillful architect can educate clients about possibilities perhaps never imagined and can develop what Bill Lam calls (in his interview in this chapter) a "shared vision of project objectives," all toward making architecture. Helmut Jahn, FAIA, of the Chicago firm of Murphy/Jahn, concludes that "Our best work comes from clients who know and support us because our goals match."

Walter Gropius, the quintessential collaborator—at least among colleagues—had a policy in his office (The Architects Collaborative or TAC) for resolving the problem of too many or conflicting ideas in the design process. Sarah Harkness (a TAC partner) has quoted Gropius as proclaiming that to "safeguard design coherence and impact, the right of making final decisions must be left exclusively to the one member who happens to be responsible for a specific job, even though his decision should run counter to the opinion of other members."

Charles Moore (whose inspiring story of designing a church together with its congregation appears next) has a slightly different take on the collaboration/compromise issue. Invoking "Goldilocks and the Three Bears," Moore has said, "The extremes (too hot/too cold, too big/too small, or too hard/too soft) can be troublesome and uncomfortable but the balanced middle ground can be a pleasing compromise [that] is for me as admirable and truthful and meaningful and pertinent as any philosophy."

COLLABORATION AT ST. MATTHEW'S

The late Charles Moore, FAIA, was perhaps the most brilliant and service-minded architect of our time. The fact that his accomplishment must be explicated in this way is a sad commentary on the public perception of what an architect is supposed to do. This image has, in no small measure, been perpetuated by the portrait of the malignantly narcissistic Howard Roark character in *The Fountainhead*. That the architect is used as vehicle for Ayn Rand's views and is so misrepresented in such a popular book (an estimated hundred thousand copies are sold annually) has, in part, resulted in an enduring focus on some of the negative aspects of the profession. (Revisit the often quoted Roark statement: "I don't intend to build in order to have clients. I intend to have clients in order to build.")

Architects who conduct themselves like Charles Moore, the antithesis of Roark, are not few and far between. His story of active client involvement in shaping the design of a church is a wonderful model: It demonstrates that beautiful architecture does not have to be created in a vacuum, does not have to be a unilateral vision of a single individual, and does, in fact, require heroism—to innovate, to compromise in some ideal sense, to learn, and to develop a meaningful, interactive relationship with the client.

Talented and secure architects are not only willing to accept clients at face value, but are also interested in eliciting input from representatives of all building users. Incorporating ongoing dialogue with the client into the design process and translating these data into an appropriate physical response are the only way a building can ultimately be considered beautiful.

Written just before he died in December 1993 (at age sixty-eight), Mr. Moore's fascinating account of a project executed with his Santa Monica–based firm, Moore Ruble Yudell, Architects & Planners, is below. (He was an AIA Gold Medalist and former dean of the

School of Architecture at Yale and chair at Berkeley, won numerous competitions and design awards, and was the author of several books including *Water and Architecture*, published in 1994.)

Around 1982, Buzz Yudell, John Ruble, and I were approached by an Episcopal congregation to design a new church in Pacific Palisades, a wealthy western suburb of Los Angeles near Malibu. Their original church had burned down in a forest fire, so they were in need of a new one. Since the parish had just emerged from a long, drawn-out conflict over the selection of a new rector (after its rector of some thirty years retired), they perceived themselves as not being able to agree about what day it was.

When the congregation started planning for the new church, they decided to include in the architect's contract a clause that any design would have to get a two-thirds vote of approval before construction could begin. We, Moore Ruble Yudell, were somehow hired with a general warning that no one would ever get a 67 percent agreement out of that parish on any subject, especially a design. We could imagine that, and thought that the only building the group would ever agree upon would be one that they had designed themselves with our professional help. The possibility of developing our own brainchild and then peddling it to them was out of the question, even if we had wanted to do that (which we didn't).

Facing such a task, we called on the services of Jim Burns, who had pioneered participatory design in his years with Lawrence Halprin. He helped us to organize and plan open design charrettes [or workshops] scheduled into four Sundays, each about a month apart. The first was spent in what Californians call an "awareness walk," looking over the site and filling notebooks with observations and possibilities for the site of their new church. Then we came back to lunch in the garden of the parish house and people worked on big scrolls of butcher paper putting down their dreams and strictures about the place they wanted. Then we went into the temporary church and brought out the materials of design and model construction: Froot Loops, cellophane, school scissors, paper, and parsley. (Parsley is great for models because it wilts quickly so nobody can get infatuated for long with what has been produced.) Froot Loops represented people, so that bits of the cereal could be easily lined up, moved around, and arranged in various seating configurations. Each person or group made a model of how the church should be, with many serious discussions about how things should relate to each other. By the end of that session, people had made quite beautiful churches.

An important discovery we made early was that when we really pushed something, we lost it. It worked best to let the parishioners generate the ideas, and then to coax them into architectural expression. We sought to translate their ideas, including the contradictions, directly into design, while giving the church a clear sense of being connected to the site and to California's arts and crafts tradition. One contradiction that we had to accommodate somehow was the longing for seating in the half round, but under a classic Latin cross plan with a nave and transept. They wanted to get as close to the altar as possible, but they didn't want to go so far around it that they were looking at each other. Another hurdle involved finding consensus between high-church parishioners and low-church parishioners. One high-church lady thought that lofty ceilings were mired in sin and offensive to God, while many low-church members vociferously wanted high acoustical ceilings to accommodate strains from the organ.

The magic moment occurred at the end of the second workshop when the participants all had the same plan. By the end of the workshop, we had a working plan that pleased everyone.

Next, we thought it might be interesting to make a kind of Rorschach test of slides, all mixed up, with two questions to be responded to for each of the eighty slides. (1) "Do you like this?" And (2) "Would you like this for St. Matthew's?" It turned out that although they had all kept saying that they wanted a dark wood church (the former church had been that), the three slides of Alvar Aalto's white church in Vuoksen-niska [Imatra, Finland] were the leading vote getters. The church that received the fewest and most negative votes—emphatically, "We do not want this for St. Matthew's"—was St. Peter's Basilica in Rome. Too Catholic, too expensive. So we at least knew something about what they did not want.

The third workshop involved our coming together with a set of building shapes in model form that would cover the plan shapes that they had come up with. The parishioners were asked to consider those and make whatever contribution of plan and enclosure that appealed to

FIGURE 3-1
Charles Moore (foreground) and members of the congregation during one of the participatory workshops for the design of St. Matthew's Parish Church in Pacific Palisades, California. Photo courtesy of Moore Ruble Yudell, Architects & Planners.

them. They came with drawings and were not afraid to give us rather strong orders: "More glass to the ground!" (The rector was opposed to this one since he didn't want his sermons to be in competition with the squirrels outside, but the feeling was very strong and he did some compromising.) But again there was almost complete agreement on what they wanted it to look like as well as what they wanted, and how they wanted it to function in plan. So we drew the results of their desires with a half-elliptical seating arrangement under a Latin cross roof with a bell wall, which has since turned into a tower, with lots of glass to the ground and a very simple interior.

We presented the drawings, made a model, and left it all for a month for the parishioners to ponder. After proposing some slight changes, they put it to vote, and we got an 87 percent positive response where we had needed 67 percent, and there was enough invested enthusiasm to propel the money raising even a little past its goals so that there were funds, for instance, for the bell tower.

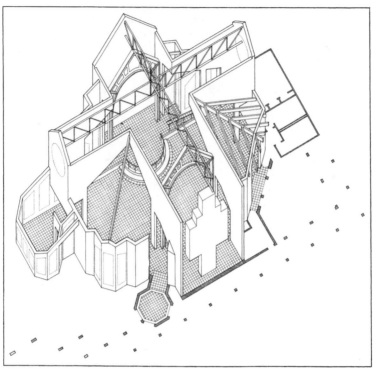

FIGURE 3-2
Axonometric drawing illustrates that there is indeed a cruciform, though masked by other forms branching out at the ground level in addition to a number of hipped roofs. This responds to the parishioners' wish for semicircular seating within a more traditional sanctuary. Drawing courtesy of Moore Ruble Yudell, Architects & Planners.

St. Matthew's is at once a simple chapel and a church with a rose window in it. It gives out double signals. On the outside, the broad, hipped roof is low at the edges, rising to a cruciform in the center, and cut away to create little courtyards and patios. Inside, the liturgical celebrations are framed by "triumphal arches" that carry visible steel trusses, with the arc of the pews mimicked above by arcs of lighting. The surfaces are made with Douglas fir battens applied to heavy plaster walls, so they are rich both visually and acoustically. With the considerable help of Tina Beebe, we made color, both painted and natural, an integral part of the church. Our goal was to balance equal amounts of artificial and natural colors—painted steel and plaster along with the Douglas fir, clay tile, and granite. Color also helped clarify the

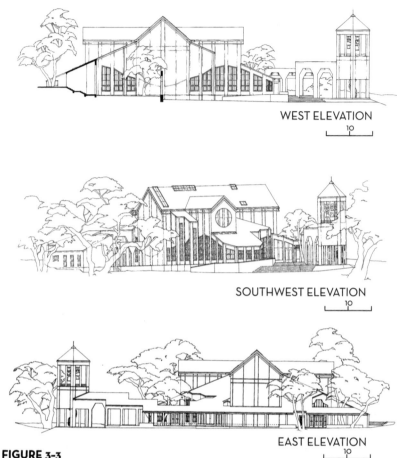

WEST ELEVATION

SOUTHWEST ELEVATION

EAST ELEVATION

FIGURE 3-3
Elevation views reveal a more domestic scale at the perimeter, ensuring a
good fit in the surrounding residential neighborhood. The contrast to the
grand scale of the sanctuary is at once intimate and awe inspiring. Drawings
courtesy of Moore Ruble Yudell, Architects & Planners.

building—green and cool on the outside, rose and warm on the inside.
We also managed to squeeze some art into the budget, so that a tree of
life, a lectern, and a crucifix add layers of Christian symbolism.

The church was built and even won an AIA award. I'm often asked if
we didn't feel a diminution of our creative satisfactions in sharing all these
design decisions, and I have to admit that part of the province left to us
involved putting a Latin cross roof over a half-elliptical floor plan, which
seemed like something Alberti would have responded to enthusiastically.

For me personally, the chance to be involved at St. Matthew's is evidence of the value in making a great paradigm shift from yang to yin or at least fanning a little bit of the wings of change. Being a part of making that church was an opportunity to work toward an architecture filled with the energies not only of architects but of inhabitants as well, and helping people to find something to which they can belong.

THE CLOSEST KIND OF COLLABORATION

When an architect's client happens to be his wife, the Fountain-headache could turn into a raging migraine. But when James Stage-berg, FAIA, a Minneapolis architect, designed a writer's retreat for his wife, Susan Allen Toth, all they found they really needed to work well together was trust, flexibility, and an occasional aspirin. Asked to comment on their collaboration, they decided to report on it directly, with equal time, in the following dialogue.

James Stageberg, principal with The Stageberg Partners in Minneapolis, Minnesota, is also a professor of architecture at the University of Minnesota. He and his wife, Susan Allen Toth, wrote *A House of One's Own: An Architect's Guide to Designing the House of Your Dreams* (Clarkson Potter, 1991). He is now working on a memoir about his life as an architect, tentatively called *Architect: A Life on the Straight Edge.*

Susan Allen Toth's latest book, *My Love Affair with England: A Traveler's Memoir* (Ballantine, 1992), was published in paperback in 1994. She is now preparing a collection of travel essays about England, many of which first appeared in the *New York Times* travel section, to which she is a regular contributor. Her other memoirs include *Blooming, Ivy Days,* and *How to Prepare for Your High-School Reunion.*

Susan Allen Toth (SUSAN): When James promised to build us a weekend retreat, a place where I could hide out and write, he asked what kind of house I'd always wanted. "An English country cottage," I told him without hesitation.

James Stageberg (JAMES): Of course I had no intention of designing something with a thatched roof and leaded windows. I'm a modernist architect, always hoping for an ideal design of simplicity, clarity, and functional elegance. But I knew what she meant. She wanted something cozy, yet distinctive. "Cozy" is a word that has become unfortunately rather unfashionable among contemporary architects. I think it means a house that is welcoming, modestly sized, warm—a shelter, not a show-off. To create that kind of cottage, without being cute about it, or phony and quaint, was a real challenge.

SUSAN: I mentioned color, too. English cottages themselves aren't usually brightly painted, but they're surrounded by wonderful gardens, jumbled-up blues, greens, yellows, pinks, and reds. Winter in the Upper Midwest has its own palette of color—grays, black, white—but that isn't enough to sustain me for months on end. I wanted color with a capital C!

JAMES: I also had to take into account our stunning site, a wooded Wisconsin bluff about four hundred feet above Lake Pepin, a widening of the Mississippi River. So I tried out many versions of a design for Wind Whistle (the name borrowed from an English pub, because of the terrific winds that often blow over the bluff). Some of these were pretty awful, some not too bad. I illustrate these try-outs in the book Susan and I wrote about Wind Whistle and house design in general, *A House of One's Own.*

SUSAN: I deliberately didn't look at any of these early versions. I didn't try to advise James on a design in any detailed way, because I just can't visualize an architect's plans in three dimensions. I had a hard enough time with plane geometry. And I trusted his skills. I'd already lived for several years with him in a house he'd designed. It was the first modern house I'd ever really liked. Most of them made me feel very cold; I can't stand a lot of chrome, icy surfaces, too much glass, no clutter. And I knew he understood how I felt about light, for instance, which I love. I did say things like, "You know I like to lie in bed and look out of a window into the trees."

JAMES: The final design has a dramatic cat-slide roof in front, swooping down over the guest bedroom. The whole roof is covered in cedar shingles that have been left to weather—about as close as I could get in a midwestern climate to the feeling of thatch. The entrance side looks out over woods and a patch of meadow, which Susan promptly began to convert to garden areas. Our own bedroom, on the river side, has two sheltered walls, but on two sides it overlooks the cliffside trees. Susan can also look up through a skylight into the top branches.

SUSAN: When I saw that swooping roof, it did make me think of an English cottage—as though a little house were tucked beneath. Inside, the spaces felt right too, not so big I'd feel lost in them, and well separated. I hate rooms that all run into each other. I want walls, doors, lots of privacy. We once toured an architect's house that had a master bathroom with side-by-side toilets. No, thanks.

JAMES: I did get some grief from Susan about her study.

SUSAN: I told James my ideal was a room of my own upstairs where I could pull up a ladder after me. Well, I didn't really expect a ladder—how would I carry a computer up and down?—but that was my vision. So he did give me a room on the second floor all by myself—it's really the only room at the top of a winding stair—but then he couldn't resist adding a small sauna for himself just above, next to a crow's nest on the roof. And I turned out to have a ladder, but it is a ladder that starts in my study and goes up to the sauna!

JAMES: Since we almost never have guests at Wind Whistle, and I'm the only one who uses the sauna, there wasn't much traffic in and out of Susan's study. But she grumped about it.

SUSAN: I also hadn't expected the number of architectural friends, potential clients, past clients, and so on who asked James to give them a tour of the house. Every architect's wife (or husband) will know what I mean. A painter has a gallery where people can look at his or her work; an architect has a house, and people have to walk through it.

JAMES: So two years ago, when we were in England, visiting Monk's House, where Virginia Woolf had once lived and worked, we saw her small studio at the back of the garden. I knew immediately that was what I had to do for Susan. When we got home, I tramped around our five-acre lot until I found a place on the wooded bluff where I could just fit a one-room studio.

SUSAN: I call it my retreat from our retreat. This time I really did get my ladder, in the form of a short bridge. It isn't a drawbridge, but it gives the same effect. *Nobody* walks across without permission.

JAMES: When we built Wind Whistle, we also had some vigorous discussion about colors.

SUSAN: It wasn't so much discussion as a confrontation between two very opinionated people. James had always preferred natural woods, and he was known for his imaginative use of different shadings and

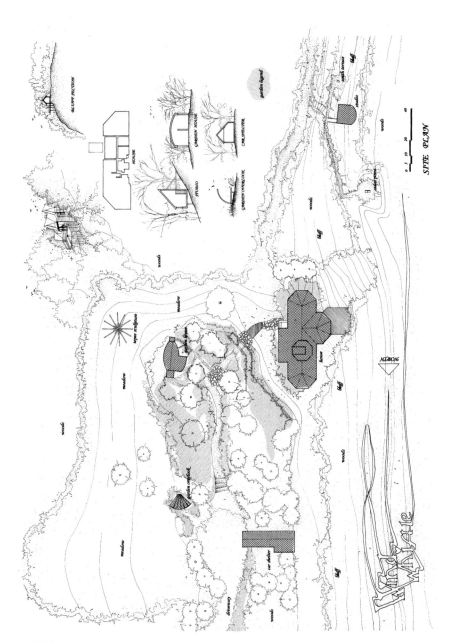

FIGURE 3-4
Collage of plans, cross sections, and perspective view of Wind Whistle.
Drawing by James Stageberg, FAIA.

COLLABORATION VERSUS COMPROMISE **69**

grains and so on. But I wanted color, outside as well as inside. I remember when the house was finally finished, ready for painting, and James and Larry, our builder-carpenter, stood outside with me, pointing out how beautiful the cedar shingles were in their natural state. Larry said, "How could you *possibly* want to put paint on that wood?" But when you live with an architect, after a while, you learn not to be easily intimidated. I pointed out that I *was* the client.

JAMES: I knew better than to push too hard. So we picked the colors together, and I hoped for the best. But the day we drove down from Minneapolis, after the exterior had been painted—lemon yellow, with apple-green trim, and accents in a sort of pinkish red and mauve—I was plenty nervous. When we walked out of the woods and stood in front of the house, I really blinked hard.

SUSAN: I loved it.

JAMES: Actually, before long, I did, too. Susan trusted me about the design, and I (mostly) trusted her sense of color. We were so relieved that we both liked the exterior that we decided to experiment with color on the interior as well. I decided to have the ceilings given an unusual treatment. They are all wood, number-two knotty pine boards. Grant, our painter, applied a colored stain, then rubbed it off, leaving a color that still revealed the graining in the wood. In the living room, the largest space, the soaring ceiling is a soft blue, like the sky. In the hall, the ceiling is green, in another room, pinkish red. I had Grant prepare different samples so Susan and I could pick the right tone. We wanted what she called "garden colors."

SUSAN: We had some discussion about wallpaper, too. Modern architects I knew never used wallpaper. It was practically a dirty word. But I wanted some floral designs on a few of the walls.

JAMES: And she got them. I told Susan that of course we'd have to agree on something special enough to justify my covering up those handsome walls. We eventually found some marvelous Swedish hand-screened wall coverings, with very clear and bright colors, one with tulips, another with peonies. I felt fine about using them—sparingly.

SUSAN: That's really how we worked most of the time. I knew James would never agree to anything that damaged his design, and he knew the general effect I was looking for. We both ended up delighted with the results.

JAMES: In fact, the only real problem with Wind Whistle is that Susan now wants to be there all the time. My office is in Minneapolis, and so we do a lot of driving back and forth.

SUSAN: I think it is a great advantage to be married to one's architect. In our case, James knew me so well he could anticipate my needs almost without my asking for them. When I did really want something, I could fight for it straight out, without feeling timid or worrying I'd be upsetting him. James can be tough-minded, but he's no Howard Roark. I read *The Fountainhead* when I was nineteen, and I thought Roark was thrilling. But he'd be hell as a husband. And actually, when I think about it, he'd be hell as an architect, too. Can you imagine what Roark would have said if I'd asked *him* for an English country cottage?

CONTEMPORARY-TRADITIONAL IN FLORIDA

ANCHORMAN: How does it feel to lose everything? You have no house, you have no transportation, you don't know if your children are alive—how does that feel?

HURRICANE VICTIM: Oh, God.

ANCHORMAN: There you have it. Reporting live from the field, only miles away from my own winter home, I'm Jim James.

It was a near-perfect commission; a call from a local celebrity, a request for help in designing a second home/dream mansion in Florida, and a budget to match the scale of the project. I say "near perfect" because the constraints were significant and would have an impact on how much freedom I would have in creating a design. Still, I jumped at the opportunity to become involved, and today, in light of the pleasure my client derives from the completed work, I have no regrets—actually, I suppose I do have a few regrets, and these have yet to be resolved.

The basic issue has to do with compromise. Is it more courageous to listen and respond to the client, or to remain unyielding in standing behind some ideal, perfect creation? As a professional who takes some pride in making the people I serve happy, I routinely compromise to some degree—perhaps the use of one color or finish over another. Until this project, I had never compromised on the core of a design concept. Assuming that it was sufficiently strong and clear, "massaging" details without sacrificing content should be feasible. At any rate, this was the philosophy I took into my first meeting with Jim James, anchorman.

One other variable in the compromise equation of this project was the novelty and importance of the work as my first house—a completely new, big building. To have this successfully executed project under my belt would be a notable credential. It is essential to refer to past experience to be taken seriously and to go after similar projects. So it would not be unreasonable to assert that I was more likely to be "flexible" in the service of designing the James house.

"Traditional home styles are preferred by three out of four respondents," I read with a sinking feeling from parts of a survey published in the *USA Today* I had picked up before boarding the flight to Orlando. Though I was grateful and even gleeful about the prospect of authoring a building, I still hoped I would have some freedom to design something really creative. At least a semitropical setting presented a very different environment for me, and Mr. James was a rare and different type in his own right. As we descended into the haze of central Florida, I was, however, decidedly uneasy about what lay ahead.

I rented a car at the airport and headed to my first meeting with Jim, at the Dolphin, one of the Disney hotels. The familiar voice was even more resonant than it was on television: "You must be the one I had Julie hire, it's Andrew, right? I remember the interview I did with your brother, what was it, a year ago, after that plane crash out at O'Hare, yep, he had good advice for those poor families of the dead."

When we finally finished with the protracted greetings and introductions, we got down to business. Jim James had photographs of neighborhood houses that he admired; he wanted a large "contemporary–traditional." The house was to serve not only as his occasional winter home, but also as a year-round getaway for the entire James clan. This rather impressive extended family included James's brother Jerry, who had three young children, a wife, a nanny, and a car dealership. The last element had something to do with a requirement for a three-car garage and on-site space for two or three other vehicles.

I returned home worried that I would design something that would be antithetical to anything Jim James would approve. I imagined a voice from *The Fountainhead*—of Roark's mentor—who warns him about the course ahead:

One day, you'll see on a piece of paper before you a building that will make you want to kneel; you won't believe that you've done it; then you'll think that the earth is beautiful and the air smells of spring and you love your fellow men. . . . And you'll set out . . . to have it erected . . . but only hear your voice begging him, pleading, your voice licking his knees, you'll loathe yourself for it, but you won't care, if only he'd let you put up that building . . . you'll want to rip your insides open to show him, because if he saw what's there he'd have to let you put it up. But he'll say that he's very sorry, only the commission has just been given to Guy Francon. . . . That's your future, Howard Roark. Now, do you want it?

In what I always regarded as not too much more than a cynical gothic romance, the two pages containing the mentor's soliloquy took on a power and meaning I had not previously appreciated. My concern began to grow into anxiety and then raw fear.

How do you hold back, how do you compromise, how do you put all of yourself behind an effort that isn't you, or, like Roark, do you simply not do it at all—or maybe you dynamite the completed work if it has been tainted? This was not the way to sit at my board and start sketching.

I was blocked, frozen by the gravity of all I had to do, by all the potentials of a first house, and by all the limitations in a task that was very much "real world." At this point, my associate came into the picture. Like the good psychologist-physician he is, Peter knows when to deliver a kick. Not only was he unsympathetic, but he also virtually ignored my tortured self-examination. The only thing he said after listening to my own soliloquy was, "Wanna play some tennis?" When this failed to elicit the desired response, he gave me the kick: "Andy, someday you'll have played the game long enough and well enough to have a chance to contribute the way you want to; in the meantime, as the folks at Nike say, 'Just do it.' Call me when you feel like hitting a few—my backhand needs work." Actually, he doesn't have a backhand and never will, but I believe he was right about me and the greater scheme of things. *Perhaps it is the very tension between practical exigencies and ideals that motivates innovation and keeps creativity tied to the solution of mundane but significant problems.*

Bold lines on yellow trace form bubbles of primitive spaces that echo the requirements of Jim James. Diagrams take shape, now superimposed

FIGURE 3-5

A napkin sketch (top) and the built project (bottom) represent alternative schemes. Common to both is a response to specific site factors: A series of hip roofs cascade down from a height of thirty feet (above the family room) to nine feet (at the garage level). The smaller roofs face the street, and echo the scale and character of adjacent houses. Sketch by Andrew Pressman; photo © Dan Forer.

FIGURE 3-6

This series of photos reveals the grand family room as focal point of the design. The skylit double-height volume is at once airy and light-filled, and secure and intimate with its framework of columns, half wall, and step-down. A second-story bridge that rings the family room serves as a dynamic connection of the master bedroom suite in one wing with the children's bedrooms in another. Photos © Dan Forer.

on the site plan. An occasional moment of inspiration leaps in with remembrance of a house designed by Frank Lloyd Wright, Charles Moore, or Richard Meier. The process of finding your way into a scheme is not linear or logical, and it is different each time you do it. The initial graphic compositions may have little to do with the final design solution, but may serve as a foundation for further exploration that does yield a key. Then, when you think you've wrestled something out of your soul and expressed it on paper, you build a model. Chipboard, Elmer's glue, scissors; rip it apart, change something, rebuild it—for me, this is the architecture of architecture.

My associate and I were back at Fred's Place, this time with chef's salads and Evian water (as we gradually aged with the practice, we became health-conscious). I talked about the project as Peter listened, nodding occasionally. My client, Jim James, was very much on my mind. He was a man who knew exactly what he wanted; I didn't elicit or detect anything other than what he dictated, and if I'd had some insight, he would not have heard my thoughts on the matter. I was an instrument, a tool for translating Jim's vision into a form acceptable to the building department. That I ended up putting heart, soul, and experience into the translation meant that it was special, professional, even though it was not close to a work of art.

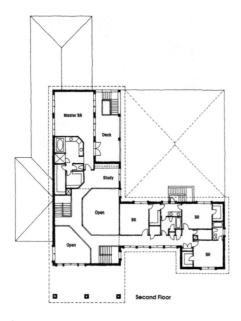

FIGURE 3-7

The L-shaped floor plans of the new sixty-five-hundred-square-foot house present narrow masses to facilitate cross-ventilation, and wrap around a screen-enclosed pool and deck. Rooms have inviting views into the pool area, promoting observation of children at play. Design and drawings by Andrew Pressman.

FIGURE 3-8
Deep overhangs reduce solar gain, and tall palms provide shade without blocking breezes at window level. Photo © Dan Forer.

While I knew that the design was not novel enough to merit coverage in one of the major journals, I was nevertheless satisfied with the work. Orchestrating the players was no small victory: The client insisted on major design changes late in the process (and even considered abandoning the project for a completed builder-home), and the contractor made unilateral decisions without appropriately consulting me. In spite of these hurdles, the house reflects a sensitivity to the client's needs and preferences, and region-specific characteristics of the site, climate, context, and construction techniques.

A COLLABORATIVE IDEAL

Bill Lam is not only a renowned lighting designer (based in Cambridge, Massachusetts) but also a consummate politician in jobs in which the client assumes an active role. What does this really mean? In many of his firm's more than two thousand projects, he has demonstrated success at educating clients about the benefits of good design. I asked Lam to elaborate on his team design process and to generalize about the roles of architects, clients, and consultants.

Client Input

"Take advantage of the client as a significant design resource," says Lam. "Sometimes there are wonderful suggestions and the design evolves into a better project." He enlists people as allies and collaborators in the design process, simultaneously educating them about time-honored design principles. Designers should *want* to make changes and disregard preconceptions if the project can be improved. Lam cites an example in which a client (the Boston Public Library) made the designers aware of historically important inscriptions that are sculpted into the frieze of the existing building. In the daytime, they are visible but not generally noticed. Rather than illuminate the façade uniformly, Lam aimed lights directly at the inscriptions, which now, for the first time, invite passersby to read them.

> If a client has a bad idea, we may still try it in model or mock-up form, or find a similar built example to analyze. If our own reasoning is sound, we should be able to demonstrate that a poor solution is indeed bad—to the satisfaction of the client.

Lam is quite frank about his methods to keep clients not only invested in the project but excited. Obviously, the client's support is critical to the success of any project. Moreover, Lam implores designers to accept the premise that most clients (the real users, owners, and decision makers) are sophisticated and should be able to understand the rationale behind design decisions. Architects have a responsibility to communicate clearly, and he says that this forces the designer to really know what he or she is talking about. According to Lam, clients should simply not accept the attitude, *Believe me because I am a great designer.* Rather, the architect's attitude should be, *I'm not doing it my way, I'm doing it* our *way.* Accountability for design decisions should be of paramount concern. Lam believes that "Clients should be wary of designers who do not want to listen to them, who would rather be secretive about the design process, and who only present their completed proposals rather than discuss alternatives with a preference articulated. The best client is a strong client who is also willing to listen."

Design by Team

Lam advocates a team approach to preliminary design, and refers to the Caudill Rowlett Scott concept of "squatters" in which client, architect, engineering consultants, and other specialists meet at the site to brainstorm. Values are clarified and design ideas are developed. Perhaps most important for complex projects, systems integration is facilitated with explicit multidisciplinary collaboration resulting from the face-to-face interactions. This bit of extra work up front promotes efficiency during the design development and construction documents phases, and a better project overall. There are inevitably fewer reversals of concepts at later stages.

On numerous occasions, Lam has challenged mechanical engineers, for example, during these early team meetings, to innovate. It is clear that integrated concepts cannot evolve successfully without the participation of all relevant disciplines. In Lam's experience, structural engineers are typically the most cooperative in working with architects, but they, too, have preconceptions about framing given a certain configuration and size of a building. What the "good ones" share is a desire for excellence; given the motivation and a shared vision of project objectives—which require designing in a nontraditional manner—they *will* collaborate in moving toward this end.

With the right mix of personalities, the team approach to design can be quite synergistic. Lam describes the ideal session:

> In most of the major projects that I've done involving complicated building systems, the essence of the design is created in the first meeting. It is enormously gratifying to be able to engage all of these people and reach agreement. We don't dismiss the design session until everyone is satisfied with their portion of the work. It does, however, require the best-qualified people, and those who can make decisions on behalf of their respective offices. These jobs are 10 percent inspiration, 90 percent perspiration, and after an exciting meeting, there is still much work to accomplish.

Therefore, rapport and sensitivity among individuals is essential so that meaningful dialogue can continue. An individual has to care more about results than his or her ego. The ideal client participant here is the real user, owner, or decision maker.

Lectures and Field Trips

The lecture and field trip are Lam's one–two punch for educating his clients, which he views as an essential first step to develop a consensus about what constitutes a good building. Only then can the principles be applied to the particular project, and be fully appreciated. Lam says that it is crucial for all the key players, including clients and consultants, to meet at the same time and develop a common language and shared values.

The field trip is typically a critical exploration of both good and bad buildings (mostly bad) that includes visits to Lam's projects. Clients are usually favorably predisposed to appreciating them, reports Lam. Clients say, "That's the kind of building we want to build." Selling and educating are dramatically *intertwined*. Moreover, the field trip serves to generate enthusiasm, overcome preconceptions, and develop an understanding of innovative design ideas—in a relatively short period of time.

The lecture with accompanying slides reinforces the learning in the field with the theoretical underpinnings and rationale of the specific design features. Lam talks about everything from what a good environment means to construction details. He adjusts comments to relate to the local experience. For example, he will take slides of buildings on the way from the airport to the client's office to illustrate principles. And Lam will utilize the lunch break for a minitour of familiar buildings to examine concepts and details. Lam attributes much of his success in dealing with clients to these lectures given at the beginning of projects.

The scale of the project and the design budget will modify but not eliminate Lam's collaborative approach. With small-scale work, his involvement is concomitantly reduced, perhaps involving only the development of concepts following a one-hour rather than one-day field trip. He feels that work in the residential arena, for example, is a huge, largely untapped market for this sort of professional consultation.

Bill Lam's greatest strength and satisfaction lie in guiding the design process—the manner in which he educates clients, and describes and

FIGURE 3-9
Washington Metropolitan Area Transit Authority illuminated presentation
model of a typical subsurface station. Lighting effects were simulated with
custom-made lengths of neon tube. Lam says, "Inexpensive study models
[such as this one] are one of the most economical means of generating
productive discussion within the design team itself." William Lam
Associates (lighting consultant), photo courtesy of Harry Weese
Associates.

then solves problems. While there are many common elements across
the body of his work, each project reflects the unique characteristics of
his client constituted by the makeup of the design team (those archi-
tects/engineers that retain him), and the particular circumstance. Lam
clearly enjoys opinionated clients who are not shy about expressing
their preferences and requirements. He feels that direct client involvement forms the basis of an appropriate design response along with his
own values and personal style. This is what distinguishes Bill Lam and
his work—and makes him both a great designer and politician.

FIGURE 3-10
The Rosslyn Station of the Washington Metro. Bill Lam's lighting system design integrates beautifully with the structure and furnishings. The brightly illuminated ceiling vault counteracts the effect of subterranean gloom, and minimizes feelings of claustrophobia and visual noise. Photo courtesy of the Washington Metropolitan Area Transit Authority.

WORKING WITH SPECIALTY CONSULTANTS

Gary W. Siebein is a registered architect, and is principal consultant with Siebein Associates, Consultants in Architectural Acoustics. He is also professor and director of the Architecture Technology Research Center, which specializes in architectural acoustics at the University of Florida.

Gary Siebein writes about the need for architects (as well as their clients) to recognize situations in which an engineering specialist would be invaluable to collaborate on design. Smart politics means that the architect, as leader of the team, surrounds him- or herself with appropriate experts. Architects are not educated to know everything; the issue of retaining consultants is not a question of diminishing the role of the architect or losing power, but is very much part of managing a complex process.[3]

> Technology has reached the stage where buildings no longer fall down: But they are often inconvenient and uncomfortable because the well-known laws of nineteenth-century physics have been ignored well into the twentieth-century.
> —Henry Cowan, *An Historical Outline of Architectural Science* (Elsevier Publishing Company, Amsterdam: 1965)

Scene 1: Who's That Knocking on My Floor?

We were hired by a condominium association to undertake field testing and expert witness work for a large, luxurious complex on a beautiful barrier island in south Florida. The condominiums had sold for $250,000 to $500,000 each. They were initially provided with a bare concrete slab for a finish floor, and the Condominium Articles prepared by the developer prior to sales stated that carpet would be installed throughout the building. Many owners did not like carpet. They wanted to install handmade tiles from Mexico, marble from Italy, exotic wood flooring from the rapidly vanishing rain forests, and other beautiful, expensive, difficult-to-install, and *noisy* flooring materials in their units. This is usually not a problem in the large single-family homes in

---

3. *An Acoustical Consultant's Perspective.* © Gary W. Siebein, 1994.

which many of these owners had previously lived. They hear only themselves walking up stairs. Many were not prepared for the realities of condominium living. The owners complained:

The guy upstairs walks across the floor with his damn golf shoes at five o'clock every morning. It sounds like he's walking in my unit.

The couple two floors up goes out dancing all the time. They come home and who knows what they do up there but her high heels make quite a racket.

Why does anyone take a shower in the middle of the night? It sounds like Niagara Falls down here when someone upstairs flushes the toilet.

The building formed an efficient, continuous sound distribution system for the footsteps on the floor, the sliding of furniture, and the vibration of plumbing pipes. The case settled out of court. The lawyers for all parties involved probably each own a new Jaguar; the architect, developer, and contractor will face an increase in their liability insurance premiums; and the people living in the buildings will probably never undertake the extensive, disruptive work needed to actually make the renovations to solve the noise problems.

SCENE 1 LESSON.
(1) Let the buyer beware. (2) Listen to buildings; they will speak to you. (3) Architect: Think of the users of the building.

Scene 2: Do People Really Want to Hear in an Auditorium?

"We spoke to the architect and he said that providing good acoustics was not within his scope of work for the project."

"What do you mean?" I responded.

My new client elaborated: "We called him because we felt he should fix this. I mean it's awful—we can't understand a word that's said in the room. He said that he designed the building, not how it sounds. That was not in our contract, it's an extra service. He didn't tell us anything about this while we were working on the project. We just want to get it fixed. We *can't* use the room the way it is."

"I think we can help," I added reassuringly.

The committee chair, in disbelief, acknowledged that his group had a brand-new building that had to be renovated before it could be used for its intended purposes.

This is how my conversation began with the chairman of the building committee of a community center with a five-hundred-seat multipurpose auditorium with a small stage. He was calling for advice on how to make his recently completed building usable (not perfect, just usable). I met him the following week during a site visit. The building was beautiful but technically deficient.

"What do you use this room for?" I asked.

"Tonight we've got bingo. The people sit right there at the center of the stage with a microphone on the table. On Friday, we're going to have a potluck dinner; on Saturday, we've got a local dance band performing on stage; and a new church is thinking of renting the room on Sunday mornings until they build a building of their own." He continued, "People can't hear very well in the building at all. It sounds all garbled, one word runs into the next. What causes this? Why does it sound so bad?"

"It's really no mystery," I said. "The high ceiling, hard building materials, and angled side wall panels create a long period of reverberation in the room. When someone speaks from the stage, the sound reverberates from every surface in the room for well over two seconds. Each syllable persists in the room long after it is spoken. This is the same thing that happens to a greater extent in a large cathedral."

I had to resist my university professor's habit of delivering a lecture on every subject discussed, including explaining the historical significance of the experiments of Wallace Sabine, a young professor at Harvard, in the late 1800s who first quantified this phenomenon and established the scientific basis for architectural acoustics. Sabine was actually presented with a room with similar acoustical problems by the president of the university, and was asked to improve its acoustical qualities. As an untenured young instructor, he worked diligently for over five years in an ambitious experimental program. He would take seat cushions from the theater across the street and place them on the walls and ceiling of the room. He would sound an organ pipe and measure with his stopwatch how long the sound reverberated in the room after the organ pipe stopped. He would work late at night so the sounds of the streetcars and other city noises would not disturb his work. Each night he would add more cushions or put them in different locations in the room. He was finally able to determine the relationship between the persistence of sound in the room and the quantity of seat cushions in the room. We know this quality as reverberation time.

I added, "When the room is used for dinners, sound from people talking to each other at the tables builds up in the large volume of the room so that they probably end up shouting back and forth. The more people there are, the louder they talk. As it gets louder in the room, they talk even more loudly so they can be heard over the din. They are also probably distracted by sounds from other tables reflecting from the angled ceiling surfaces. These sounds compete with their own conversations and disorient them as to the location and content of their dialogues."

Should the acoustical qualities of the room be the responsibility of the architect? No one asked us; but our answer would have been a resounding *yes!* The acoustical qualities of rooms are a direct result of their architectural design: The shape, materials, volume, and so on all influence the sound of the room. It was the architect's responsibility either to deal with these issues herself or to engage the services of a specialty consultant to assist in these matters.

Unfortunately, many of these problems could not be corrected at the stage of the project when we were first consulted—only symptomatic improvements could be made. An extensive diagnostic procedure involving field measurements and computer simulations identified problem surfaces and materials in the room. The sound system was redesigned. Several months later, after this additional work was completed, the community had a building they could use and enjoy. During the initial design, had someone considered that people may actually want to hear each other in an auditorium, an even better room could have been built for less money, and the community could have been using it all along.

SCENE 2 LESSON.

Too often, specialty consultants are not part of the design team for many projects. Acoustics are considered only in "problem" buildings such as open-plan offices, factories, hotels near airports, and so on, or in special buildings such as radio stations and theaters.

Every building has an acoustical environment that is designed as the building is designed. Sometimes this is designed with specific intentions and sometimes it is left to chance. When it is left to chance, the results are usually less than satisfactory. Look for specialty consultants to help the owner, users, and designers achieve the goals to which they aspire on each project. A carefully chosen consultant will complement the assets the owner and the architect bring to the project.

Most important, learn to know what you do not know! In other words, be keenly aware of situations that require additional assistance in a specialty discipline even on seemingly simple projects such as the one described above.

Scene 3: The Vacuum Cleaner Analogy

"If it doesn't make a lot of noise, people won't think it cleans."
—anonymous vacuum cleaner salesman when asked by the author if a quieter model was available

The building was completed. The contractor wanted to receive a Certificate of Substantial Completion. The owner would not accept the building because of excessive noise from the heating, ventilating, and air-conditioning system in all rooms. This problem took five years of design and construction to create. The owner expected an "expert" from out of town to come in and solve the extensive noise problems in five days with little cost and no modifications to the building so they could move in right away.

SCENE 3 LESSON.

You don't have to hear it to be cool. A frustrating part of a consultant's work is the renovation of recently completed buildings to meet the expectations of owners and users of the buildings under very tense situations.

The role of the consultant and the probable success of the project are severely compromised in these situations. The retrofits are expensive and time consuming. Walls that have already been built are taken down. New walls are built. The building cannot be used for some periods of time. The results are never the same as if the issues had been considered within the context of the total design solution from the beginning; and they are always more expensive.

Doing It the Right Way from the Beginning

A much-preferred role is for the consultant to be involved with the design team from the beginning of the project. Often, acoustical design concepts, if discussed during programming or in a schematic design meeting, can result in simple changes to a design that can improve the acoustical qualities of the building and also improve the overall design with little or no cost. The consultant's participation in job meetings is essential. A specialty consultant can translate the qualitative statements of the owner or user into design criteria, organizational concepts, and building systems that can be used in the design of the building.

During design development, the consultant works to implement these goals in planning and zoning the building in concept, preliminary selection of construction assemblies, and preliminary design of sound systems and other equipment; participate in budget reviews and value engineering (cost cutting) meetings; and provide a general review of the overall architectural and engineering scheme to ensure that it meets the programmed intentions.

During the construction documents phase, the consultant will produce special details where required, specify sound system and other specialty equipment, continue participation in budget reviews, and review the work of the rest of the design team so that the total building package will meet the design criteria and concepts formed during programming and schematic design.

Construction administration is also necessary from the consultant's perspective. Meeting with the contractors who will perform sound insulation details is helpful to teach them the importance of attention to the details of sealing and penetrations in walls, floors, and so on.

Architects will frequently wait until the construction documents phase to engage a consultant. They mistakenly think this will save some of their hard-earned fee for themselves. Unfortunately, the results are often more time consuming for all involved because the design scheme must be substantially revised late in the process. It is also embarrassing for an architect to approach a client shortly before bid date with organizational revisions to an already accepted scheme that are required to solve acoustical problems.

In summary, learn to work productively with consultants as important members of the design team. Don't try to save money by waiting until late in the design process to hire consultants, who will then be unable to satisfy the needs of the project. Hire the consultants for full services for programming through construction administration. Listen to the consultants' recommendations carefully, especially regarding the necessary scope of work and the difficult trade-offs that are often required between the many complex factors in every architectural project.

CHAPTER 4

FOREIGN AFFAIRS

Globalization of architecture has become a reality: American firms are following their clients and designing buildings all over the world. And just as American businesses are expanding internationally, so too are foreign entities conducting business and requiring facilities in this country. Washington, DC, area architect Marvin Cantor, FAIA, tells a once-in-a-lifetime story of a foreign government awarding him a commission to design a chancery in the heart of the district.

A special kind of political understanding and conduct is essential to successful navigation of local ways and customs. Roger K. Lewis, FAIA, writes about his stint in the Peace Corps—also a singular and enlightening experience.

In the first section, Stanley Tigerman, FAIA, has assembled several amazing vignettes from over thirty years of practice. Only the last one is a foreign affair. The other three are set stateside, but are sufficiently exotic that they earned a place in this section.

EMOTION AND ETHICS IN ARCHITECTURE

Perhaps one of the most thoughtful and reflective architects of our time, Stanley Tigerman, FAIA, has written and built extremely provocative work worldwide. He was more than a little upset with what he perceived to be a negative connotation in the theme of *Curing the Fountainheadache*. Tigerman has said that *The Fountainhead* was and continues to be influential in his life. It is the heroism of going against the grain that motivates him to sometimes outrageous and often noble goals, as he illustrates below.

Tigerman is a partner, with his wife, in the Chicago-based architecture firm Tigerman McCurry. He has taught widely in the United

States and abroad; he has written four books, including *The Archi-tecture of Exile* (1988), and there have been numerous books and articles on his award-winning projects.

We all have war stories, horror stories, wonderful stories about clients, situations, buildings—things that we've been engaged with as architects. But rather than dwell on, as you called it, "the Fountain-headache" side of things—architecture is too optimistic for me to find "downers" or, even worse, ways of mocking situations and so forth. So I would rather just tell you a whole bunch of vignettes of the *really good* things that have happened to me because, for me, these thirty-plus years that I've been in my own practice have *not* been a "Fountainheadache." They are actually a fulfillment of the raw, unbridled optimism that I always saw in the book *The Fountainhead*.

Two projects that have wonderful stories associated with them occurred fairly early in my practice, and involved remodeling barns into houses. The first barn, in Wisconsin, was done for a couple who had inherited a piece of land near Burlington, Wisconsin, that had a barn on it. They came to me to remodel the barn into a house. I did. They loved it. They spent a lot of time there; they lived in Chicago, but it was a weekend house for them.

Over time, in one of life's tragedies, she contracted an incurable disease very prematurely in her life. Then, the most remarkable thing happened. As she began to disintegrate, she still looked terrific, but her husband, knowing that she was going to die, started to lose weight, became increasingly morose, and generally looked terrible. Everyone around him knew (and certainly as the architect, I knew) what was happening.

The woman did an extraordinary thing, right out of a movie from the late 1930s or early 1940s with Myrna Loy in which she played the part of a woman who was dying. Her husband, who loved her very much, started to go to pieces. Seeing this, she fixed him up with their daughter's piano teacher, making sure that the teacher was invited to various dinners and was seated next to her husband—while the wife was still alive. There was a kind of transition between the wife and this other woman—a passing of the baton.

It worked in the movie. It worked in real life too, because the wife, observing her husband deteriorate, found a young woman colleague whom she situated in proximity to her husband. At one point when her condition was irredeemable, the wife took a one-way plane trip to Switzerland, checked into a hospice, and died with dignity. Sure enough, the husband, as he experienced this tragedy, became closer to this young woman, and they ultimately married. This is the kind of story that I like.

The second story involves another barn conversion in Michigan that I did in the late 1960s/early 1970s. It was actually one of the nicest projects I had ever done for two of the very nicest people I have ever known. We got along wonderfully—they were fabulous clients.

When the job was finished, I came to my office one day and there was a big crate from them with a little envelope—a bread-and-butter thank-you note. I opened the crate, and it was a case of 1936 Château Lafite-Rothschild, which in 1970 was worth a ton of money. The note said how unhappy they were now that this was all finished and they were disappointed that we just could not continue. This is the kind of story that I frankly cherish!

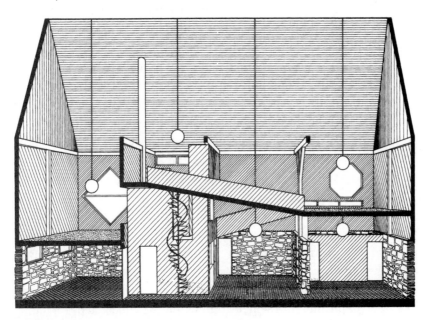

FIGURE 4-1
Barn conversion into a weekend retreat in Burlington, Wisconsin, for a Chicago couple (1969–1972). Section-perspective drawing courtesy of Stanley Tigerman.

You see, for me, architecture is the kind of discipline wherein you are supposed to bring joy to people. When they respond and correspondingly return that joy to the architect, those are the sort of things I choose to remember. I'm not sure that I would want to relate so-called horror stories. Books are read by lots of people and rather than be amusing and clever, considering that some young person might pick up a book like this, I would want some stories (albeit perhaps in the minority) of at least one architect who gave and received a lot of joy. So if there is a legacy that I'm going to leave, I would want others to follow in those footsteps. We are supposed to bring each other joy in this world. And architecture is one of those things that can actually do it. You can create pain and difficulties, or you can create joy. It's not that my life or my practice is problem-free, but this business of the architect playing the villain—the arrogant bastard—who is arcane and does not communicate is not my idea of architecture.

Another story involves a guy who came to me in the middle 1970s wanting to do a house in Indiana in the Dunes. He was crude and crass, and he owned strip joints in Calumet City and formerly in Key West. More impressively, he recently had a double colostomy, which was the manifestation of terminal intestinal cancer. He wanted to build a house for himself and his wife and two daughters. I thought that was fabulous. I didn't know what to do in the beginning. I didn't know how to handle it. Nobody ever came to me to do a house when they were dying, for God's sake. I ultimately came to realize that this was wonderful (talk about optimism!). It was a constructive act of a person who, even if he knew exactly how far down the tunnel the light was, nonetheless was going to go out in a blast. So what do you do for a guy like that? What kind of house do you do?

I designed this vulgar, so-called pornographic house that I took a great deal of joy in doing because *it made the guy laugh,* and that was the point of it. It brought a lot of joy to him at the end of his life. He was difficult—aren't we all?—he knew he was dying. He was very demanding. But this house really made him happy: It was erotic; it was shaped like an erect phallus with semen coming out the end as steps cascading down the hill. But the house had a certain "stylishness" that was almost therapeutic, if you can imagine such a thing. He loved recounting what that house meant, and the fact that it made him chuckle. That's the kind of stuff, as far as I'm concerned, that's really important to do.

FIGURE 4-2
"Frog Hollow," barn/house conversion in Berrien Springs, Michigan
(1973-1974). Sketch by Stanley Tigerman.

Sometimes what you do as an architect and as a person that is really important is at a much larger level or scope. For example, for a period of ten years, I worked on a series of polytechnic institutes in what is now Bangladesh, but I began the project when it was East Pakistan. I worked collaboratively with a wonderful man who was my classmate in my master's program at Yale in 1961.

As all young people in graduate school often do when they are really good friends albeit halfway around the world from each other, we swore that we would find some way to spend more time and work together. Sure enough, he structured a situation that brought me to Dacca in 1964 through the vehicle of the World Bank, which was in the process of funding these five vocational training institutes in five jungle villages with the government of East Pakistan.

The years passed. In 1971, our five projects were under construction in the five different locations. In 1971, the struggle for liberation in East Pakistan began against Islamabad and what was then West Pakistan to attain independence in what has since has become the People's Republic of Bangladesh. During the course of that struggle, my friend had been instrumental in engaging in dialogue with a certain sheik, using his

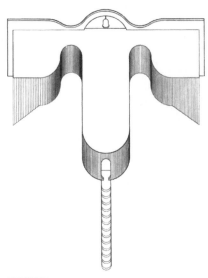

FIGURE 4-3
"Daisy House," a private residence in Porter, Indiana (1975-1978). Entrance axonometric drawing courtesy of Stanley Tigerman.

office as a place to coalesce ideas and even to foment revolution. I was witness to many of these proceedings.

When the actual war began, I was back in Chicago and I started getting correspondence from our various site offices of what the revolution really meant with respect to the projects. One of the workers was killed, several of the staff at different sites were beaten up by the Pakistan army, and so forth. I decided that I couldn't engage in that any longer, so I wrote a letter to my classmate, who by then had fled to Calcutta. I said that I thought I was going to resign the commission because I couldn't maintain the kind of distance you have to maintain working for a government—West Pakistan—which was in the process of reducing East Pakistan to an agricultural land by killing the intellectuals by genocide.

I then founded the Bangladesh Defense League, I raised money for guns for Bangladesh, and finally, in September 1971, I went to Dacca and I told our Pakistani client that I just couldn't continue anymore, that I was very upset, and that I was going to resign the commissions. I took a plane to Bangkok and then doubled back to Calcutta to see my classmate, who had arranged a press conference. I resigned. I said that it wasn't my role nor that of any architect to structure situations in which people who are employed by me are killed as a part of another agenda.

I added that I hoped that when Bangladesh became a free state I could finish the projects.

By December of that year and into January 1972, it finally became an independent Bangladesh. One of the first acts that transpired was to get me reappointed. But the World Bank (I think under pressure from the U.S. government) had not liked the fact that I had resigned, in other words, that I had become, to use their term, "political." They resisted my reappointment. But in any case, the People's Republic of Bangladesh prevailed, and I was in fact reappointed.

I finished the projects, and there are two postscripts that are very interesting in my view: One is an "upper" and one a "downer"; one occurred almost immediately and one occurred practically yesterday. The upper happened in 1974 when I went back for my last trip to see the projects inhabited and participate in a bunch of ceremonies announcing the beginning of the operations of the polytechnic institutes. I'll never forget in Pabna, on one of the sites where a ceremony was taking place, a young boy, a student who had no arms and had only one leg, presented me with a plaque for my courage in speaking out on their behalf. Mind you, I was able-bodied—he was practically destroyed by that war, and he was congratulating *me*. You can imagine the emotion that I felt.

The downer occurred recently when a professor of urban planning from Calcutta came to Chicago in 1993 to invite me to a conference there. He had actually invited me two years earlier but presumably because of the Persian Gulf war, the conference was postponed, or, in any case, the funding from the USIA was curtailed using the rationale of the Gulf war. This gentleman told me, just recently, that the reason that my funding didn't come through was because the U.S. government did not want me to go back because they felt that I had been "political."

If these stories are useful, maybe they stand in counterpoint to others who will be happier to tell horror stories and war stories in their practice and in their career. I think architecture is obligated to try to heal, to put Humpty-Dumpty back together again. These little vignettes are examples of many more that I could tell you. They are very important in understanding how these experiences have shaped my belief in a moral and ethical basis that underpins a discipline like architecture. If that basis does not exist, there really is no promise in something that is detached from human emotion. Architecture is supposed to reinforce those human emotions and our optimistic belief in the perpetuation of the species—not our belief in the bomb. I think it is a field that, at its best, ignites passion from a moral and ethical foundation.

A PROJECT DIES BECAUSE A COUNTRY DISAPPEARS

Marvin J. Cantor, FAIA, has been a principal in private practice since 1960 in the Washington, DC, region. His clients have included many foreign governments for projects related to their operations and activities in the District of Columbia. Mr. Cantor has been honored by the American Institute of Architects with many leadership and service awards. Also noteworthy is his sense of humor, which in no small way must account for his success and longevity in the profession.

In Mr. Cantor's tale about the design of a chancery for a foreign government, worldwide political events collide with the politics of the architect–client relationship. The message here is that while two parties may communicate and compromise quite ideally, there are forces over which no one has control, and these will occasionally determine the fate of any project.

We have all heard the stories of projects failing because of the client's inability to secure financing, the city's zoning board denying a sought-after variance, the market demand drying up, and so on. But how often does a project evaporate because the client, a sovereign nation, disappears from the world map? This is one such story in a lifetime.

By 1981, the German Democratic Republic (GDR), popularly known as East Germany, had logged diplomatic relations with the United States for more than twenty years. East German officials decided it was time to investigate moving out of an eighth-floor office rental space in downtown Washington, DC, and into an impressive new chancery building ("as would befit a first-class sovereign country") in the international center of Washington. Accordingly, the office of Marvin J. Cantor, FAIA, Architect, was retained to start preliminary planning for this effort. The start was auspicious, but shortly thereafter, a combination of world events brought the project to a standstill: the Soviet occupation of Afghanistan, the increasingly harsh enforcement of the Berlin Wall barricade . . . the cold war heated up, and international relations with the Eastern Bloc sunk to the barest minimum short of breaking off diplomatic relations. The project entered a deep freeze!

In 1985, a fresh breeze blew into the Soviet Union. Mikhail Gorbachev became the country's new leader, and embarked on his famous policy of *glasnost* and *perestroika*. In 1986, Gorbachev paid a visit to President Reagan, taking time off to stop his motorcade on Connecticut Avenue and shake hands with DC citizens, and a new era of "friendship" with the Eastern Bloc countries began. Early 1987 brought renewed interest in the GDR's proposed chancery, and once again, Cantor's office began the planning process. This time, however, following a period of international unrest that had terrorists targeting all types of establishments, with embassies and chanceries heading the list, the GDR foreign office supplied what it felt was an appropriate architectural solution to its Washington Chancery (see Figure 4-4).

The fortresslike, mausoleum quality of the design could not be overlooked, and Cantor, realizing that the Washington, DC, Office of Planning, the National Capitol Planning Commission, and the Commission on Fine Arts would all have to approve the project eventually, immediately turned the proposed design down, indicating that it, "Just would not fly in DC." Instead, he came up with a new design (see Figure 4-5) that resolved the problem of security for the sensitive offices while maintaining an open and inviting "office building" type of exterior that would still possess the monumentality a foreign country might like to achieve in its proposed new mission outpost.

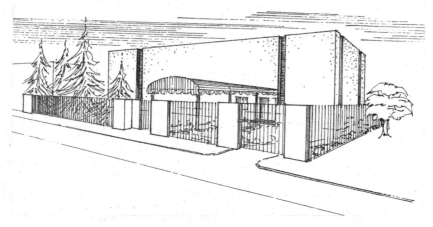

FIGURE 4-4
Preliminary design sketch of the proposed chancery developed by the German Democratic Republic's foreign office.

FIGURE 4-5

Design of the proposed chancery of the German Democratic Republic in Washington, DC, by the office of Marvin J. Cantor, FAIA, Architect, of Fairfax, Virginia. Rendering by Hossein Rashtian.

The design was essentially a square doughnut organization with the most sensitive offices opening from a central atrium, and protected around the outer perimeter of the building by corridors and nonsensitive spaces. The vertical circulation and service cores were located at the building corners, whose windowless façades served to anchor the building and provide the grand scale that the clients demanded.

From early 1987 until late 1989, the planning process moved forward; the government agencies mentioned earlier had all given the green light to the preliminary designs, and construction documents were then started, and finally completed in early 1990.

But in November 1989, the Berlin Wall came down! How, why, and when are subjects that will occupy historians for decades to come, but the inescapable fact was that the wall came down! Now talk of unification of East and West Germany started to emanate from both countries; however, without question this would be years, even decades into the future. At a diplomatic reception in December 1989, when then GDR ambassador Gerhardt Herder was asked about it, his reply (roughly paraphrased) was, "It will be a long, arduous process; we are two separate people with two distinctly separate forms of governments, two different ideologies, and dramatically different responsibilities for World War II. [It seems that all of the unrepentant Nazis went to West Germany, and all that was left in East Germany were those Germans who never really were in favor of Hitler's policies or actions.] Unification is but a dream, now we must proceed without question on the chancery to its completion!"

In May 1990 the construction documents were completed, the bid invitations were prepared, and the bidders' list was narrowed to those who would be asked to submit prices on the building's construction. All that was necessary was the final United States State Department clearance to issue the plans. However, between January and May of that year, events in the two Germanies were moving with unprecedented speed and surprise! And at the end of May, the earthshaking announcement that the USSR would not oppose the unification process put the final piece of the puzzle in place. Unification had become not only a viable future dream, but an almost immediate reality! No plans were issued, and when East German marks were converted to West German currency on July 1, 1990, the official word came down that the GDR was on its way to extinction. The impressive and detailed model of the building was returned to the architect (where it now resides in silent splendor), the final contractual fees were paid in full (as client, the architect felt that they had behaved in the finest tradition), and the project was consigned to the dustbin of history!

THE HOSPITABLE TUNISIANS

In the first of several intriguing contributions to *Curing the Fountainheadache*, Roger K. Lewis, FAIA, describes a truly unique and memorable relationship with clients in an international arena.

Roger K. Lewis is a practicing architect in Washington, DC, and a professor of architecture at the University of Maryland. His weekly column, "Shaping the City," appears in the *Washington Post*. Professor Lewis authored *Architect? A Candid Guide to the Profession*, first published in 1985 by The MIT Press. His projects have received many AIA design awards and have been cited in both the popular and professional press. (His cartoons are a personal favorite of mine, and are scattered throughout *Curing the Fountainheadache.*)

Of all the clients I have ever worked with, my favorite were those I served when I was in the Peace Corps in Tunisia.

Just out of architecture school, inexperienced yet eager and self-confident, I spent two formative years—from 1964 to 1966—as a volunteer architect working for the Tunisian Ministry of Public Works.

I was among the first architects stationed in the ministry's regional office in the small town of Nabeul, the seat of government of one of Tunisia's fourteen provinces. For many years there had been no architects, private or public, in this region of the country, the North African peninsula reaching northeastwardly toward Sicily. When Tunisia gained its independence from France in 1956, most of the country's French and Italian architects returned to Europe, leaving Tunisia with no one to design buildings. Thus local officials who governed the province and its towns waited enthusiastically, project commissions and funding in hand, for architects to arrive.

Almost weekly, mayors, provincial delegates, and directors of various civic organizations walked into our office and, after the requisite salutations, proceeded to describe their site and what they wanted built on it. Then they departed with the expectation that, within days, the ministry and its youthful American architects would complete the necessary designs, produce construction drawings and cost estimates, and initiate project construction. Sometimes it actually happened this quickly.

In less than two years, I designed more than thirty projects, half of which were either built completely or under construction before I left the country in June 1966.

A special kind of mutual understanding existed between the Peace Corps volunteer architects and our Tunisian clients. The Tunisians were our hosts as well as the people we served. They had invited us to come there to help them build. Most important, they believed that we had been chosen and sent because we were professional experts, university graduates armed with knowledge and talent, notwithstanding our youth. Our status seemed assured when we were given the exalted title "architecte-urbaniste."

From our simultaneously idealistic and pragmatic perspective, we were there as volunteers, minimally compensated, funded by the American government, able to choose to leave at any time should circumstances warrant. The Tunisians were our clients, but they weren't really paying us. We were committed to living like Tunisians live, not like tourists or diplomats, yet we still were different, still guests. And we knew, and we knew that the Tunisians knew, that we could make proposals, offer advice, and take actions that a Tunisian employed by the ministry never could. We were expected to be polite, but we could be fearlessly candid.

The consequence of this unusual relationship was that we enjoyed remarkable credibility. My Tunisian clients would look at preliminary sketches and, after some explanation and general discussion, ask how soon I could put dimensions on the drawings so the contractor could break ground. After presenting a design, I rarely had to defend it against the usual challenges concerning costs, materials, functional efficiency, or stylistic mannerisms. Never was I asked to explore additional, fruitless alternatives once a design direction was adequately explained and justified. Reasonable aesthetic innovation was welcomed, although certain cultural traditions—for example, buildings always were finished with white stucco—and technical and economic imperatives had to be respected.

Occasionally, a client would voice skepticism about a design idea, usually related to finishes or details. To win them over, I would make a deal. "Build the project as designed and if the outcome proves unsatisfactory, I will gladly authorize changing it." Such an offer was feasible because labor and local materials in Tunisia were inexpensive. The strategy succeeded; no project was changed after it was built.

The usually positive chemistry between my Tunisian clients and me reflected a combination of mutually understood motivations and clarity of means. First, Tunisia's agenda was clear: They needed projects—civic auditoriums, schools, libraries, clinics, public parks, hotels, shopping facilities, housing—designed and built quickly. And they were able to articulate their purposes sufficiently for me to respond, even if I was playing by ear much of the time. Second, available technology was simple and readily mobilized. With limited choices to make, we could focus on basic formal issues of space making, massing, and structural geometry.

With rare exceptions, Tunisians dealt with me as a professional, believing that I was at least a competent designer and, at best, an inspired one. And in aesthetic matters, my judgment was regularly sought and faithfully carried out. It was the best of times, a time before I had learned that, in the United States, clients are not always so believing or respectful.

CHAPTER 5

IS THE CAMEL
A HORSE DESIGNED
BY COMMITTEE?

Roger K. Lewis invokes the camel cliché later in this chapter in a scene in which the building committee of an institutional client has retained a weak-willed architect. Howard Roark from *The Fountainhead* would sooner set fire to the camel then let it live in full glory. So how should architects deal with committees, and vice versa, to produce excellent buildings?

Professor Lewis points out that it is *not sufficient* to meet budget, program, and schedule—you can still end up with a camel. Concern for humanism and client needs are obviously crucial to the success of any project, but, as Robert Marquis has said, they should not be used as an excuse for average or poor work.

It is the architect's *personal relationship* with committee members that can reach beyond the bureaucratic politics that grind design projects toward mediocrity. Leslie Wexner (for whom the Wexner Center for the Visual Arts at Ohio State is named) is a noteworthy patron of architecture. His attitude in working with the best architects is that "great architecture is produced by great artists, not by laypeople who critique and edit the work." Howard Roark would surely agree.

THE CLIENT OF MANY MINDS

Roger K. Lewis, FAIA, contributes this incisive piece regarding the myriad interests of design committee members, and the importance of strong leadership on the part of the client in producing high-quality architecture. (The biography for Roger Lewis appears in "The Hospitable Tunisians" in Chapter 4.)

Perhaps the most throbbing kind of headache for architects accompanies designing projects such as schools, hospitals, museums, or churches. Common to this type of client—the public or civic institution—is the existence of a constituency of individuals, each of whom has a legitimate and direct stake in the outcome of the design process. Each also has a legitimate voice but invariably a different point of view about what matters architecturally. Consequently, the architect must try to satisfy often conflicting desires and needs of many: overseers, administrators, users, members, donors, and the community served. Often the

architect works with a building committee, most of whose members have never before built anything.

Like corporate clients, institutions develop their own internal cultures of power and competition, notwithstanding the shared values and goals of the organization's constituents. And the architect must comprehend this internal culture. Yet even when the political landscape of the institution is understood, traversing it unscathed is difficult. No strong architectural advocacy will please everybody. Aesthetic and functional compromises, usually driven by economic and operational considerations, have to be made. Not everyone represented on the building committee will get everything he or she wants.

Not surprisingly, timid or obsequious architects frequently find themselves producing the most mediocre architecture as they struggle to satisfy equally every condition imposed. Given the opportunity, the institutional client—represented by the building committee—will have its way totally, bullying and badgering the architect until it gets a building that responds perfectly to the budget and program, no matter how ugly or poorly detailed the building might be. This is the proverbial camel, a horse designed by a committee.

When institutional architecture achieves aesthetic as well as functional and financial success, it reflects not only skillful work by the architect, but also strong, individual leadership within the institution— by a board or committee chairman, an executive director, a president, or an outspoken and active benefactor. The right kind of wise and inspired leadership brings to the process a compelling vision for the institution, a set of aspirations that can invigorate architecture. These aspirations transcend program and budget. When such leadership exists, the architect's job becomes much easier.

DESIGN WITH COMMITTEES

We know that architects do their best work when the client is a strong, open-minded individual with vision. Architects must also work with design committees. In this interesting discourse by Kent Larson, the anatomy of committee dynamics is presented in explicit terms.

Kent Larson has practiced architecture in New York City since 1980 as partner with Peter L. Gluck and Partners, Architects. He is partner-in-charge of much of the private and institutional work of the firm, and has written regularly for *Progressive Architecture* and other publications.

Committees are a fact of life with institutional design projects. It is the rare architect who can play the many roles required to avoid all conflict with a committee *and* make good architecture. In spite of having little or no formal training in group dynamics or communications, the architect must become a hybrid of leader, persuader, arbitrator, creator, improviser, technical and legal expert, showman, patient listener, and, at times, therapist. Many of the great twentieth-century architects experienced major problems with design committees, lacking one or more of these skills. The best presentations to a group are often more theater than an enumeration of the architectural ideas. It is common for large firms to have front men skilled in the art of presentation—who seldom design and spend most of their time wooing clients, entertaining, and eating lunch.

Each committee situation is unique. Our most complicated process was for the design of a Presbyterian church, with its separate design committee, interior design subcommittee, pipe organ subcommittee, liturgical committee, stained glass subcommittee, grounds committee, and construction committee. At the other extreme was a no-nonsense group for the design of Columbia University's Graduate School of Business addition (to Uris Hall) who wanted to be involved with only the most major decisions. The unusual committee experience was a nonlinear process with constantly shifting budget, program, and committee membership for the design of a new synagogue. All had their difficult moments, but the design was, by and large, successful in the end.

We have found that it helps to keep a few things in mind while navigating through the logistical, political, and personal minefields of committee-based architectural design:

Motivations Vary: Members give up valuable family, work, or television time to attend committee meetings, which are often held at night. Most join in the selfless interest of helping a valued institution. Some are reluctant members who just couldn't say no. A few volunteer to gain or exercise power, stroke their egos, or develop contacts with powerful people. Understanding why each person joined a committee is the first step in working successfully with the group.

FIGURE 5-1
Addition to Uris Hall, Graduate School of Business, Columbia University. Designing with a committee can produce excellent results. Kent Larson, partner-in-charge, Peter L. Gluck and Partners, Architects. Photo by Paul Warchol, courtesy of Peter L. Gluck and Partners, Architects.

Skills and Interests Are Very Different: Committee members seem to fall into one of two groups: lawyers and everyone else. Lawyers are often articulate and persuasive, and function well as strategists and spokespeople. They frequently don't have a clue about architecture (and the best will admit this). The rest can range from CEOs to homemakers to architects. The latter are by far the worst to work with because they cannot help but impose their own agenda. Homemakers are often the most sensitive to the subtleties of a design and the most open to new ideas. Some members have only pragmatic planning concerns, some are interested only in controlling the money, some focus on the approval strategy, and some are bored with anything but aesthetic issues. Sometimes a strong leader will emerge who becomes, in effect, the client through the influence over others. This, of course, can go either way—it is all in the luck of the draw.

The Path of Least Resistance Is Banality: Strong ideas will elicit powerful emotional responses pro and con. Weak design work is the easiest to get a committee to approve. Since it is always less risky to oppose something than to support it, the strongest forces will push toward the weakening of an idea—away from anything perceived as unconventional or with rough edges. It seems, however, that opponents of a proposal usually approve the finished product if it remains fundamentally uncompromised. An architect must keep in mind that it is easy to give in, but hard to make good architecture.

Prima Donnas Don't Go Far with Committees: While it is important to keep a design from being undermined, it is the kiss of death to become labeled as an unsympathetic artist who is unconcerned with the needs and wishes of the client. Good ideas must be adopted without hesitation, and the larger architectural goals must be reinforced over and over. Members can more easily accept the rejection of a suggestion if they understand the design values. Life can be miserable for the architect if an influential committee member is actively opposed to a proposal. An architect should cultivate working relationships with the people of influence on a committee. Make allies, not enemies.

Pick the Battles: Committee work always involves compromise. A good architect will know when to compromise and when to stand firm. A few inappropriate suggestions must be accepted at times if they do not affect the core elements of a design. In other words, lose the little fights but win the big ones.

Large Committees Are Often More Manageable: It is true that a committee of more than five can do little work. Design committees, however, are not formed to do any work, but to review, recommend, and approve. A smaller committee often begins to micromanage the design process, leading to interminable meetings dealing with trivial detail. With a large committee, it is much easier for the architect to call for a vote up or down—and then move on to the next issue. If the matter is critical, however, the architect should be fairly certain of winning. It is difficult to revisit an issue after rejection.

Use Minutes to Help Control the Process: Minutes of meetings are one of the great inventions of committee-based architecture. They bring order to the process, focus attention, minimize misunderstandings, and save a great deal of time.

Make Decisions Stick: Few committee members make every meeting. Some will expect a recap of previous presentations they missed, in spite of the minutes. Some will arrive late and ask that the meeting begin again for their benefit. On occasion, members will feel that decisions made at meetings they didn't attend (they are always men) are null and void because the group did not benefit from their greater experience. Patience is a virtue in these circumstances, but the process quickly becomes unmanageable, and time is wasted when this becomes a pattern. Rules must be established at the outset to deal with these problems. Rule number one: Those present are empowered to make decisions for those not present.

Protect Clients from Themselves: There is a trap that every architect eventually falls into: Certain members will insist that the budget is fixed and can't be exceeded, while others will insist that additional items are absolutely essential regardless of their cost. A committee will rarely come to terms with this contradiction internally—leaving the architect caught in the middle. This is a no-win situation, with people upset if expectations must be lowered to meet the budget, and others upset if the budget must be raised to fulfill wishes. The problem is often compounded by an architect's natural inclination to gravitate to the more ambitious scheme, and to optimistically assume that costs will be lower than is realistic. It is far easier to postpone a reckoning than to face it head-on, but the price is reduced credibility when reality hits (bids). It must be made clear that a client cannot set the budget *and* the scope *and* the quality of the work. The architect has the responsibility to see that the client takes responsibility for the limitations of their budget. Architects must be many things, but magician is not a required role.

There is no doubt that a building designed with a committee is typically a bit more compromised and less adventurous than other work, but there are unique rewards. Chief among them is the pleasure of working closely with a diverse group of people to turn their seemingly contradictory requirements and wishes into a strong, well-conceived, satisfying solution.

INSTITUTIONS, CLIENTS, AND SERVICE

An integral aspect of functioning in any political scene is the degree to which the constituent publics and special interest groups are identified and served. Norman Rosenfeld, FAIA, describes below the unique nature of services to one such special group—institutional clients—and the committees that represent them.

Mr. Rosenfeld is the founding principal of Norman Rosenfeld, FAIA, Architects, a New York City–based architectural firm, since 1969 specializing in the programming, planning, and design for health care, education, and commercial projects. He has lectured widely and taught hospital planning and design courses for graduate students and architects.

Institutional clients are a breed apart. Because health care, educational, and cultural institutions are such complex building types run by multifaceted constituencies of administrators, professionals, and technicians, providing architectural services to these institutions is an extraordinarily demanding professional challenge. This is not a complaint but simply a realistic observation on a very special architect–client niche relationship.

Architects practicing in the institutional field need highly developed skills in a multitude of disciplines. A validation (I am delighted to share) of a successful client relationship is evidenced in this hospital client's reference letter for my firm:

> Norman and his associates are more than architects—they are systems consultants, public relations advisors, historians, mechanics, decorators, designers, and fierce advocates of our hospital's physical plants, which will long survive us all.

While it does make me blush more than a little, this client understands and values what we try to do. The projects we have done for them have been successful—even the ones not yet built have served the institutional purpose of satisfying the board and the medical staff that administration is sensitive to facility needs and seeking to improve image, environment, and bottom line. It is enormously rewarding to be an architect in this professional environment in which we are called on to satisfy vying needs, to work with bright and dedicated staff, to accommodate requirements for cutting-edge technology, to meet stringent and often conflicting codes, and to ultimately provide an environment, in this case, for healing, that satisfies staff and patients and gives us a sense of pride in our practice.

FIGURE 5-2
A COMMUNITY GENERAL HOSPITAL
Funding needed for facility improvements in a financially distressed hospital. This project was planned to improve the antiquated diagnostic and treatment departments of this aging community general hospital. Physician support and patient occupancy were falling off. To finance the capital program, the hospital had to transfer ownership from the city to a voluntary status to access the financial market. The new front entrance and radiology, surgery, laboratory, and emergency departments have reversed the hospital's image and finances, bringing in new physicians and improved health care delivery. Photo by Norman McGrath, courtesy of Norman Rosenfeld, FAIA, Architects.

The selection process for institutional architects is complex. There isn't one entrepreneur CEO who decides. Often it is a committee process established to ensure representation of many constituencies. In the final analysis, the selection of an architect requires a good deal of courage and an equal amount of faith. After all, an architectural project is among the largest investments made by an individual, a corporation, or an institution. The selection of an architect to conceive of and guide this investment is a weighty choice.

Retaining the services of an architect is a unique experience, even to those institutional leaders who may be accustomed to "purchasing" all sorts of things. The product of an architect's services is not something for which you can "kick the tires" or "compare sticker prices" before you

FIGURE 5-3
A GOVERNMENT HOSPITAL
Persistence, patience, and "stay with it" can produce good architecture.
Government agency clients present unique architect–client relations. This
project extended ten years from initial contact to completion. The project
passed through three changes of management in the central office and four
site facility directors. Each new participant voiced somewhat different
views of the developing project. At a considerable hardship, the architect,
the only constant in the ten-year process, remained a strong advocate for
the integrity of the initial design concepts. Photo courtesy of Norman
Rosenfeld, FAIA, Architects.

buy. Unlike the purchase of an automobile, buyers have little ability to
judge the quality of the building on which they may be expending
hundreds of thousands of dollars in professional fees to design and
millions of dollars to construct—before the project is completed.

Frequently, institutional administrators and trustees hire architects
who are "problem solvers." Sounds impressive. Afterward, those same
administrators remark that the consultant team solved the problems,
addressed the needs, but ultimately—something was missing. Louis
Kahn, one of America's most historically eminent architects, once said,
"Need is just so many bananas." What separates great architecture from
"building" is the ability to encapsulate desire. Great architecture
expresses the aspirations of an institution, while it solves basic needs.
The architectural design process should reveal windows of opportunity

not previously contemplated and thereby provide solutions that will enhance operations in an uplifting environment. We call this approach "value added" services—but a building should also motivate and inspire the people within. This is particularly relevant to institutional projects where the complexity of space needs, functional adjacencies, technological imperative, and regulatory constraints provide an often nightmarish challenge even to the best of architects. But succeed they do!

[Norman Rosenfeld is one who succeeds often in creating beautiful buildings for this client type. Some examples of his projects are given in Figures 5-2, 5-3, and 5-4.]

FIGURE 5-4
HOSPITAL OUTPATIENT DEPARTMENT
Judicious use of limited funds can provide superior environments.
Outpatient departments often serve the medically indigent in a community. The architect's challenge here was to provide a dignified, functional, and maintainable physical environment within a very low capital budget. Through the use of plastic laminate, painted gypsum board, and vinyl composition tile enhanced by selected wood detailing and special lighting, this hospital-based clinic experienced an increase in its projected annual visits from 90,000 to 120,000 after its first year in new quarters. We would like to believe the physical environment contributed something to this success. Photo courtesy of Norman Rosenfeld, FAIA, Architects.

PATIENCE IS A VIRTUE

Within a given institution, there are opportunities for a diversity of architectural projects—from low-end maintenance to high-end design of new buildings. Politically astute architects such as Cathy Simon, FAIA (who writes, in the following contribution, about a prestigious private school), know how to establish and maintain excellent working relationships with clients. These relationships support the provision of high-quality service and further enhance the likelihood that the architect will be considered for the institution's next project.

Cathy J. Simon is the director of architecture and one of five founding principals of Simon Martin-Vegue Winkelstein Moris (SMWM). Under Ms. Simon's leadership, the San Francisco architecture, interior design, and planning firm has established itself locally and nationally with an expertise in institutional, educational, and civic design projects. Ms. Simon, former president of the Harvard Graduate School of Design Alumni Council, is currently a Distinguished Visiting Professor at the University of California at Berkeley.

In 1989, my firm (SMWM) was contacted by Lick-Wilmerding High School, one of San Francisco's premier educational institutions, to present our qualifications for a range of architectural services. Two projects were in the offing: The first was utilitarian in the extreme; the second was so attractive as to render the first a necessary evil. After a successful interview process, SMWM entered into an intriguing evolution of architect–client relations that has resulted in four years of steady improvement for the school. The intrigue lies in the journey traveled between the first and second projects.

Contrary to my hopes of an expansive first project, our work with Lick-Wilmerding began with a mundane series of quick fixes. Twenty years earlier a freeway, I-280, had been cut through the southern part of the city, along the school's eastern property line. Finally, after years of intrusive traffic disruption, funds for noise abatement had been made available through CALTRANS, California's mega-agency that controls transportation infrastructure. CALTRANS had performed an acoustical study and had developed a cost-driven strategy that suggested sealing all the operable windows in the school and providing mechanical ventilation, but no new ceilings, no new lighting, no new finishes.

Lick-Wilmerding's Board of Trustees considered the noise abatement projects to be the school's highest priority. The second and, in the board's view, slightly peripheral task involved preparing a master plan for future development of the school. When Lick-Wilmerding first contacted us, they informed us of both tasks (in that order). As design-oriented architects, we found it difficult to embrace the challenges afforded by the narrowly defined noise abatement project, but the prospect of designing a master plan for a wonderful school on a large, open urban site was utterly irresistible. We also knew that the potential of the master plan project was evident to Al Adams, the visionary headmaster of Lick-Wilmerding and the driving force behind the project, and to David Plant, a brilliant, service-oriented builder and alumnus of the school. There is no doubt that we were hired in part for our experience with the State of California, but principally because we were inspired by the opportunity to create a place for learning that matched the extraordinary goals of the school.

We enthusiastically embarked on the immediate tasks, interacting with CALTRANS on the one hand, and the school administration and faculty on the other. True to our profession, we attacked the pragmatic and mundane physical needs of the school, and at the same time began to establish a physical development path for it. For the former, we relied on CALTRANS's acoustical study of environmental noise; for the latter, we solicited information from the administration and teachers in an open-ended collaborative process. As we jumped through bureaucratic hoops and calculated cubic feet of air per minute and noise reduction coefficients, we also speculated about the future shape of the school, marrying philosophy with physical design. As architects of this vision, we viewed the shortcomings of the school as opportunities to redefine the campus image and create a sense of place where previously none had existed.

Part of the CALTRANS work involved evaluating existing facilities: seismicity, deferred maintenance, environmental quality, visual characteristics, and use of space. For example, our condition assessment revealed that one of the school's four principal structures, a wood frame industrial building housing wood, metal, and machine shops and the drafting studio, was "seismically nonexistent." We therefore optimistically proposed replacing it with a new shop building on an adjacent site, to help define the campus edges while allowing ongoing programs to continue during construction. In place of the existing shop building, we proposed a new library/student center to provide a physical and metaphorical, intellectual, and social link between the technical and liberal arts on the campus.

The reaction to our proposal was unexpected. While appreciating the thinking and work that had informed our suggestions, the Board of Trustees did not readily accept the scope of change that we envisioned. During the process, they had little opportunity to interact with us, and therefore did not "own" the proposal. Rather than support our concept to replace the shop building that summer, they hastily agreed to upgrade the existing shop building, paying for the work out of the endowment funds, and therefore tacitly agreeing to keep the structure for a long time. (Independent schools, in my experience, are loath to spend money on temporary improvements.) The following summer, the CALTRANS noise abatement proceeded concurrently with seismic, life safety, and handicapped access remediation of the existing classroom building.

Ironically, these pragmatic projects—seismic upgrades triggered by the existing facilities assessment, funds for noise abatement becoming available through CALTRANS, and the presence of a handicapped student who needed to be accommodated—were a catalyst for renewed thinking on the part of both the board and administration. The moment had arrived to address profound and complex needs for the school. These were several: the inadequacy of student seating and the collection space in the library, the lack of a student center, a misplaced student cafeteria, cramped quarters for both general classrooms and the visual and performing arts, little flexibility in room sizes to enable the emerging variety of teaching styles, poor acoustical adjacencies (math classes next to instrumental music classes), and dysfunctional intellectual adjacencies (foreign-language departmental offices next to shops).

Thus in 1993, four years and several projects later, having learned from the previous experience, we embarked on a master plan study. This time, we created a methodology that involved full participation of the board, faculty, administration, and students. The process was intriguing,

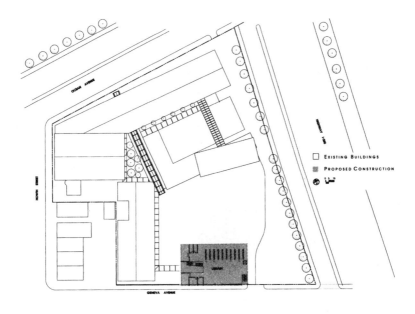

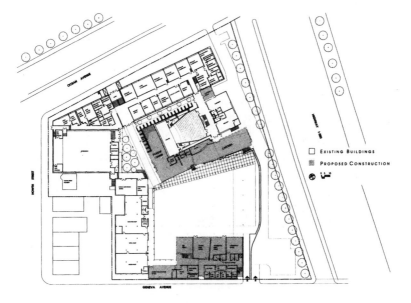

FIGURE 5-5
The master plan of Lick-Wilmerding High School in San Francisco, showing existing buildings and proposed construction. Bottom plan is first level; top plan is upper level. Drawings courtesy of SMWM.

FIGURE 5-6
Model photos reveal the three-dimensional expression of the proposed master plan. Bottom is an aerial view looking west; top is an eye-level view of the new cafeteria in the foreground with studios and library beyond. Photos by Gerald Ratto Photography, courtesy of SMWM.

synthetic, iterative, and rewarding. Interestingly, the students, all of whom are required to study architecture as freshmen, were some of the most acute, intelligent, insightful, and outspoken clients I have known. The master plan, which will be implemented over time, allows for flexible phasing and integration of emerging technologies. It envisions a new image for the school that builds on the tradition of the comfortable and unassuming existing buildings that characterize the Lick-Wilmerding present campus.

The proposed design is in every way a physical manifestation of the school's mission, purpose, and curriculum. Lick-Wilmerding's educational program is based on its dictum, "Head, Heart, Hands." (Head: The education of the mind. Heart: The nurturing of a social conscience. Hands: The training of applied skills.) For example, our master plan specified the use of exposed structure and assembled industrial skin, as a continued reflection of the hands-on teaching at the center of the school's curriculum. To accommodate the three-tiered structure of the Lick-Wilmerding program, we included in the master plan a variety of settings from large lecture rooms to small group study/conference spaces in which the rich and diverse education proposed by the school can generously take place. The plan recognizes the validity of the departmental identities while making numerous explicit and implicit connections among disciplines.

Interestingly, it took the existing-facilities assessment and the various practical remodeling steps to realize this new vision. For the school and the architect as well, the process unfolded with a life of its own; now it has assumed the conventional fund-raising implementation rhythm so familiar in independent institutional contexts. We expect our relationship with Lick-Wilmerding to be very rewarding and very long. We hope that realizing the master plan will result in an educational environment as inventive and multivalent as the students, faculty, and administration at the school.

CHAPTER 6

THE POLITICS OF DESIGN: RACE AND GENDER

Race and gender appear to be increasingly appreciated as mediators of the relationship between architects and clients. The contributors to this chapter are extraordinary pioneers in architecture's effort to shed light on some very uncomfortable but crucially important issues.

While exploring and analyzing the specific problems posed by certain kinds of discriminatory patterns, there is the added benefit of simultaneously achieving a fuller understanding of how bureaucracies behave in the most general sense. In the following material, Jack Travis poignantly states, "The biggest disadvantage [to being black or female] is that the captains of industry, the people who are in the power positions, are white males who give work to architects who are in a traditionally white male–dominated profession. So all of us have to fight."

A BLACK ARCHITECT ON A MISSION

Jack Travis is a black architect on a mission.

It was early spring when I visited Jack in his office on West 29th Street in Manhattan. A friendly and frenzied staff, curvilinear perforated sheet metal partitions, exposed concrete block, and African furnishings signaled a workplace that was busy, with a unique design flair.

Jack Travis's book, *African American Architects in Current Practice* (Princeton Architectural Press, New York, 1991), was reviewed in *Progressive Architecture* in March 1993. I was quite intrigued with the review, and subsequently the impressive quality and message of the book itself. It is the first book to promote the identity and work of black architects practicing today.

I wanted to learn more about the meaning of "mainstream practice" from Jack's perspective, and how he concurrently maintains a strong cultural identity. I asked him for an interesting architect–client story, and, more generally, what motivates his practice, writing, and teaching.

What especially struck me about our conversation was his characterization of the specific and very personal nature of the relationship between architect and client. Travis highlighted the frequent struggles for control and the challenges to communication as independent of the more globally important themes involving race and ethnicity in America today. In the instance presented here, the politics of architect–client relations are as crucial a factor in a successful outcome as is attention from both architect and client to the politics of race relations and achievement of social and cultural parity.

The following story from my conversation with Jack Travis revolves around his design of the renovation of filmmaker Spike Lee's home in Brooklyn, New York.

A Brownstone Grows in Brooklyn

Andrew Pressman (AP): Can you tell me how you met Spike Lee, and how he subsequently selected you as the architect to design his new home?

Jack Travis (JT): The day I met Spike Lee, on that Monday, I was sitting for two hours because they were already doing the first readings for the movie *Jungle Fever*. Then Spike came down, he walked past me once or twice, and didn't know who I was. Then he asked Wesley Snipes [the star of the movie], "Where's the architect, man?"

"He's right there, fool!"

"Man, I'm sorry. I didn't know who you were." Then I looked at Spike. Here was this man who had three calls waiting—one from

Warner Brothers for the movie *Malcolm X*, another from the Teamsters for a quarter of a million dollars on equipment to use in the street scenes for *Jungle Fever*, and I can't remember the other. And this man was talking to me! Hold on those other phone calls!

Spike had on open Nikes, he was short, he had the ugliest knees I'd ever seen in life, and I thought this is a CEO from a major company doing high-quality work, dressing the way he wants to dress, and running his business. As long as you can produce and deliver, you can be yourself.

AP: How did your relationship start?

JT: It all started when Wynn Thomas, Spike's set designer, discovered an article illustrating one of my projects: It was the Giorgio Armani Boutique—the Emporium Boutique—on Fifth Avenue and 16th Street in New York City, and was featured in the September 1989 issue of *Interior Design*.

Wesley and Spike had been collaborating on this new movie at the time, *Jungle Fever*. Wesley asked Spike if he could get an architect with whom he could mentor, because Wesley did not know any black architects and he wanted to make the part believable to young, black architects. Spike then asked Wynn Thomas to find someone, and Wynn then called us.

At first Wynn suggested that they film part of the movie in my office—and I said, "Fine!" So he came to my office; it was another office—not this one—and he said, "Nooo, I don't think so, this is not quite what we had in mind. But maybe you could work with Wesley."

Wesley came over one evening. We hit it off immediately. Within a week, I was called out to Brooklyn to Forty Acres and a Mule Film Works, Inc., to meet Spike. All the actors and actresses were present, and, of course, I was blown away—it was incredible! When I returned to my office, I had a message on my machine from Spike, and it said, "Jack, I need a black architect. Come over to see my house." So I went back to Brooklyn to see Spike's newly purchased brownstone. I sent him a proposal for services and he said it was fine, and I knew he never even read it. He said, "Just do it. We can have this done in a month, right?"

"In a month?"

"Yeah, gotta move in!"

I said, "*Sure*, we can have it done in a month—I don't know exactly *what* will be done in a month, but we can do it." When I tried to explain to him exactly what it entailed, he said, "Oh, how long?"

"Well . . ."

"How long?" he insisted.

"Probably take a year."

Spike paused and said, "All right, when can you get started?" Just like that. So I knew from that point on, he'd be a very easy person to work with. All of my staff working on this project were black, and one was Puerto Rican—it was a good team including Vincent Nealy, Adegboyega Adefope, and Buster Tiangco. Spike was very positive.

The Design

AP: In your initial meetings with Spike, did he tell you exactly what he wanted, give you a program?

JT: The first thing Spike said to us was, "I want you guys to respect the house." It was a circa-1868 High Victorian era brownstone. It's probably one of the top three or four brownstones on Washington Park in Fort Greene, Brooklyn—and all of them are fairly magnificent—but his was really wonderful. To me it seemed that he was not sure how to make the transition from the existing detail to the kinds of imagery that he wanted for the spaces. So we were supposed to be the mediators to make that change.

Our approach was to come up with a concept and a direction. The relationships of the rooms [to each other] were of course already set. So we thought we would go in and bombard Spike with a great deal of information and show him what we wanted to do—*Wrong!* We went in there wearing suits and everything; we were going to intimidate this guy—*Wrong!* He looked at what we wanted to do and said, "I like that, you can do that, don't do this, I'm not listening to that, but this is okay, I don't care about that." He just snapped his fingers—within minutes—he knew what he wanted.

AP: How did you respond to such an opinionated reaction?

JT: We needed to regroup. We went back in and said, "Spike, this is High Victorian," and we wanted to show him what the traditional style was, and he said, "No!" We replied, "Good! Now just let us kind of hang loose and go with the flow."

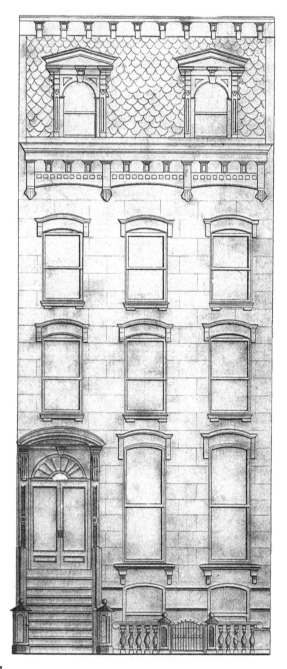

FIGURE 6-1
Front elevation view of Spike Lee's renovated brownstone in Brooklyn by the New York City firm Jack Travis, Architect. Drawing courtesy of Jack Travis.

He loved our next presentation. We just loosened things up; we did not design the spaces fully. Rather, we allowed him to come in with certain imagery and ideas—mostly art—what he thought he should live with including pieces that would be compatible to the transition from the existing envelope to the new imagery. It was a marriage after that—a full go-ahead—that was about four months into the project.

The Contractor

AP: Did the process continue smoothly through bidding and construction administration phases?

JT: Drawings were completed about six months into the project. They went out to bid and Spike asked, "Who are these drawings going to?"

I said, "I've worked for five years with Giorgio Armani with Herbert Construction as the contractor. They're a very good firm, they'll do the job, and I can beat up on them if I have to in case there are mistakes or if there are cost overruns, or problems like that."

Spike inquired, "Black-owned?"

"No."

Spike repeated: "Black-owned."

I said, "I don't know any black contractors in New York City that could do this level of work at this point in time"—which is a ludicrous statement—although it was true. I just did not know anyone; it was ludicrous on my own part, and this is New York City where there are the biggest black talent markets in the country, and still we didn't know anybody. And that pretty much says where African Americans are: I thought we have to do something about that, and Spike was absolutely right. So we went out looking. Then I went back to him and said, "I found a couple of people but they can't show me any work of this level. Quite frankly, I'm concerned about that because this is my first job with you; I want to work with you and I want this job to be the best that it can be."

"Well, I want black contractors."

I said, "Let me tell you about Herbert Construction. They do have a black person on the executive committee, he's a good friend of mine. He's the estimator."

Spike responded: "*One?* Out of how many?"

"Seventy."

"No. Un-uh. Un-uh. I don't want that. If they're going to be working on my house, they're all going to be black-owned firms, including the subcontractors. Go out and find them."

So we went out and now we have a list of all these black contractors and subcontractors, which is really wonderful. But when it came to marble and plaster work—there are no African Americans in this work. Spike understands that and then it's, "Okay get the best."

AP: The next step was selecting the general contractor?

JT: We ended up using a friend of his as the general contractor who had done some work for him before, and without drawings. The work, in my opinion, was not great but I had faith in these people after speaking to them that I could talk to them and communicate the kind of quality that I wanted. Of course, this would be very good for them because it would be their biggest job to date and again *it was what Spike's philosophy was all about: helping black owners catapult to the next level of professional accomplishment.*

The Need for Better Communication

AP: As the project was nearing completion, did any conflicts arise between you and Spike?

JT: We had only one major argument with Spike: It was about the move-in date. He chose a date that was inopportune for us; and we had given him three dates before that on which he had agreed to move—and did not tell us otherwise. We had no chance to regroup. I had another project going, I had to be out of town on the weekend he decided to move in, and he gave us only a couple of days' prior warning. It was disastrous. There are always those little things that never come together but ideally *can* come together with a little bit of supervision and coordination. Because I wasn't there initially, there were workers coming in and out for two or three months—decisions were made by Spike to do things that should have been made by Spike *with* me. Things like furniture: There were some fairly large items that needed to be coordinated and it could have ended much better.

The lines of communication simply broke down. If I had been able to be there—if he had moved in on one of those agreed-to dates—or if I could have canceled my plans when he did move, it would have ended better. I think we could have made a list together, and I could have explained to him why things are the way they are and I could have then given him a schedule, and of course held to that schedule. With other business commitments, I was never able to connect with him and get the schedule down.

AP: Was he inaccessible to you because of his celebrity status?

JT: Absolutely. He had final editing, distribution, and publicity to deal with on *Jungle Fever*. Then *Malcolm X* was gearing up big time. It was going to be the biggest thing of his career, and he was just not available. The house was not a major part of his agenda at that time. In his mind, it was very important, but he never understood the full scope of work until very late in the process.

Spike had a *ton* of stuff! He was living in one garden apartment about six doors down from the new place and we thought, okay, he's moving into five stories now, how much could he have? Immediately, when he moved in, the plan was obsolete. The man had thirty-six pairs of glasses, over two hundred pairs of sweats, and a hundred pairs of sneakers. How is he going to get married and raise a family in here?

AP: You were surprised!

JT: We should have tried to elicit all this much earlier in the process. I have learned my lesson. Now we stop and take a detailed look at inventory. We set up a clear, detailed schedule and if clients are not available, then we add time to the schedule, and that has to ultimately add fee. Spike put up with us, too. There were things we did not coordinate and things we could have done better. I think our drawings were three weeks late. I was editing my book at that time. He was very nice about it. We asked for payments at the most inopportune times for him and there was no more than a word and he found a way to get them to us. When I gave him the biggest invoice, which was when the construction drawings were done, and he hadn't seen them at that point, a *big* invoice, he looked at it and said, "If I pay you tomorrow, is that okay?"

AP: Spike seems like a remarkable and even an eccentric individual.

JT: When I hear people say, "He's a racist, isn't he?," my response is that you're reading white media coverage. If you look at what happens in *Ebony* or *Jet* about this man, does it say that he's a racist? You're reading the *New York Times* or listening to network news—if you listen to *Tony Brown's Journal*, if you listen to *BET News*—black people know what this man is trying to do. There's no other black entrepreneur doing it to his level.

Now we're doing other projects for Spike including showroom space for his record and fashion companies, and we have some inner-city kids involved—kids who are from troubled, disadvantaged families—who are going to help us do the interior work. We've set aside some areas for them to work on.

On Black Architects Today

AP: Who has had great influence on your career in architecture?

JT: Spike, my mother, and Rushia Fellows are my wake-up call. Rushia Fellows was the first black architect that I ever met. I was in third-year architecture school before I met my first black architect—able to do all the things my white counterparts could do. How can that be? It hit me like a ton of bricks.

AP: What can you say about the advantages and disadvantages of being an African American architect, and does race enter into the politics of architect–client interaction?

JT: I don't know if there are any advantages to being black in the profession of architecture today. Architecture is still so white male dominated. I equate the profession of architecture to the professions in general—like the sport of golf is to sports in general. White people play golf. I think that white men do architecture now, although it's changing, more so for women, in the schools.

The biggest disadvantage is that the captains of industry, the people who are in power positions, are white males who give work to architects who are in a traditionally white male–dominated profession. So all of us have to fight. It is very tough to fight because there is a network, there is a subconscious network setup where white men just seem to relate, get along better with other white men, and they take it for granted that this is the way things should be. And when a person of color or a female comes into it, many of them are kind of surprised, not prejudiced, but really uncomfortable. Then there are people who are outright prejudiced and then there are just a very few people who will give it a go. I'm talking about the people who are the problem—and there are a few of them but they happen to be in the very powerful positions. It's difficult to get to these people. Then once a person comes in, he or she is representative of her whole gender or race. So if you screw up, even a little bit, or if you make them uncomfortable, that's it. They're not going to try again. They go back to white men, and even if the white men screw up, they're at least comfortable.

AP: What's really shocking to me is the number of black architects—what is it—1 percent? How can we address the problem?

JT: African Americans represent less than 1 percent of all architects practicing today. There should be twelve times as many black architects. Blacks are 13 percent of the country—twenty-nine million blacks in America—the second largest population of Africans outside of Africa.

What I'm challenged by most is the architectural curriculum in the schools, and the way students are taught. There are a lot of issues that are not being addressed, particularly the urban context and interior design—which is how people relate to buildings. Cultural aspects of architecture and the architect's responsibility to society are, for the most part, ignored. Studios should be provided where students have an alternative to explore issues that are socially and culturally based, along with the existing studios that are design or formalist based. The schools have to broaden their whole outlook, where architecture programs energetically promote urban planning, environmental design, landscape architecture, and interior design in the same complex. It's now primarily all about form—and that's not what people really relate to—people relate to the sensual feel of the space, and all five senses play a role.

We need writers, editors, photographers, and so on to come out of the architectural curriculum. We need to have a place for people who are not going to do new buildings, but who are going to talk about how the environment needs to come together and how we can look at the environment in a more positive way.

I lecture frequently in the schools. When I mention Giorgio Armani and show slides of my work for him, the white male population listens. When I mention Spike Lee and describe my work for him, the black population listens. You have to be able to touch people on all bases, and then you can hit them with your message!

POLITICALLY INCORRECT IN WICHITA

Charles F. McAfee, FAIA, NOMA, is a distinguished black architect with a gleam in his eye that is apparent even through the telephone lines. Like Jack Travis's, McAfee's discussion (below) has the personal and professional transactions between an architect and a fine client superimposed upon an enduring and pervasive societal racism.

While illustrating how a successful project and satisfied client very much result from genuine connections between individuals, it is also disturbingly clear that cultural differences and the associated prejudice can creep into and weaken the best of relationships, and create a special brand of politics we must strive to recognize and ultimately avoid.

Mr. McAfee has had an eminent career in architecture. His firm (Charles F. McAfee, Architects/Planners) was one of four selected to lead the programming, design, and construction management for the 1996 Olympics in Atlanta. He recently won three design awards from the Kansas Society of the American Institute of Architects, he was past president of the National Organization of Minority Architects, and he has lectured nationwide and served on the boards of numerous civic organizations. McAfee is based in Wichita with branch offices in Dallas, Atlanta, and Oklahoma City.

One day with a big sky over Wichita, I had a call from Britt Brown, a client that I had for about three months. We'd discussed an addition for a new computer center for the Wichita Eagle and Beacon Publishing Company.

I went to Britt's office as requested with a blank AIA contract (one of the Standard Forms of Contract between Owner and Architect). The program had grown to include the business department, library, editorial department, Britt's executive offices, and complete remodeling to the balance of the third floor. During a conversation that lasted approximately five minutes, he had penciled in the blanks for the fee and the retainer, and called his secretary and instructed her to type the contract and bring a check for the retainer. I had only been in business for a short time, and this was my first major client. I thought that this was the way the process was supposed to proceed.

I designed the addition, and Britt approved everything. He called his secretary once again and instructed her to send me a check. We started

FIGURE 6-2
New computer center addition for the Wichita Eagle and Beacon
Publishing Company. Photo courtesy of Charles F. McAfee, FAIA, NOMA,
Architects/Planners.

construction and Britt left Wichita to write news articles about the war
in Vietnam.

We finished the project a couple of weeks before Britt returned.
Shortly thereafter, I received a phone call. Same instructions: Bring a
blank contract. I asked Britt, "What are you going to do now?"

He responded, "Just bring the contract."

I arrived at Britt's office; he pushed the controls on his desk to open
the drapes and said, "You see those railroad tracks?" (It was a double
track that dead-ended at the front property line.) I commented that I
had seen those tracks before, and Britt continued, "I bought the tracks
and we are going to design a building over them."

As usual he was in a hurry, and I worked all week to design this five-
story addition with a full basement to receive and store newsprint, move
it to the presses, then back to the second level for processing and
delivery. The design was approved in seven days—after a five-minute

presentation, a check, and instructions to proceed with construction documents. I thought, "Right!"

We started construction soon after and then one day I got this rather emotional call from Britt: "Can you have lunch with me?" When I arrived on time, he had already finished his first scotch and water and had ordered a second. I asked what was wrong. He was furious.

He said that he had been out to his club, the one I could not belong to, and had been asked, "Brown, what do you mean hiring the nigger to do your work?" As I sat there, Brown continued, "I won't mention his name, but he's one of our so-called leaders. My answer to him was, 'First of all the nigger, as you call him, is the best architect in town and second, it's my money.' " I thought, "This is indeed the right answer, but I know this was very tough for you—the racism of your own people is challenging your loyalty to me and to your social priorities. What a sad commentary."

One day I drove to the site to check on the progress of construction. I had parked my car and headed toward the building. Britt's uncle, the chairman of the board, came out of the building and was also looking around. He had reached an age of forgetfulness and, with this look of bewilderment on his face, asked if I knew where his car was. It was right in his parking space where he had put it. Then he said, "Mr. McAfee, would you mind driving me to my barbershop?" This guileless, almost childlike request led to many subsequent philosophical discussions on education, business, sports, the Kansas history of each other's ancestors, and how our respective families thought about problems confronting the races.

I was jolted back to reality one day as I was reading the morning paper. I saw a page that made me very annoyed. I called Britt to see if he was in and went to his office. I showed him the page on which the only two articles about black people in the newspaper appeared. One article was a story about Dr. Martin Luther King Jr. receiving the Nobel Peace Prize, and next to that a picture of Sammy Davis Jr. kissing May Britt.

Later, a very small article full of falsehoods about me appeared in the paper. I was furious. I called and again went to Britt's office. I asked if he had read the article. He said he had not seen it, called the newsroom, and asked the reporter to come to his office. This "journalist" arrived immediately. Britt asked, "Where did you get your information?"

FIGURE 6-3

(left) View of entry reveals sculptural massing as addition joins the existing building. (right) Detail of board-formed concrete finish. Photos courtesy of Charles F. McAfee, FAIA, NOMA, Architects/Planners.

He answered: "A reliable source."

"Did you call Mr. McAfee?"

"No."

"Meet Mr. McAfee."

This episode underscores the importance of addressing and resolving any political issue as it arises within the architect–client relationship to ensure an ongoing and truly collaborative partnership.

GENDER, MARKETING, AND A CLIENT'S FAITH

Carol Ross Barney, FAIA, is a very talented architect, who, through political savvy, is able to create opportunities for her firm. She recounts one such effort and clearly demonstrates that design ability alone is not adequate to establish and maintain a viable practice.

Ms. Ross Barney is president of the Chicago architectural firm Ross Barney Jankowski, Inc. She recently served as the chair of the

AIA Women in Architecture Committee, and her firm is the recipient of numerous National Honor Awards from the American Institute of Architects.

The Selection

Among the many, sundry, and generally minor subjects that are not covered in architecture school is the nature of clients. Clients, from a student's perspective, are always benevolent and highly principled, and the selection process is fair. By extrapolation, we are taught to expect that our clients will select architects based on their creativeness and ethical purity. Since most architects are attracted to their profession for reasons that include a societal consciousness and rarely include economics, it is not a big surprise that we also run our businesses with a great deal of naïveté.

I started my own firm in 1981, following a mutual parting of the ways with my employer. While I contemplated my future, two of my former clients called to inquire if I would continue working for them. So without any planning, I was in business.

Those first few months were flush. Another client called. Soon four of us were working, just out of my two-story house, and shortly after that offices in a building I had designed for my previous employer. Unfortunately, after about six months, it seemed that everyone who had ever wanted me as their architect had already called.

In desperation, I began my search for clients, an epic undertaking that continues to dominate my time a dozen years later. I quickly learned some basic rules. Projects do not select architects, people do. Therefore, you need to know people who will build projects, not projects that are going to be built. First, volume counts. There is no way you ever make enough calls or write too many proposals. Second, quantity and not quality is often the deciding factor in architect selection. For example, people are more comfortable with a designer of fifty mediocre buildings rather than ten great projects. Most people prefer to work with someone they already know. Accordingly, my search for work concentrated on my former clients.

I had worked for the United States Postal Service (USPS) while I was with other firms, and they built almost constantly. USPS was a natural for me to pursue, I thought.

The federal government is mandated to procure all contracts over twenty-five thousand dollars with public announcements. In the case of architect/engineer services, the procuring agency places an advertisement in the federally published *Commerce Business Daily,* advertising the project and the criteria by which the architect will be selected. Interested firms respond by submitting two Standard Forms, SF254 and SF255. In bureaucracies, at least, one might avoid the high stakes wine-and-dine circuit of commercial real estate or the campaign contribution chicken dinner sieve of local government work.

And so my quest for postal work began. I sent in SF254 and SF255 and about six weeks later received a two-paragraph response thanking me for my interest but explaining that my firm had not been selected. That was okay; I did not expect a direct hit on the first shot. Twelve months and as many SF254/SF255s later, my frustration was growing.

I called the local USPS real estate office. They said that the chair of the slating committee could tell me more. I called each chair. I learned that there were criteria that were not published in the *Commerce Business Daily.* The typical ad was answered by seventy-five to a hundred firms. It was hard for the slating committee to cut the field down to five or so for the interview; therefore they added qualifications to more easily cull the group down. Only firms in or adjacent to the zip code where the project was located were considered. Since all the projects were mostly in Chicago suburban communities, and most architect/engineers were in Chicago's "Loop" central business district, this worked neatly for them.

Other common added criteria were a minimum of five years in business and twenty-five employees. This one also worked well, since 85 percent of architect/engineers employ fewer than ten architects. (Two to three architects typically handle a job this size.)

Since the projects were generally within thirty miles of the Loop and under two million dollars, neither one of these list-shortening criteria seemed particularly relevant. My protests were politely considered and I continued to receive the two-paragraph rejection letters. I did notice, however, that some of the advertisements stated that preference would be given to firms owned by minorities. When I asked my USPS contacts about the rationale behind the preference, they told me it was necessary because the minority firms were disadvantaged and were generally fewer than twenty-five employees and less than five years old and therefore didn't meet criteria, and were almost certainly not located in the suburbs.

The explanation did give me a valuable idea. I inquired whether they ever hired women architects and politely pointed out that women-owned firms wouldn't meet the criteria, either. When I asked if they could give preference to women-owned firms, my question was kicked up to the regional manager and finally the headquarters.

Not much after that, an advertisement appeared in the *Commerce Business Daily* for a new post office with preference for minority- *and* women-owned firms. I sent in my SF254/255, was slated for an interview, *and* got the commission for a new branch post office in Glendale Heights, Illinois.

The Design

The Glendale Heights facility was pretty typical for suburban branches. The program included a large workroom where the mail is sorted, offices, locker rooms, a service lobby, and a lockbox lobby. Our project manager, Fred Gleave, provided a "functional design" plan that established the critical adjacencies.

Glendale Heights is a medium-size, blue-collar suburb. Developed in the 1960s and 1970s, Glendale Heights doesn't have a traditional downtown or village center. Shopping and fast foods are located at the heavily commercialized intersection of two major arterial streets.

The Postal Service had selected a site about half a mile from this intersection in an industrial park. At that time, the Postal Service required the architect to present three alternative designs based on the functional design plan. Because the plan was more or less set, the alternatives were reduced to elevation studies of color and materials.

We visited the Glendale site and other recently completed branch facilities, including some in industrial parks. The most lasting impression we had of the new buildings was that they were so similar in expression to their office/warehouse neighbors that they were hardly recognizable as public buildings. We discussed our impressions with Fred and he agreed.

So we concentrated our three alternatives on designs that would distinguish the new post office from its surroundings. Our first inclination was to use forms and details that were "governmental," a common

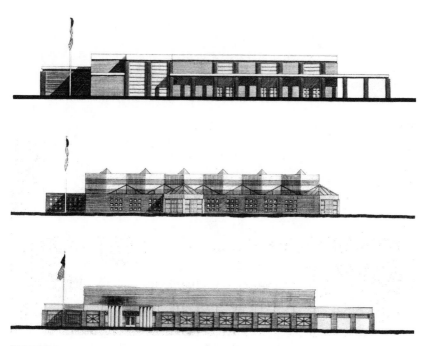

FIGURE 6-4
The three elevation studies for the Glendale Heights Branch Post Office.
Drawings courtesy of Ross Barney Jankowski Inc., Architects.

1980s approach, often called postmodern by critics. But since most detail is of pedestrian scale and our site was viewed at forty-five miles per hour from an arterial street, this approach was less than ideal. We briefly considered overscaled detail.

Our second attempt also relied on providing more visual interest to the façade than the typical office warehouse. The third design rejected the notion of using familiar detail and form to distinguish the building. The theory was to use the materials already present in the industrial park but to combine them in unexpected ways. Using the existing white and red brick palette of surrounding structures, we created a bold striped façade that enclosed the workroom. The customer lobby was clad in striking blue glazed brick, giving the building a flaglike appearance (see Figure 6-5). The illusion was completed by adding gold chevrons on the parapet that functioned as skylights and scuppers.

When we presented the three schemes to Fred, we thought he would appreciate the third but opt for the first. After our presentation, he

FIGURE 6-5
The flaglike Glendale Heights Post Office. Photo by Barry Rustin
Photography, courtesy of Ross Barney Jankowski, Inc., Architects.

asked which we wanted to build. We answered the flag scheme, and he approved it without hesitation.

Fred's confidence in our solution was to become invaluable during the development of the design. He stalwartly defended us to his own colleagues, the USPS operations people, and the Village of Glendale Heights.

Other team members were invaluable to the completion. The USPS construction representative, architect Craig Sharp, was less convinced than Fred, but also a staunch team player. The general contractor's superintendent, Nick Karas, was as responsible for the quality of the design as anyone by the end of the project.

As the building neared completion, it began to attract attention (not surprising, since that was the premise of the design). Most of the attention was very favorable, culminating with a Presidential Design Award from the National Endowment for the Arts and an Honor Award from the American Institute of Architects, which is generally regarded as the most prestigious American architectural prize.

Happily, Fred got to receive all the awards for the Postal Service. To this day, the higher-ups at the USPS remain mystified by the attention and praise generated for the building.

Lessons to Learn

Shortly after our commission, the Postal Service developed their "Kit of Parts" approach to design, so the days of uniquely designed facilities are, at least temporarily, over. Consequently, we haven't been asked to design another post office. However, we occasionally use our post office "guerrilla style" marketing approach. These tactics aside, the most important element is the trust and confidence of the individual client representatives. This is a rare condition and one that we will always be looking for and trying to inspire.

CHAPTER 7

ALL ABOUT COMMUNICATION

One of the most fundamental elements in making good architecture is *communication* between client and architect through all phases of a project, from conception to construction. Communication is traditionally defined as "a giving or exchanging of information by talk, gestures, writing, etc."; a "close, sympathetic or meaningful relationship." Usually, there is a direct correspondence between quality of dialogue and quality of architecture. This is such a basic truth, yet communicating well is frankly elusive for many architects.

How can architects facilitate "meaningful" communication? Certainly clients should bear some of the responsibility as party to the transaction, but *the architect is the professional*, and therefore it behooves him or her to ensure success. As part of the architect selection process, clients (and architects) should weigh the chemistry factor heavily; if it is nonexistent, then it is likely client and architect will never be "on the same page."

In this chapter, Jeremiah Eck draws an analogy to the medical profession and proposes that architects think about clients as if they were patients to effect better communication; Kirby Lockard believes that architects owe their clients a "careful explanation of the intentions and rationale for a building's design"; Bob Greenstreet tells us how to avoid legal squabbles by communicating well; and stories with happy and sad endings by CRSS Architects and Roger K. Lewis, respectively, begin and end the chapter.

IF THEY DON'T UNDERSTAND YOU,
YOU HAVEN'T SAID ANYTHING[4]

The firm of CRSS Architects, Inc. (now joined with and operating as HOK) has a long history of providing superb comprehensive services worldwide. On their behalf, Renate Schweiger contributes the following story that exemplifies the ease with which "politics," in the worst sense of that term, may be a direct result of faulty communication between architect and client. The position illustrated here is that power struggle occurs when the principal parties don't understand each other and the only reaction is an escalating defensiveness and a fear that agendas simply cannot be met.

Since its founding in 1946, CRSS has won more than 350 national and international design awards. In 1985, the American Institute of Architects posthumously awarded its Gold Medal to CRSS founder Bill Caudill. The firm pioneered a number of programming and project delivery processes including the intensive on-site work sessions ("squatters") to help clients build consensus among diverse special interest groups.

Every architect has a story of spending time and money producing elaborate plans and models of a building that will never be built. Faced with this possibility due to a severe communication problem, CRSS Architects was lucky enough to get a second chance. What we did with that chance astounded both ourselves and our clients.

We were doing work with an international automobile manufacturer to develop an automotive retail design for a nationwide installation program. Our role was not to design individual dealerships, but to create a prototype that local architects would use. We had a concept we called "branding" that linked design to brand identity through a series of branded elements. Having reached a relatively detailed level of design, it was time to present to the client. The "client" in this case was

---

4. From The TIBs of Bill Caudill: "Last night during a school for instrument pilots sponsored by the Houston Traffic Control Center, FAA, I heard one of the controllers explain the importance of two-way communicators with this astute remark:

IF THEY DON'T UNDERSTAND YOU,
YOU HAVEN'T SAID ANYTHING.

That's the essence of communication."

The Architect and Client Communicating

not one or two individuals, but a group of about thirty people. Within this group there were people from four different countries, speaking three different languages. We were working with foreign clients, and we were having a fairly large communication problem.

We had prepared the traditional architectural presentation. There were plans, sections, elevations, and models. In terms of a typical presentation, we had a lot of good information. The client looked and listened . . . and didn't understand.

A main issue was that we designed some sculptural-type walls in the interior space. The problem was, when we said "walls," the client saw walls in isolation, and the immediate reaction was: "It's going to be claustrophobic. It's going to feel enclosed. The customers won't come in. It's not inviting. We don't want walls!"

The idea was to create a specific customer experience through a sequence of branded elements—as the customer moves from exterior through the interior, these objects build on each other, terminating at the feature product display piece. We were using the sculptural walls to define special areas within the larger space. The client could see the objects as "things," but they couldn't see beyond these objects to the experience of the interior space that the sequence of objects created. They became fixated on the walls.

In the first presentation, we were trying communicate the quality of the experience of the interior space more than just the details of the solution—this layout, this material, this finish, this color, and so on. While we knew the principles operating here would work, it was apparent that many in our audience found it hard to match what we were showing and describing to them with their own internal picture of what they wanted. The ideas we were presenting through traditional media did not bring the understanding that we'd hoped for. Instead, the presentation had severely biased the client.

This was a problem because we couldn't begin work on the prototype until we got them to agree on the fundamentals. Because we were working on a prototyping project, it was not typical project delivery. Instead, we were designing a concept that would be rolled out on a national basis. We knew we had a good idea and if they saw it built, if they could "experience" it, they would like it.

The audience made their perceptions very clear. At one point, the vice president began to talk about a dealership he had seen in Los Angeles: "It was all glass. Beautiful. Everything in the building was glass."

"But look," we said, "that's the way dealerships are now. We are challenging that." But if we couldn't get them to agree to the logic of what we were trying to do, there would never be a prototype built.

They gave us another chance. "We've looked at models; we've looked at drawings; we've looked at perspectives, but we still don't get it." They asked: "What can you do?" In fact, they pleaded with us to find a better

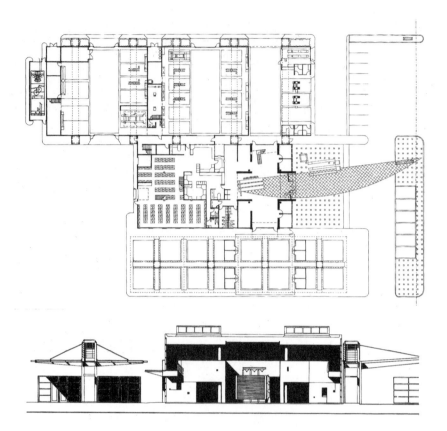

FIGURE 7-1
Floor plan (top) and front elevation (bottom) of the automobile dealership prototype. Drawings courtesy of CRSS Architects, Inc.

way to communicate. All they wanted to see was how they could sell more cars.

Whatever it was we were going to do, they had given us only three weeks to do it. If we didn't solve this communication problem, the project would be over.

Design director Douglas Oliver got the team together: "We know what the client's requirements are. We know that we have the details that fit the requirements. Let's take the viewpoint of the client and imagine ourselves in their place. Let's try to answer their questions and concerns in a way they can understand. If we can do that, we will have a project that not only is satisfying to imagine, but also has a chance of becoming an outstanding reality."

We could have removed the walls, put in a lot of glass, and made some other openings. But, as a team, we decided that what we had was good. Communication was the real problem for us to solve.

It was the early days of our use of computerized visualization, but we decided to take the gamble. "I was skeptical," said Oliver, "that we could actually do it in the three-week time frame." We started with a series of stills and strategized how we could show the buildup of the experience without visualization. Then we created the animation and transferred the animated output to video.

We produced a five-minute video showing the buildup of the concept in an existing dealership. Photorealistic images tracked the sun and changed daytime shadows; the structure was viewed from all directions with texture, reflective surfaces, and multiple light sources; and a walk-through was created following a typical customer path.

"But as far as the design goes, we didn't change anything," said Oliver. "We literally just re-created the design in visualization."

"This is going to be the thing that puts us over the top," Oliver told the team. "If this doesn't communicate what we are trying to do, then there's nothing we can do short of building it. Or starting over."

We began our "last chance" presentation the same way we had done the first presentation, by going through the logic using traditional media. When they started the attack, we said: "If you'll hold your questions for a minute, we have one final tool to show you."

We showed the video on a twenty-foot screen, and two things happened. First, they stood up and applauded. The executive vice president of international operations said, "For the first time in my career, I have completely understood a design presentation." In fact, the same expression was overheard around the room: "Now I understand what you've been saying." Not only had they finally understood the design concept, but they were genuinely excited about the presentation experience.

Second, and more important, is that they decided right there to build two buildings.

"I was dumbfounded," said Oliver. "We had not changed anything on the design." It confirmed what we believed—that the ideas were good, that the client would like them *when they understood them.*

"The thing about visualization," said Oliver, "is what it does for client communication. It's like nothing else I've ever seen." Its real power in

FIGURE 7-2
Interior detail of customer center of the automobile dealership prototype.
Photo courtesy of CRSS Architects, Inc.

terms of communicating a design is that it dispels clients' fears. Most clients can't read drawings; but what's even worse, they think they can. Like the wall in our design, they get fixated on something in isolation and it becomes impossible to alter their perceptions. But doing a "walkthrough" in visualization exposes them to a more complete design experience. By obtaining a higher level of comprehension, the client gets a level of comfort from knowing that what is going to be built is what they understood—no surprises.

In 1973, Bill Caudill spoke about what was then a new design and communications tool that CRSS was attempting to use: video. "It's a great design tool," he admitted. "But it takes too much expensive equipment. We got back in bed with drawings and models. We were ten years too soon. I've often wondered, had we stuck to this tool [videotape], how would that have altered our practice?"

Twenty years and many advancements later, video is proving to be one of the most powerful tools for communicating design ideas to all types of audiences. Visualization technology has taken our profession into a brave new world of communication.

By definition, visualization is a form of communication: to form an image that allows us to share with others. And the medium used to share that image is videotape. Utilizing a combination of live video, computer graphics, sound, and animation, the design business is adopting techniques used by the entertainment industry. The by-products of visualization, in this case, the video, gave us a badly needed tool to communicate with our multicultural, multiheaded clients. In the ever-expanding global marketplace, visualization becomes a very effective communication tool that transcends barriers between multicultural teams and clients.

And more to the story. We recently attended the grand opening of one of the two completed dealerships. Everyone who had been at the presentation was there. They were extremely pleased with the results: "All of the things you told us it would do, it does. The things we thought were going to be problems are not." Through the dynamic, realistic imagery of the presentation media, the clients' understanding of the design was so complete that, upon seeing the built product, their comment was: "We've already seen this."

For us, it was a breakthrough in communicating a very complex concept to what is, in more and more cases, a very diverse client group with very complex problems. Architects like to communicate with drawings. But that is not how most clients perceive. Not everyone can read a blueprint; everyone can watch television. It is very important that we explore ways to go beyond our drawings and look through our clients' eyes at how they will perceive something. Visualization is one of the many emergent technologies that affect the way we work and communicate.

TREATING CLIENTS AS PATIENTS

Without being at all patronizing, architect Jeremiah Eck invokes a clinical metaphor in doing architecture, and proposes that this approach has a profound influence on the politics of the architect–client relationship. He suggests that there is less of a power struggle if the architect thinks of him- or herself as a clinician.

In a recent issue of *Contract Design*, Editor-in-Chief Roger Yee extended the metaphor: "A lesson we might draw from [a failure in] the doctor's office is that taking time to communicate with the client represents a highly visible and symbolic show of concern that also happens to be quite useful. Shouldn't it be obvious that showing more interest in the client's needs convinces the client of his importance to us—just as knowing more about the client's needs helps us solve them better? We should take the time to listen."

Jeremiah Eck is lecturer in the Department of Architecture at the Harvard University Graduate School of Design, faculty director of the Career Discovery Program at the GSD, and a practicing architect in Boston, Massachusetts. His residential works have won numerous awards and have been featured in more than forty national and international publications including *Architectural Record*, *Architecture and Urbanism*, *Fine Homebuilding*, *The Christian Science Monitor*, and the *Boston Globe*.

It has become increasingly clear to me over the last few years of practice that architectural clients are in many ways similar to medical patients. Or perhaps put a better way, that architects might regard their clients more as patients who come to them with a health-threatening problem that requires a solution.

How many of us actually think of a problem to be solved when we first procure a commission? Or rather, do we think of an opportunity to use the financial capacity or program of a client to create or satisfy our own architectural fantasies? I'm convinced that if we instead think of a client as a patient with a specific problem, we are more likely to produce a good building, and that the desired concomitant result—a beautiful building—will also quite naturally follow.

This approach has other implications, since treating or understanding a client as a patient is not always easy. I'm a strong believer in the theory that good clients make good architecture. But what is a good client? Unfortunately, they can be both easy or difficult to work with. Some clients may have only a cold but a rotten disposition; others may have pneumonia and a good disposition. I've had my share of both. To underscore my point, one of my most difficult clients produced one of my best, award-winning projects.

Their project was a very small house; the fee had to be fixed and they had already "fired" two previous architects (which I didn't discover until after the project was complete). But the site was extraordinarily beautiful

FIGURE 7-3
The small house, on an island site. Photo courtesy of Jeremiah Eck Architect.

and on an island; and at the same time, it seemed to me to be just the right kind of project to fill out my built project types. In other words, I love doing small houses and this one seemed like a special opportunity. One could easily say I had already made a number of classic errors—at least from a business point of view—but that's a discussion for another story.

From the start they were very difficult, demanding innumerable options. I vividly remember sitting across the dining table, usually at night, discussing the house with them and thinking to myself, *How can they be so demanding—and frankly, so cheap?* I struggled with them both and their needs. It was a marathon that I can honestly say I almost didn't finish. But then one day in the office—I can remember it clearly—the design fell into place. Their problem had been solved, their difficult needs had been satisfied. I'm sure you've all had similar experiences. Of course the relationship and the problem solving were hardly over. Each construction detail was analyzed and put to the "what if" test. And later when the bid documents came out, the contractor was asked to lower his price, too.

Though somewhat counterprofessional, that contractor and I held a mutual respect for each other's tolerance of our shared client. Then, three-quarters of the way through construction, the hitherto low-budget clients "found" some additional money for some of their last-minute additional needs. No money was available, of course, for any additional fees for either the architect or contractor.

When it was all over, the house was extraordinarily simple and elegant, and it won a number of awards for me. All of the Sisyphean efforts had, in some ways, paid off. I've had easier clients since then and more award-winning houses, so I've often asked myself why that one was so difficult. The truth is that I've never really been able to answer the question. Just the particular mix, I guess. As I mentioned earlier, I did learn subsequently that there had been two other architects before me. So was I totally off the mark? I doubt it!

The lesson to learn perhaps is that a good client is not just an easy client, but one that brings the best out in us to perform our service as problem solvers. Each client—or patient—has their own particular needs and point of view, and some are more or less difficult than others. Each of us as architects remains the same, tempered by our experiences. So it is really up to us to adjust our services accordingly. Indeed, one of the most difficult aspects of practicing architecture is the need to reinvent the wheel each time for each new client. Why can't they just let us do our jobs as we have learned to do over many years of practice?

The answer of course is that each client has a fundamental right to ask you to solve a problem first, a problem and process that they have never been through before. Like a patient with a doctor, if the health problem is not diagnosed and solved correctly, the doctor has not done his or her job. Thinking of the architectural process in this *clinical* fashion has allowed me to profoundly temper my relationship with most clients. In many ways, our common goal is achieved through a process struggle not a power struggle. If, like a doctor, we begin to think of clients as patients, we may begin to overlook their particular personalities and our idiosyncratic needs, and begin to produce responsive and beautiful buildings again.

ARCHITECTS AS GREAT COMMUNICATORS

William Kirby Lockard, FAIA, reiterates below the need for architects to understand how to communicate effectively with clients (and constructors) as basic to providing professional services. He calls for distinct phases of communication that should ideally correspond to phases of the design and construction process.

Professor Lockard has taught for thirty years at the University of Arizona, and has his own practice in Tucson. His books, including *Design Drawing*, are classics in the field.

One of my most satisfying experiences in communicating with clients came while taking a group of my design students on a field trip to a church I had designed some fifteen years earlier. We were met by the young pastor, who had come to serve the church five years or so after it was built. He asked if it would be all right with me if he showed my students around the church. I was amazed to hear him explain the building, especially the sanctuary and the way it reflects the Lutheran liturgy, in almost exactly the way I had explained it to the original pastor, building committee, and congregation fifteen years earlier, using many of the same phrases and analogies.

I have since come to believe that such a verbal explanation of the intentions and rationale for a building's design are a very important part of any architect's professional service. We owe our clients that careful explanation. I even believe the explanation should be an integral part of the cover sheets of our construction documents, so that all those who help build the building have a better understanding of the design's intentions.

We have been slow to realize that architect–client communication is absolutely crucial to the success of any architect, any building project, and, altogether, to the success of our profession as a whole. Our greatest architects have always been great communicators and spent an enormous amount of energy in their effort to understand and be understood. Frank Lloyd Wright's voluminous correspondence and his ability to charm and persuade clients, even when his purposes were questionable, remain truly impressive.

Three years ago, at the University of Arizona where I teach, we initiated a graduate concentration in design communication and, having taught the graduate seminar in that concentration and helped several graduate students in their research projects, I have come to two interesting conclusions.

My first conclusion is that, aside from the rich and extensive anecdotal literature about the communications between architects and their clients, there is almost no research on the subject. And further, we are finding that many of the traditional and most strongly held opinions that architects have about communicating with clients are not supported by research. They are just flat wrong. We have found, for instance, that clients are much less impressed and persuaded by elaborate drawings than most architects suppose. Architects have continued to make those beautiful drawings for one another, as a kind of ritual, without ever bothering to find out if they were efficient communications.

Another interesting result of one graduate student's research concerns the ethics of client communication. In extensive interviews with individual members of public client–architect selection committees, one of our master's students found that architects' "free" sketches, presented at job interviews, were almost never perceived as unethical or inappropriate, but simply as a convincing indication of interest in the project.

The second realization that is unmistakably indicated is that, just as we have a lot to learn about successful communication, if we take our understanding of it seriously, we will have a great deal to contribute to communication theory. This potential theoretical contribution is based on the uniquely complex and changing way we must communicate during the process of the design and construction of a building. The context changes from the tentative, questioning, listening communication of programming through the explanation of schematic alternatives to the dialogue of change and refinement to the confident, convincing, persuasive communications that seek approval of the final design; and the media changes just as drastically, from verbal and numerical expressions of needs to two-dimensional conceptual diagrams to complex three-dimensional drawings and models, to intricately detailed construction documents and, finally, to the design intentions that communicate in the masonry, steel, and concrete of the finished building.

We need to be masters of communication and it is time we realized that communication, considered broadly, is perhaps our most essential professional skill.

LEGAL PITFALLS OF POOR COMMUNICATION

Robert C. Greenstreet, RIBA, PhD, is dean of the School of Architecture and Urban Planning at the University of Wisconsin–Milwaukee, and has written the following cogent essay regarding the architect–client relationship. He is an architect specializing in legal aspects of professional practice, and has also written extensively on presentation techniques and graphics. He has authored or coauthored the following books: *Legal and Contractual Procedures for Architects* (Fifth Edition, Architectural Press, 2004), *Architectural Representation* (Prentice-Hall, 1991), *The Architect's Guide to Law and Practice* (Van Nostrand Reinhold, 1984) and *Law and Practice for Architects* (Architectural Press, 2005).

While the architect–client relationship can be viewed from any number of perspectives, one that is perhaps given too little attention is the legal bond that ties the two parties together. This is not surprising, given the less-than-stimulating content of most contractual arrangements, but it is a factor that is ignored at the peril of both parties, as recent statistical reviews show. During the 1980s, legal action against architects reached an all-time high, with 43 percent of insured architects reporting a claim against them in the year of 1984. This alarming statistic did not include uninsured architects or those who settled prior to the claim reaching the insurer's ears. Of these many legal suits, over half of them were brought by clients against their architects and, while the overall number of annual suits against insured architects has dropped to 27.2 percent in 1993, there is still a high proportion of legal action generated during the architect–client relationship.

Why do so many relationships, presumably originally founded on trust and faith, deteriorate into legal squabbles? An extensive review of decided cases including clients and their architects suggests that poor communication, particularly during programming and the estimation of projected costs, lie at the heart of many disputes. The Farnsworth House, for example, is a world-renowned icon of modern architecture and yet was the catalyst for a nasty fight between Mies van der Rohe and Dr. Edith Farnsworth. He sued for mechanic's lien foreclosure on the architectural masterpiece to recover $28,000 in unpaid fees, while she countersued for $33,000, the exact amount by which she claimed Mies exceeded his original estimate. Too much focus on the *product* of the relationship, the building, and not enough focus on the *process* of getting it built—which includes constant client updating and involvement on all issues—lead to such problems.

Strong and successful architect–client relationships in which legal action is minimized seem to be rooted in solid, well-constructed agreements in which the rights and responsibilities of each side are clearly understood and a meeting of the minds has been reached. With clients inexperienced in construction matters, the onus is upon the architect to take the lead in educating the client as to the contractual process and the building process that will be necessary in bringing a building project to successful fruition. This is not a patronizing task, but one where the importance of owner participation in decision making and dealing with unexpected change is emphasized so that the client is a deliberate participant in the process. In this way, the client is likely to experience fewer nasty surprises—budget extras, time delays, and so on—or at least be prepared for them and therefore less prone to blame the architect immediately for issues beyond his or her control.

How can this state of grace, a meeting of the minds, be best achieved? Standard Forms of Contract, while an anathema to many attorneys and derided as inflexible or insufficiently advantageous to the client, have the distinct advantage of containing articles and language that are generally understood throughout the construction industry. American Institute of Architects Standard Forms, for example, have been modified through as many as thirteen editions by groups representing architects, clients, contractors, and consultants, and offer a relatively level playing field, complete with rules of the game, upon which the parties can establish, define, and comprehend their relationships.

Beyond the contractual capacity they offer, Standard Forms, which come in a range of abbreviated or customized variants, can be very useful as a means of education, enabling an architect to walk a potential client through the contents and enlighten them on the process of construction that is ahead. It's a lot less fun than scribbling pictures on the back of a napkin, but does provide a structured education to a client on the role he or she is expected to play in the upcoming adventure.

Of course, the really important aspect of the architect–client relationship is the success of the building itself, its contribution to the built environment, and the satisfaction of its inhabitants. This endeavor can only be enhanced by a successful interaction between the parties based on a sound contractual footing. This reduces the likelihood of legal action against the architect, increases the prospect of a satisfied client, and therefore a happy and well-paid architect—while over 75 percent of architects who sue clients for their fees win, the cost in legal fees, reputation, and bother hardly seem to make it worthwhile. Consequently, the success of the architect–client relationship, the cornerstone of the building process, needs to be firmly established on a professional footing where the need or threat for legal action is substantially minimized.

THE MERCURIAL CLIENT

A vivid example of a client failing to communicate—or at least not listening well—is presented by Roger K. Lewis, FAIA. Alas, in some circumstances, going to court (or at least the threat of legal action) is indeed the only option to reconcile opposing viewpoints. (The biography for Roger Lewis appears in "The Hospitable Tunisians" in Chapter 4.)

At our very first meeting, he exclaimed: "I want this project to be one I can someday show with pride to my grandchildren! That's why I want you to be my architects." We architects smiled, admiring and sharing this residential developer's infectious enthusiasm and can-do aspirations after hearing him describe what he sought to accomplish. He was looking for award-winning architecture.

Our client was the prototype of an entrepreneurial, 1970s would-be iconoclast well into middle age: mod clothes, open shirt and leather vest, gold chain necklace and copper bracelets, stylishly long and thick well-coiffed hair. He was constantly in motion, full of nervous energy, always talking and gesturing exuberantly, reviewing design ideas and issuing approvals as he cheered on the architects. "These houses must be top quality, great spaces, finest materials, latest amenities."

For many months, we worked diligently together. He and I became friends, visiting each other's homes and meeting each other's families. Sometimes we would meet in the evening at the trendy restaurant where he regularly held court. He began dating one of my secretaries and didn't hesitate to drop by my office without an appointment, both to visit her and to check the progress of his projects. He was a bright and engaging person, a memorable character in a city of bureaucrats and conformity.

I should have known better. We ended up embittered adversaries in court three years later.

I was the plaintiff—he had refused to pay the last portion of the fee that I was owed. His defense was that my firm had failed to perform adequately. Thirty minutes before the trial, both his and my attorneys persuaded him to settle and pay up. That morning at the courthouse, he and I never spoke to each other, never exchanged glances, our connections long ago severed. Surrounded by his entourage of lawyers and witnesses, he purposely stayed out of sight while I, my attorney, and my project manager sat in the courthouse lobby deliberating our strategy and negotiating with his representatives, to whom it became increasingly obvious that their client would probably lose.

The schism had occurred many months earlier, when final plans had been completed and the developer had hired an independent, professional estimator to prepare construction cost estimates. The estimator telephoned and, audibly distressed, asked me to come immediately to his office to meet with him and our client. I knew something was seriously amiss. When I arrived with two of my associates, our client was on the verge of losing control. Sitting mutely, tensely, his lips pursed and his face exuding anger, he exploded into a fit of rage. Shouting and screaming, he condemned me and my staff for designing houses that were too expensive to build. Moreover, amid the yelling were accusations that I had been neglectful and inattentive, too busy doing work other than his. In his view, I and my office staff had prepared incomplete and inadequate documents lacking sufficient information for estimating and construction. Also included in his ranting and raving were repeated assertions that he hadn't gotten what he was entitled to and had paid for.

Trying to look squarely at him, his face still flushed with anger but the tension beginning to dissipate just a fraction, I told him that I was leaving, that I refused to be subjected to his abusive language and hysterics, and that I would discuss his concerns only in a rational manner when he calmed down. We left immediately, knowing that the relationship was forever finished.

What had transpired and led to this confrontation?

We had designed the project exactly as required, not only complying with all of our client's initial requirements and subsequent requests, but also apprising him continually of the economic consequences of every design decision along the way. The cost estimates came as no surprise to us. The surprise was that our client, a professional and presumably experienced builder, was surprised. Since undertaking the project, national and local economic conditions had changed dramatically—interest rates and construction costs had risen and, most important, the real estate market had weakened substantially. Rather than accepting responsibility for his own specifications, approvals, and economic misjudgments, he chose instead to lay blame for his current financial dilemma entirely at the feet of the architects. He had conveniently forgotten all of our advice and warnings month after month about rising costs. And he was unconcerned that we had, in fact, expended far more time perfecting the designs—with his continual involvement—than was normally required, certainly more than we were being paid for.

His behavior was symptomatic of someone whose ego and sense of self-righteousness made it difficult, if not impossible, to acknowledge his own shortcomings or fallibility. Having received bad news, he needed to blame someone other than himself. And this was exacerbated by manic-depressive tendencies. I had seen hints of his mood swings, but had never appreciated how potentially volatile he really was.

After getting over the initial shock of our encounter at the estimator's office, I rebutted his indictments in writing, completed the work remaining under our contract, and hoped that he would pay his debts.

The experience was so distasteful that I chose not to meet with him again. Indeed, when he later refused to make final payment, I was at first reluctant to sue him, fearing that it might provoke another explosive outburst, or worse. Yet I also felt compelled not to let him intimidate me or my colleagues—I learned that he had abused, both verbally and financially, numerous other architects and engineers whom he had hired previously. In my case, his bullying wouldn't work.

Despite the outcome, I still recall the promises and aspirations expressed at the outset of the relationship. They were just too seductive to resist.

CHAPTER 8

CORPORATE POLITICS

Few things in life are more political than the workplace. Maalox consumption is but one testament to the universality of covert executive agendas. How then can architects identify their real clients in this context, the movers and shakers of corporate America, much less uncover the pressing tasks to be accomplished? In the first part of this chapter, Roger K. Lewis deftly analyzes the nature of the power structure in corporations and how it impacts on the architect.

Gene Kohn of Kohn Pedersen Fox Associates discusses several projects in which sophisticated, intelligent clients who appreciate the value of high-quality design are able to reconcile the seemingly contradictory goals of making money and being socially responsible. Kohn refreshingly credits his clients as the significant driving force shaping their award-winning buildings.

Closing the chapter is Cambridge, Massachusetts, architect Thomas Bakalars, who describes a comical case of mistaken identity. Sometimes luck (when combined with talent and ability) is more important than politics, relationships, or antacids.

THE POWER STRUCTURE

Roger K. Lewis, FAIA, pens this next piece on how corporate politics influences the architect–client relationship. (The biography for Roger Lewis appears in "The Hospitable Tunisians" in Chapter 4.)

Consider some of my corporate clients: development companies replete with multiple partners or stockholders, boards of directors, chief executive officers, vice presidents, project managers, construction managers, sales and marketing managers, purchasing agents, accountants and bookkeepers, and, of course, attorneys. To deal effectively with such clients, the architect must get beyond the corporation's organizational chart.

Normally the corporation's designated project manager is the architect's primary point of contact, the person from whom the architect officially receives instructions. But periodic meetings attended by other corporate officials inevitably reveal that, in fact, there exists a complex political structure internal to the corporation. The architect must seek to understand this structure—the power structure—if he is to achieve his architectural objectives. Accordingly, he must pose and extract answers to several crucial questions.

What really is the corporate pecking order? Who is really the boss? Who proactively leads and who passively follows? Who, if anybody, is the innovator, the risk taker, and the experimenter? Who obstructs? Are there cliques? And most difficult to fathom but always critical: What are the interpersonal relationships among corporate officials—who is competing with whom, who dislikes whom, who is trying to subvert whom?

Ideally, decisions about architectural propositions shouldn't have much to do with corporate politics. One would think that once project goals, sites, programs, and budgets are adopted, corporation officials would unemotionally allow the architect to carry out and execute the project. But this is rarely the case, especially when powerful and persuasive individuals within the corporation choose to exert substantial influence over the design process. This is even more challenging for the architect when a multitude of such interested and potentially competing officials enter into the fray.

The architect may become a mediator, or may be subjected to lobbying, usually in private and off the record, by individual corporate executives anxious to build a direct alliance with the architect. Especially tricky for the architect is receiving conflicting signals, opinions, or instructions. Since an official line of authority and responsibility is normally established, the architect may be placed in an awkward position if someone bypasses the official line with a request that contradicts what someone else requested. When this occurs, the architect must very carefully navigate his course. He must act ethically and not violate contractual obligations but, at the same time, must avoid entanglements in corporate politics.

Of course, beyond figuring out the power structure of a corporate client, there is one other corporate issue on which architects must focus: Who's in charge of accounts payable?

RESOLVING PROFIT WITH SOCIAL RESPONSIBILITY

Rarely in architectural life does a figure appear of such charisma as Gene Kohn of Kohn Pedersen Fox Associates in New York. Kohn speaks openly (below) about operationalizing his strongly held ideals on a canvas of huge economic risks and potential rewards.

Bringing Religion to the Client

Consider the buildings that comprise most cities: commercial office towers, hotels, retail complexes, apartment buildings, and light industrial warehouse and manufacturing centers. The common thread that links these building types is *profit*. They are, for the most part, built by commercial developers to generate income. More important, though, these buildings have shaped and continue to shape our cities. For that very reason, it is the challenge of every architect to approach the process of working with a commercial client-developer with an overriding sense of great responsibility. Our cities and their architecture share a symbiotic relationship fostering progress that is essential to human vitality and survival. In this context, the politics of architect–client relations deserves special scrutiny.

A city's civic quality and sensibility are dependent upon a common understanding of goals shared by the architect, developer, corporate leader, and agencies such as planning and zoning departments. Historically, architectural design for a developer client is an aspect of our profession that has been heavily criticized. The esoteric architectural community, to a great extent (although now changing), has viewed the commercial building as something other than architecture. This, however, could not be farther from the truth. Our challenge as architects is to "bring religion" to the client and to illustrate the impact and contribution a building can have beyond its mere boundaries.

The first major surge in urban American, postwar commercial development occurred in the late 1950s, the 1960s, and early 1970s. Much of what was built lacked a sense of design consciousness. Many of the early developers entered the real estate field from other businesses without being trained or educated relative to the responsibility at hand. Today's commercial clients are more knowledgeable and conscientious than their predecessors, because of lessons learned from the past and the availability of high-caliber university programs specializing in real estate development.

What *has not* changed is the ultimate goal of the developer client: profit. The potential for profitability controls the budget and schedule of the project—it dictates the type and size of the building within the established ordinances, and is influenced by the amount of financing the project will receive. Admittedly, a struggle often exists to achieve architectural quality in the face of budget constraints; outstanding design services are often viewed as expensive and/or unnecessary by some commercial clients. Since the early 1980s, though, the "signature" architect-designed building, speculative or otherwise, has become more commonplace. Educated, visionary developers have some notion that "architecture" will ultimately benefit their cause. The names of leading, well-recognized design firms are often used to attract financial institutions for equity participation, and to market the building to prospective tenants. As a result there has been, until the economic downturn of the 1990s, a constant competition among design firms and their developer clients to elevate the level of buildings in today's urban centers. This can be seen as good for all those involved, particularly the city and its citizens.

Gerald Hines, president of Gerald Hines Interests, Houston, and George Klein, chairman of Park Tower, New York, are excellent examples of "architecturally aware" commercial clients. They consistently use the "signature" firms to design their buildings. In turn, the quality of their buildings allows for higher rents as tenants are willing to pay more to be associated with a building that has a high profile and *engages its surroundings*. Critics cite the "snob appeal," but in actuality it works to benefit all parties involved: the owner, the user, the architect, and the passerby. It forces us and our clients to think critically about what is being designed, where, for whom, and *how it relates to its immediate context,* specifically its neighbors and community.

The Power of Architects' Patience and Clients' Faith

In 1976, senior-level executives of the American Broadcasting Companies—New York, who had made the acquaintance of Sheldon Fox and myself several years earlier, selected Kohn Pedersen Fox (for its first commission) to complete a series of master planning studies for their operation located on Manhattan's Upper West Side. Soon after we completed the New York study, Thomas Klutznick, president, and George Darrel, vice president, of Urban Investment & Development (now a division of JMB Realty Corporation) contacted us. They had learned that ABC—Chicago was looking for new studio and office space. They asked us to prepare a design proposal for a one-million-square-foot office building that would house at its lower levels a new home for ABC—Chicago.

The site was a unique edge location where the orthogonal city grid met the bend of the Chicago River, creating a triangular parcel. We saw it as one with tremendous opportunity, where opposing forces of the rigid urban matrix and of the flowing, curvilinear waterway offered the perfect setting for a bold, significant architectural statement. From a development point of view, though, the site was considered to be in a "soft" location—meaning the area immediately surrounding it was underdeveloped and less desirable than others in the Loop.

Tom Klutznick had a great vision of the building he wanted to erect on the site. He was willing to risk the location issue because he was convinced a successful building would generate future development. It would help turn the area around and reconnect it to the city fabric. His commitment to the city of Chicago, concern regarding urbanistic issues, and desire to add to its community were unyielding. Some time passed after we submitted our proposal. ABC was to be the major tenant with office, studio, and technical space located at the lower six levels, one of which was below grade, providing easy access to Lower Wacker Drive and the environs of Chicago beyond. Ultimately, though, they decided against relocating.

For the following year, a finely crafted, small-scale model of our scheme sat on a shelf in Klutznick's office. He reflected, and increasingly recognized and appreciated the merits of the design, knowing that even without ABC, the concept of the proposed building (which he helped to form) held together very well. In 1981, he called to tell us he wanted to go ahead with the project as a speculative venture—and the rest is history. The building, 333 Wacker Drive, has in many ways become the definitive example of Chicago's most recent architectural surge. Its symbolic, curvilinear front is highly visible and well articulated. The

FIGURE 8-1
View of 333 Wacker Drive from across the Chicago River. Photo by Barbara Karant, courtesy of Kohn Pedersen Fox Associates.

building relates to the adjacent Loop surroundings, while majestically asserting itself on the city skyline by reflecting the changing light of day. Its success lies in the strength and simplicity of its form, and is largely responsible for KPF's rapid ascent to architectural notoriety. Klutznick and Darrel were courageous enough to place the utmost confidence in our young, relatively untested firm. It was one of several successful risks they took. The process and personalities involved proved to be the catalyst for good design. With 333 Wacker Drive as an inspiring force, surrounding sites have been developed, adding to the cohesiveness of Chicago and its urban experience along the river's edge.

Making Profit and Urban Redevelopment Consubstantial

Similarly, our work at One Logan Square deals with challenging site issues and concerned and competent clients. Philadelphia is my hometown, and as a result I felt a great sense of responsibility to this project. The site was the last undeveloped parcel on Logan Square, which dates back to William Penn's original master plan of 1683 for Philadelphia. Since the City Beautiful Movement, the square has served as the institutional node of the city. For thirty-three years it was a parking lot, and while a number of suggestions, studies, and proposals had been considered, no action was ever taken.

We believed that the difficulty of this project was that this site, which we referred to as "the missing tooth," was very important to Philadelphians for a variety of reasons. Many different interests had to be satisfied due to the rising influence and power of planning, preservation, community, arts, traffic, and political commissions. This was a complex task that required substantial planning and creative thinking; five years' worth of earlier proposals for the site by other noteworthy architects were rejected.

In 1979, KPF was approached by PIC/Cigna Insurance, the owners of the site, and asked to complete a proposal within a month; they knew of an established law firm, Morgan Lewis & Bockius, that was aggressively looking to relocate to new office space. PIC/Cigna asked for a development with one million square feet of office and hotel space. We worked closely with the city in our planning and design, and in one month we had a scheme that all the involved parties favored. Soon after the lead tenant, Morgan Lewis & Bockius, committed to the building, Urban Investment & Development Co. (of 333 Wacker Drive fame) joined the team and brought with them their commercial urban development expertise. As well, The Four Seasons Hotels Limited was selected to participate in the project and manage the hotel.

In five months, we had received all the necessary approvals from the city agencies involved, and construction began soon thereafter. The end result, a low-rise luxury hotel directly on the square and a high-rise

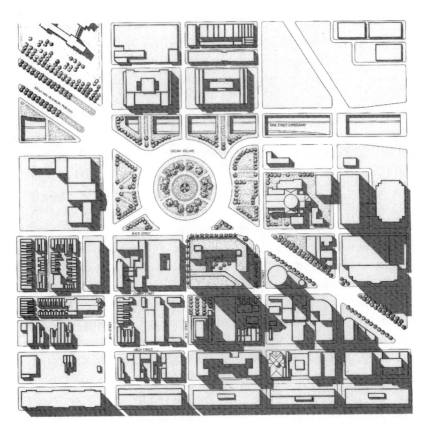

FIGURE 8-2
Site plan of Logan Square, Philadelphia, Pennsylvania. Drawing courtesy of
Kohn Pedersen Fox Associates.

commercial office tower set back two hundred feet linked by a large
courtyard, is a hybrid expression that completes the square while
respecting the historical significance of the immediate surroundings:
The square is in the front and the downtown business district in the
back. The true success of this project is marked by the *teamwork, vision,
and cooperation of all the parties involved.* We arrived at a means to
achieve an appropriate architectural fit, all the while keeping sight of
the client's need to generate profit and the city's desire to retain the
classic character of the site. One Logan Square is the only commercial
building on the square, yet it is reserved and subdued enough to accord
with the harmonious, institutional climate of its setting.

FIGURE 8-3

View of hotel façade from Logan Square. Photo by Norman McGrath, courtesy of Kohn Pedersen Fox Associates.

The Value of the Demanding Client

KPF's professional relationship with the Procter & Gamble Company for the design of their new consolidated world headquarters in Cincinnati, Ohio, in 1985, best illustrates how well this type of relationship can work. The scope of this project involved adding 800,000 square feet of office space to an existing complex of 600,000 square feet for the consumer products giant. P&G strongly identified with the city of Cincinnati—it had been home to their very conservative, diverse international operation since the founding of the company some 150 years earlier. They were committed to maintaining their low profile and to being sensitive to the culture and traditions of their city.

Their project team started by composing a list of many different firms that they believed were capable of achieving their goals. These firms were presented a questionnaire and, based on their responses, P&G reduced the list to twelve firms. Preliminary interviews were conducted at which they discussed each office's philosophical approach to the project, which narrowed the list to eight firms that were then interviewed in their respective offices. The P&G project team decided on three final firms to be considered for the commission, all of which were from New York City: SOM, I. M. Pei & Partners, and us, KPF.

We were asked to give our views and ideas relative to a master plan adopted a year earlier by the P&G expansion committee, which called for the new construction to be contained within a forty-story office tower. Our objective was to site the tower at the P&G complex, establishing an appropriate rapport with their existing eleven-story building. We worked alongside the Rockefeller Center Development Corporation, which had been advising P&G for nearly a year, as did the other two architectural firms. We presented our proposal, and were then asked to travel to Cincinnati to meet with P&G chairman John Smale and president Brad Butler. At the meeting, Bill Pedersen and I elaborated on our firm's design philosophy and spoke about the needs of their employees, their work environment, the building's image in Cincinnati, and what opportunities P&G would have to give back to their city through the new construction. As we left the meeting, we really had no idea of where we stood. We were very confident with our presentation, and I was particularly impressed with P&G's "hands-on" approach—they were genuinely interested in our proposed process of designing and the more esoteric issues surrounding the project.

We were leaving the building for the airport when Brad Butler caught up to us in the lobby; he explained that he wanted us to have a good trip home, and then told us we had been selected as the architects for P&G's new corporate headquarters. I have since joked that Bill and I were so excited and relieved that we flew home to New York but without the plane. At that time, we were still a relatively young firm and, as a result, we saw this project as the commission of a lifetime.

We were intent on approaching the process with as much intensity and enthusiasm as expressed by our client. We presented several different alternatives to the tower scheme. John Smale did not respond well to our first six or seven schemes. He was concerned that the designs did not provide a sense of unity between the old and new structures. He made it clear that the existing building would have to be totally integrated—he did not want it to appear, or its employees to feel, second class. His comments triggered Bill's final scheme, which called for a large, public garden space to serve as the focal point to the entire complex. It gave equal footing to both the old and the new structures by

FIGURE 8-4
Procter & Gamble Consolidated World Headquarters, Cincinnati, Ohio.
(top) View from public garden. (bottom) View from northeast toward
downtown Cincinnati. Photos by J. Pottle/Esto, courtesy of Kohn Pedersen
Fox Associates.

unifying the newly created L-shaped complex and establishing a sense of place. The ceremonial entrance to the site was located at the base of twin sixteen-story towers that anchored the overall site and served as the eastern gateway to the city. The issue of domination by a single tower was resolved by the scale of the two smaller towers that worked much better with the existing P&G building and with the context of the city of Cincinnati.

In our experience with P&G, the overall success was to their credit as much as our own. They were excellent clients because they demanded the best solution and took the needed time to work closely with us. We held bimonthly meetings with their project group, headed by Don Lowly, senior vice president, David Crafts, vice president, and John Lehigh, project manager, where they tested and questioned everything we presented. We found their curiosity and commitment to thoughtful problem solving inspiring. These characteristics were largely responsible for our intensive working meetings, where everybody, particularly John Smale, with their sleeves rolled up, stayed late in the day in order to move the project forward. The comprehensive nature of this commission made it the kind that most firms could only dream about. We knew this was an extraordinary opportunity to work with an exceptional corporate client and I believe our accomplishments and the mutual high regard shared to this day demonstrate what can be accomplished with sensitivity, talent, dedication, and commitment.

Relationship with Client Also Means Relationship with a Community and Context

Our affiliation with the American Broadcasting Companies, Inc., has spanned seventeen years and sixteen commissions, including programming, master planning and feasibility studies, interior architecture, and nine building projects. ABC, like any other corporate entity, develops its facilities with success in mind; in most cases the priority concern is for financial success, but in the case of ABC—New York, it has also been necessary to successfully compromise and integrate with the established neighborhood and community at large.

Their operation, occupying most of the block between 66th and 67th Streets and Central Park West and Columbus Avenue, is set in the midst of one of the city's more elegant residential areas. Its residents have consistently and properly fought to prevent the intervention of a major corporate presence in their once tranquil enclave. Our challenge with the ABC—New York projects has been to *respect the existing architectural context while establishing a strong visual corporate identity for ABC*.

At the same time, we have had to integrate complex programming requirements such as television studios, technical support, and office and production space, all the while working to win the approval of an influential community of upper-middle-class professionals. All of the ABC building projects have been implemented *piece by piece*, in which we have had to make use of a concept known as "checkerboard" expansion. It stresses *preplanning*, where redevelopment is considered relative to the client's and the community's projected needs and business. Coordination of any needed demolition, construction, and move-in is arranged so that activities on and around the site are never interrupted. From what on many occasions over the years seemed to be irreconcilable differences between the client and the community, we (ABC, the community, and KPF) were able to arrive at architectural solutions designed with the utmost of concern for the early-twentieth-century architectural context of the neighborhood *and* the commercial needs of ABC.

The association of the commercial client and the architect is complex and nonexclusive; many other entities such as financial institutions, community boards, and planning and zoning commissions are involved with and affect the professional dealings. Often, the interests of the client do not coincide with those of all or even one of the other involved parties. In such cases, the architect must serve as "quarterback," with the challenge of trying to bring all the represented groups, with their wants and needs, into a realistic form of agreement without losing sight of the design issues at hand.

Building in our urban areas is particularly difficult. In general, people are resistant to change; negative responses are seemingly at every turn when attempting to add to the city, even if for the better. The need for more office space will continue to cause new construction at some point in the future. Albeit subjective and difficult to quantify, good architecture has made a name for itself, and corporate executives and commercial developers know this. The benefits a well-designed building offers, such as addressing its surroundings, increasing employee productivity, enhancing the corporate image, and creating spaces and properties that will lease or sell at higher rates, are long term.

FIGURE 8-5
Various ABC—New York projects: Oblique view of ABC Phase II, Phase III
(ABC/Capital Cities Headquarters), and Phase IV (ABC—Healy Building)
from 66th Street looking west toward Columbus Avenue. Photo by J. Pottle,
courtesy of Kohn Pedersen Fox Associates.

When architects and commercial clients work together toward
common goals and objectives, great things can happen in our cities,
towns, and communities. The 333 Wacker Drive project illustrates how
an intuitive developer, by taking a sizable speculative risk, added to and in
turn upgraded and enhanced a weak area of the core of Chicago. One
Logan Square in Philadelphia, a group venture with profit-based building

types as its focus, successfully integrated with the surrounding institutional setting to complete William Penn's classically inspired Logan Square. For the design of their new world headquarters in Cincinnati, the Procter & Gamble Company matched our every step in terms of commitment and intensity. Our long-term rapport with ABC demonstrates that designing specialized architecture for a corporate body in a densely urban residential environment, as improbable as that seems, can be accomplished to the benefit of all the parties involved.

Architecture is a multifaceted pursuit. It is not just external trimmings or a shell and a core. A building has to address numerous issues beyond its own enclosure. Most important, it needs to be responsive to the context in which it will stand. It must appeal to the needs not only of its users but also its streets, neighbors, history, and the community and city at large. Great commercial/corporate architecture is not always easy to come by. It is the result of the vision and willingness to risk of the developer and the talent, inspiration, enthusiasm, and execution of the architect, the client, and the community.

IT'S ALL IN A NAME

Thomas Bakalars's amusing tale about receiving a commission to convert an 1892 bank building into a headquarters for a prestigious nonprofit organization is not only a model for adaptive reuse but also an example of the impact of bureaucratic error on architect–client relations.

Mr. Bakalars is president and founder of Thomas Bakalars Architects, PC, in Cambridge, Massachusetts. His work includes projects for some of the largest cinema corporations: Hoyts, Paramount, and General Cinema. The firm's residential and commercial work has been featured in *Good Housekeeping, Variety,* and other professional and trade journals.

It's 1985. I am a recent graduate of the Harvard Graduate School of Design called in by Henry Cobb [then chairman of the Department of Architecture] to rewrite my review of a faculty member up for tenure (which is another story). As I dutifully recant, Mr. Cobb mentions that an organization called the Two/Ten Foundation is renovating a nineteenth-century bank building in Watertown, Massachusetts, and is looking for someone to do the design work. Would I be interested?

Fred Bloom is the one who actually hires me after an initial meeting. He is a professional fund-raiser, still pushing his compact sixtyish body through endless rounds of lunches, dinners, and cocktail parties. He seems really happy, I mean *really* happy, to meet me. We talk for quite a while about modern art, which is an avocation of mine. Now, I didn't know this at the time, but Bloom is now convinced that I am some relation of David Bakalar, a significant patron of the arts in the Boston area.

The contract is a done deal before Bloom sits back and gives me a wink.

"So, how is your father?" he asks.

"My father?"

"Yes." He claps me on the back. "How is he?"

"Well, he's fine, thank you."

"And how is business?"

"Good. The market is looking up in Wisconsin." My father is a retired professor turned developer.

Bloom's face falls. "You're *not* related to David Bakalar?"

Well, what could I do?

The Two/Ten International Footwear Foundation, founded in 1939, is a privately funded nonprofit charity for the benefit of retailers, manufacturers, distributors, and importers of footwear. The foundation's good works include social services, job placement assistance, and a popular scholarship program. Its original location was 210 Lincoln Street in Boston; hence the name.

The building they have acquired is very clean structurally, and very well maintained. The real issues are in space planning and furniture, finishes, and equipment. The 1892 bank building must be turned into offices; the existing furniture is a hodgepodge of ugly design spanning twenty or thirty years. Nothing matches and none of it presents the desired image. The budget I am originally presented with is modest, and I put in long hours working to squeeze the most out of every available dollar.

Meanwhile, Bloom and his band of fund-raisers are making donation history. I eat out a lot during the schematic design phase, sitting at Bloom's side as he sweet-talks the wealthy members. By the time he's through, the foundation has raised five times the budgeted amount for the project. Simple enough, the board thinks—divert the excess into the

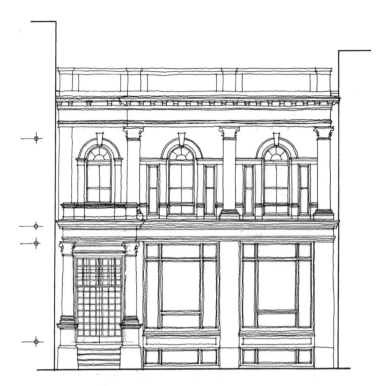

FIGURE 8-6
The forty-four-hundred-square-foot existing building for Two/Ten Charity Trust, Inc., is located in Watertown, Massachusetts. The design team's task involved an exterior restoration and interior rehabilitation of the entire structure. Drawing courtesy of Thomas Bakalars Architects PC.

scholarship fund or operating budget. Wrong, say the lawyers. The money has to be used on the building or it has to be returned.

Suddenly, this is a lavish project. Even after a generous building maintenance fund is established, I've got something like one million dollars to play with.

"Will you be able to spend the money?" the board implores.

No problem.

"We don't want to appear . . . ostentatious."

The renovation is all understated elegance. The exterior is restored to its original state (Figure 8-6); we replace the west bays and pediment that were removed in 1928. We resolve public sequencing and establish the cellular plan mandated by the Building Committee to facilitate

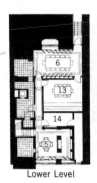

Lower Level	Main Level	Upper Level

1. Entry Hall
2. Reception
3. Waiting Room
4. Service Office
5. Library
6. Conference Room
7. Executive Office
8. Executive Conference
9. Clerical
10. Office Manager
11. Staff Office
12. Computer Room
13. Employee Lunch Room
14. Mechanical

FIGURE 8-7

The cellular nature of the plans was mandated by the Two/Ten Charity Trust Building Committee to facilitate donations for sponsorship of defined areas. Drawing courtesy of Thomas Bakalars Architects PC.

donations (Figure 8-7). The remaining funds go to custom interior window and partition detailing, an elegant reception desk, display cases, recessed blinds, very durable fine furniture, etching on the mirror over the mantel, and on really nice plaques (slate with gold leaf, to be precise) identifying the major donors. Every room, every corridor, and every floor has a GIFT OF plaque. With furnishings, the cost per square foot comes in at five hundred dollars.

The open house when the project is completed is thrilling for me. This is my first built project. Kitty Dukakis is there, and I am appointed to give her a private tour. I discover that "private" is a relative term and that I can scarcely get a word in edgewise with the entourage tagging along with us. Finally, she turns to me and smiles, asking me to give her regards to Sandy.

Sandy?

Sandy Bakalar. You must be related? she asks.

Wouldn't you know Michael Dukakis dated Sandy Bakalar in high school? (She was Sandy Cohen back then.) Sandy set Michael and Kitty up on their first date! It's the mistaken identity thing all over again.

Later that night, a dinner for four hundred is held in a hotel in downtown Boston. When Mel Sherman, the chairman of the board, introduces me, the audience gives me a standing ovation. Seeing all these heads of corporations and generally powerful people clapping for me, I am really looking forward to the rest of my career, let me tell you. I expected to sit back and let the skyscraper commissions roll in.

Well, nothing like that happened. As far as I can tell, I never got one lead out of that project. And that big budget, all that surplus funding? I renegotiated my fee as only a brand-new graduate could. I guess I earned about four dollars an hour.

CHAPTER 9

ALL PROJECTS GREAT AND SMALL

Just do it . . . yourself. The phrase can evoke anything from the fitness of the long-distance runner to five years of weekends fixing up a back room. Much of this chapter examines the small-scale project, and explores aspects of participation of both architects and clients in its design and construction. Apart from the vagaries of the spectrum of small projects, what links them all is an intensely personal, emotional, and idiosyncratic quality—one that must at least be recognized if not understood in order to achieve success.

Summer vacations (leaving client and builder *home alone*—without the architect), collecting fees, and the personality-laden clients and character-rich spaces of independent bookstores round out the material in this chapter.

MEASURE TWICE, CUT ONCE: ARCHITECTS AND APHORISMS— THERAPY IN THE SPOKEN WORD

Architect Duo Dickinson's humor is clearly informed by many years of experience working with clients and builders. In the wise and entertaining essay that follows, he captures the poetry and angst of the day-to-day struggles of an architect.

Dickinson, a Cornell University graduate, is principal of his own five-person office in Madison, Connecticut. He has written five books on architecture, including *Small Houses for the Next Century,*

published by McGraw-Hill in 1994. Mr. Dickinson has taught at Yale College and Roger Williams University. His work has been featured in more than forty national and international magazines, including an *Architectural Record* House award for his own residence in 1985.

"Measure twice, cut once."

If a television program can synopsize our willingness as a culture to substitute clichés for substance it is *This Old House*. When architects watch this show (usually for vicarious thrills during a recession—at least we can *see* somebody building *something*), they cringe at the lack of insight and innovation presented by all parties concerned—but especially by the architects as presented to the audience by the producers. At the appropriate moment their concerned faces spout sound bites with just enough aphoristic clout to have the tiniest bit of resonance. The collective wit and wisdom of this program has been distilled to the commonsense comment "Measure twice, cut once." This quote has been emblazoned on millions of T-shirts and coffee mugs owned by public television elitists.

The real world of design and construction presents far more unpredictable, ambiguous, and just plain stupid vignettes. Televised craftsmanship is sterile when compared to the lack of pretense and self-imbued ego that are present when people of goodwill get together to build something. Witness the anti-cliché spouted to me by a carpenter with a vague smell of Miller on his breath on a hot summer job site at about one fifteen in the afternoon:

"I've cut it three times and it's still too short."

Given the ups and downs and vagaries of the design/build process where the motivation to build things is seldom limited to the basic human need for shelter, and given the lack of a rule book to tell us exactly what to do at any given moment, there is a lot to be learned from the collected wisdoms of those who have distilled their humor and knowledge into *meaningful* sound bites from which anyone can learn.

"I have a porch addition—and some smaller projects."

This quote has been ascribed to a young Michael Graves—an architect who presumably now looks upon porches as infinitesimal specks of graphite dust on gigantic plans for huge projects—elements that have now probably fallen from his consciousness. But within this quote lies a subtle commentary about the latent outlook of most architects. We try to put our best foot forward and convince the world (and mostly ourselves) that there is actually a real, viable, professional future in designing things for people. "God is in the details" *especially* when *all* you have the opportunity to design is detail work.

It is this sort of gallows humor that provides architects and builders with some of their best lines. This attitude reminds me of a phrase from a 1974 *National Lampoon* magazine depicting a parody of a Pillsbury advertisement for its crescent rolls. In this case it was for "Nilsbury"— and showed the classic Dough Boy figure (but in this case with ribs showing) staring vacantly into an empty cardboard tube that once held crescent roll dough and supposedly murmuring the phrase:

"Nothing says nothing like nothing from the oven."

As bleak as this is, it does allow us to laugh at a hopeless situation when there is very little in the real world that makes sense (darkly enough in this case, the Biafran famine). So it can be with architecture. Phrases that are literally cynical become almost hopeful in their irony.

"Free advice and worth every penny."

So said a young architect-builder in giving a time-consumptive bid that I was extraordinarily grateful to receive. He put a spin on his services that allowed me to appreciate their *real* value despite all his hard work. In the construction industry, all professionals involved risk their time in trying to *get work,* and clients are often all too willing to take advantage of this willingness to pick the brains of those who desperately want to execute their project. A valuable lesson to be learned from this young builder is that the budgeting and planning work that architects and builders do *before* things actually come out of the ground are inherently flawed and conceptual.

When I use this phrase to conclude my sales pitch to potential clients who are interviewing me, they often look blank and then giggle—realizing that I've acknowledged that any thoughts I give them with such limited data on a first-blush basis are inherently incomplete and it would be silly of them to hold any view offered up in such a vacuum as anything other than a personal reaction. In this way, humor casts the bright light of truth on the presumptions of everyone concerned. It's humor born of experience that can guide architects and clients into understanding that the business of design has very little *tangible* value and a great deal of *perceived* value that is derived from experience, trust, and the indefinable belief that aesthetics have meaning.

"A good architect can turn a screwup into a feature."

So spake architect David Sellers—someone who might describe himself as relatively "out there," beyond the world of architectural normalcy. His quote is the natural progression of the previous quote—merely that it is extraordinarily easy to offer up a design or an aesthetic construct based on imprecise data. Anything that exists on paper always *evolves* as it begins to become a physical reality. There are often extraordinarily lyric and poignant architectural elements that evidence the

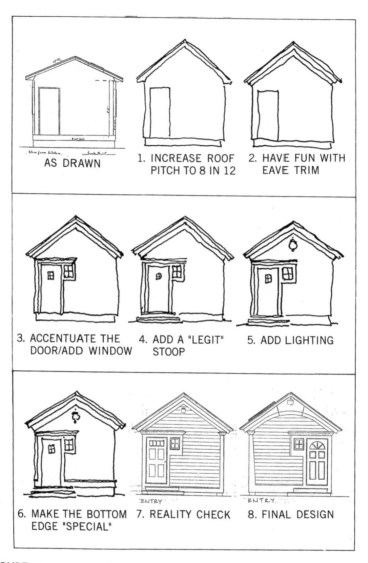

FIGURE 9-1

Images showing the progression between a builder's sketch and the final design for an outbuilding in New Canaan, Connecticut. In some respects these sketches present an answer to the cliché query, "Why the hell hire an architect, anyway?" That's the way I used them when the client came to me and asked, "Does it make sense to hire you?" I responded, "No job too small, no fee too high," and proceeded to transform the builder's rude image into a semi-expressive little box. Drawing courtesy of Duo Dickinson, Architect.

greatest level of skill because they *compensate* for something that was completely unanticipated.

A flowing stair that I executed in a project in New York could be said to be curvilinear counterpoint to an angular context—inserting lush ash and walnut steps into a preexisting world of unfinished redwood—but in truth we saved twenty thousand dollars by *not moving* a four-hundred-amp electrical power box (discovered once we removed part of the house that surrounded it). Should we have known that power box was there before demolition? In the best of all possible worlds, yes. Does the final product look like we did not anticipate that potentially costly feature? Hopefully not.

> "Good, fast, and cheap—you can only have two—
> the third is always excluded."

Think about it: If a project is "good" (high-quality, lustrous materials) and "fast" (executed quickly), it involves the highest level of skill and resources, and is always relatively costly—it *won't* be "cheap."

If a project is "fast" and "cheap," odds are it *won't* be "good."

If a project is "good" and "cheap," it almost always takes a *long* time to execute—skill levels are low, or there is little or no "organization" behind the construction—hence it *won't* be "fast."

Since a builder revealed this construct to me, it has been claimed by clients of mine who are in advertising and other industries involving money and schedules.

More money can save time and facilitate quality. *More* time can compensate for less money. These are simple truths that provide perspective beyond the 1980s cliché, "You can't have it all."

> "It'll get done before it's too late."

So said a hardwood sawmill owner to stair maker Richard Walston. He'd asked for a *date* when he could pick up his material—having waited months when weeks were quoted. When asked how *long* he'd have to wait "before it's too late," Walston was asked:

> "How long is a piece of string?"

Building anything that has *not* been built before makes timing and costs virtually incalculable in any finite terms. Rather than let the angst get you down, these vagaries are used to spawn humor that is both cautionary and therapeutic.

Words and architecture don't mix very well. Architects are infamous for obfuscatory polysyllabic nomenclature (and I just proved it!). So it's often left to these seemingly jaded phrasings to capture the true essence of what makes architecture so tough to describe—both as art and as a profession.

> "There are three rules of architecture:
> (1) Get the job, (2) get the job, and (3) get the job."

This has been ascribed to architect Vincent Kling of Philadelphia, but it conveys (not unlike the three rules of real estate, "location, location, location") a universal truth. In this case the point is if you design without clients and are without work to *build*, you are a dilettante. An architect *builds* by "getting the job"; a dilettante makes excuses, feels bitter, and does not practice architecture so much as conceptual art. Without "jobs" to execute, there is no *architecture*—only aesthetic ideas that may (or may not) apply to building something.

Architectural theory constantly flails about, trying to locate its hard edge (or edges). Definition of aesthetic theory is akin to catching springwater in your cupped hands—you get only a little of it and it's never easy to hold on to. Aphorisms invalidate the pretensions of the theoretical by casting the bright light of a reality on fuzzy concepts often based on nonarchitectural values set amid personal jealousies. The more we expose pretense, the thinner the emperor's garments become.

LESS MAY ACTUALLY BE MORE: THE POLITICS OF THE SMALL PROJECT

Architect Joe Harris has said, "What sets successful architects apart is producing a good concept within the confines of the opportunity an owner has given them." This is a profound statement in view of the following four projects, all tiny in scale and low in cost, and each for a very distinctive client.

The opportunities presented by the clients in these stories, were, in fact, huge. Each client was eager to empower the architect with creative control at the outset, along with a set of needs and preferences. Once the program was set, including functional requirements and general intent, the architect was free to design, unencumbered by changes or questions along the way.

In most cases an ongoing dialogue between architect and client is not only politically or diplomatically desirable but crucial to the creativity in developing the most responsive schemes for tough challenges. (This is perhaps why design competitions, in general, are severely flawed—no communication and no give-and-take between designer and client are allowed during the design process.) When considering architecture applied to residential work at the scale of a room, a playhouse, a kitchen, or an entry, all within a modest budget, the design process must be further adjusted. An architectural *consultation*, to develop concepts and to suggest the general means of implementation, is probably the best (and the only practical) utilization of both the professional's time and the client's dollar. In other words, consultation as opposed to comprehensive services is the most efficient, effective, and politically manageable approach in the small-project realm. Michael Crosbie, a leading architectural journalist, affirms this sentiment by stating that it's time architects surrendered their all-or-nothing design ethic (epitomized by Howard Roark in *The Fountainhead*). Crosbie believes, "The trouble is, we're trained to get a death grip on a project and wrestle it away from the client ... architects should be more helpful."

There is a surprising level of design and meaning in the architecture to be created from small projects. With great ease and passion, we all throw ourselves into the big, high-profile jobs; it's surely axiomatic that we also tend to disdain the ordinary and relatively small endeavor. Mundane little projects, however, may loom very large for those of us who will live with them. The following case illustrations demonstrate some of the typical feelings of, and interactions among, client and architect both struggling toward their common good.

(1) Making an Entrance

"All the world's a stage,
    And all the men and women merely players:
    They have their exits and their entrances ..."
    —William Shakespeare

It was bad enough working late and having to negotiate a particularly intense Beltway that night. Then, to find herself unable to recognize the place she had lived for this past year was something else again. With a thin cover of snow and minimal street lighting, every house in the new suburban subdivision seemed identical. The row of standardized façades by day blurred into a block-long monolith by night.

More from habit than visual cue, home was identified. Fumbling with her keys and the alarm system in the ever-darkening evening, our heroine took a step up as she pushed open the front door. At the same time, she slipped on the frozen slush, and briefcase and purse went flying into the Maryland night.

So went the story of Matilda Wu, a young lawyer whose campaign preparations for state representative had been somewhat thwarted by a small assortment of fractured limbs and ribs.

Matilda sat at my conference table, crutches to her left, leather-trimmed backpack on the floor to her right. With a very serious expression, she summarized: "I want to be able to find my house in the middle of the night when I'm very tired and preoccupied, and in bad weather I want my front steps protected, and whatever you do, it *can't* be distinctive: I want to preserve my anonymity; I certainly don't want the house to stick out like a sore thumb."

I commented, "Mmm—bold yet demure, tall yet short, omnipresent yet somehow absent." Fortunately, Matilda cracked a smile and replied, "Yeah, that sounds about right." (Humor is sometimes *the* most valuable political device.)

I reassured Matilda that I could offer a happy ending for her all-too-common story. With its potentials for both functionally and aesthetically transforming a façade, the modestly scaled entry is, ironically, perhaps the single most powerful residential addition that can be undertaken.

Matilda continued to detail her goals for the project: "I do want more than a cute little nose job on the face of the house, and I do want something more than an unobtrusive bit of shelter with storage for a snow shovel. I want a real place of transition—from which I gear up for 'big entrances' into the political arena on the way to work, and then collapse back into when I'm ready to return home. Just walking up Independence Avenue, you know, with the Capitol on the left and the House office buildings on the right, and all the young-ambitious, and the old-powerful striding and strolling—it's exhilarating and scary at the same time, and I'll tell you, it requires some kind of performance to navigate the day. Before I moved here from San Francisco, I visited the district a lot, and my firm would always get me a room at the Mayflower or the Willard. When you walk out of those lobbies, well, you're somehow prepared, energized, walking The Walk, you know what I mean?"

I said, "Of course. You want your entry to give you a cue, to signal the change of ambiance, to help you take a deep breath and let it out slowly, to turn on the right mental tapes, all as you leave to face the day and make the move on stage." (A good politician not only understands the constituency, but also helps the constituency to *feel* understood.)

"That's it," Matilda said. "That's exactly it, and I appreciate your application of the stage metaphor. Then after I've survived the matinee and perhaps an evening show as well, I want to be able to come home and reverse the process."

I tried to clarify further. "You mean, get the cue for warming-down and becoming yourself again."

"Yes, something like that, like a lobby that now says, 'time for a change of pace': You can cease being brilliant and glamorous, and put on sweats, and go get a bowl of Häagen-Dazs."

I now had to comment about harsh reality: "Obviously, you can't have the lobby of an elegant hotel—the scale, the opulent finishes, the feelings of calm and power. I can certainly avoid designing an addition that looks like a restaurant kitchen exhaust vent, and I may be able to realize some of the very genuine potentials for a residential entry—it will undoubtedly be a place of transition—we're good at integrating sculptural form, storage areas, materials, even plants. But it's too easy to get carried away."

In a role reversal that was a first for me, Matilda insisted that her project *"was not to be trivialized,"* and might in fact hold even more promise than I could ever imagine. She said, "You've got me intrigued and ready to spend some money—don't destroy my dreams!"

I replied, "I merely want to suggest that expectations remain in the realm of practical possibilities. I certainly reach for the theoretical ideal, but"—I searched for the right words—"in politics, you wouldn't want to

FIGURE 9-2

(left) "Before"—A rather dull, flat façade with a front door fully exposed to the elements. (right) "After"—As a natural extension of the original house, the entry adds a third dimension that strengthens the natural focus on the front door, and provides protection from wind, rain, and snow. A transition between inside and outside, the new entry was conceived as an outdoor foyer with concealed glare-free lighting, room for plants, and a built-in mailbox. Side walls can be oversize to incorporate storage cabinets, planters, and benches. An added trellis offset from the wall can blend the boundary between the landscape and the house. Design and drawings by Andrew Pressman.

make a speech in which you identify all kinds of idealistic goals and imply a promise that you'll deliver. You promise you'll do your best to *try* to deliver on those goals, right? I think that architecture is probably similar to politics in this regard. I've been upset too many times because it's so easy to pledge everything and sometimes even deliver—and then the client fires you because in his or her mind, even the goals and promises suddenly appear alien. So please don't get me wrong; all I ask is that we all agree on some rather simple, concrete goals, and if we exceed our hopes, then we've all collaborated to produce a little magic—that is, architecture."

The final design for the entry turned out to be modest, buildable, and pleasing to the client. Several years and elections later, Congresswoman Wu remains happy with her entry. I suppose we actually did produce a little magic after all, and in no small way because of an enlightened and energetic political transaction.

(II) Do-It-Yourself

Friends of friends referred a nice couple in their early forties to me. Harvey and Patrice were established as physical therapists with their own practice. They had three boys who ranged from four to eight years of age. The two family cars never saw the garage, which was filled with bicycles, toys, pet paraphernalia, and residuals of skiing and barbecuing.

With the children's arrival at school and wild growth and development phases, Harvey and Pat realized that they needed more space. The couple came to me with this problem, and another: "We have no money right now." Unlike some who say the words and then spend tens of thousands of dollars on renovation or addition, Harvey and Pat actually had little more than fifteen hundred dollars "to play with."

Our mutual friends had talked about me as being creative and able to stretch a budget, and Harvey was more than half serious about devising some kind of storage tent in the backyard. In her resulting panic, Pat insisted that they at least present their problem to me and see what I might propose.

Pat would turn out to be the key to the success of this project in more ways than just seeing to it that an architect was involved. She immediately volunteered herself as general contractor, saying, a little tongue-in-cheek, "I do everything else around here, why not carpentry, too?"

I was certainly interested, and Harvey seemed somewhat relieved. He related a comical but nightmarish dream in which he was totally alone in a do-it-yourself theme park. Unfinished and obviously botched home handyman projects surrounded him. The devil, looking like Bob Vila, appeared and commanded Harvey to complete the entire array of projects; otherwise he would remain in the park for eternity. Harvey felt he had already developed a classic case of "construction performance anxiety."

Pat went on to speculate that the possibility for involving the children in the construction seemed attractive from a number of standpoints: It would help keep them busy, maybe they would learn a bit about teamwork, acquire a few skills, and derive satisfaction from seeing the results of their work. Moreover, their involvement in the early stages of any project might ensure that they would take better care of the final product.

The concept for the project emerged as a playhouse for the kids that could do double duty as storage space for yard tools, outdoor furniture,

FIGURE 9-3
Sketches of the fantasy playhouse: A multilevel plywood castle that
doubles as storage for yard equipment. It is intended to elicit imaginative
play, and provide a visual lesson in geometry, space, and scale. Design and
drawings by Andrew Pressman.

and so on. The element we strived to develop was the fantasy clubhouse
feeling that seems to drive the best imaginative play. I recalled my childhood wanderings among the fabulous playhouses on display at FAO
Schwarz in New York City. After some happy reminiscing, we conceived
a plywood castle with balcony, parapet, ladder, gates, arches, grand hall,
window, and sand parlor. It was to rest on concrete pier blocks, and sit
up against a rear wall of Harvey and Pat's house, looking out at the full
expanse of backyard.

FIGURE 9-4

The built work has a central interior space (a simple shed), and is flanked by
a sandbox and a tower with balcony accessible by ladder. Big arches and
squares are easy to cut out of five-eighth-inch plywood panels that wrap
the shed. Masonry block is used as an apron in front of the shed doors to
extend the play area into the yard when doors are open. Design by Andrew
Pressman. Photo © Chris Eden/Eden Arts.

A Word on the Pitfall of "PC"

As excited as I was about this little exercise (and the associated local
publicity), there was something else gnawing at me. It was not so much
about this particular project, but about what it came to represent or
misrepresent. I felt that the entire do-it-yourself movement was great
except when it becomes so "politically correct" that there is a blind spot
for *craftsmanship and craftspeople*. Simply and resolutely deciding to

wallpaper your kitchen or install a tile floor is a far cry from accomplishing those tasks with a special competence and flair that may actually "touch the soul," as Charles Moore has said. Much of the enthusiasm for do-it-yourself home improvement is undoubtedly influenced by the economy, and we all must do what is necessary to get by—but it is presumptuous to foster the belief that the handiwork we young urban professionals may do is anywhere near the quality of that which professional craftspeople are capable. Talent, training, apprenticeship, and experience are special commodities and we should respect the results.

(III) Good Guest Rooms Make Good Guests

George was pleased with himself. He had completed the mission: He had met the challenge of scooping up his mother-in-law from the North Terminal. As he accelerated into the southbound traffic, his passenger turned and smiled. Things were going well this time—then, without warning, the spell was broken: "George, will I be staying in the sunroom again? You know, that cot you have does give me such a backache. And the kids' toys, do you know how many times I've tripped and nearly fallen over that stuff? And I feel so self-conscious trooping upstairs to use your bathroom. I don't mean to be difficult, George, but you really should do something—especially now that I'm a *frequent flier.*"

The crowd roared as George sprinted the last hundred meters of the race. He would be the oldest Olympic gold medalist in history. Suddenly, he was pushed hard from his left. Opening his eyes, George saw his wife's face and heard her say, "Wake up, you're kicking me!"

"Oh, sorry, I'm sorry," he responded, breathless. George's wife had collapsed back to sleep and George, try as he might, could not follow suit. So he decided to do what any typical American male would: He started toward the kitchen. Through the bedroom door and one stride into the living room, he remembered the cousins. Too late. Catching his right foot on a corner of the futon that was unfolded on the floor, George went sprawling, bouncing first off one sleeping cousin, then the other. Barney, the sheepdog, began barking maniacally and rushed headlong toward what he thought was the clear path to safety under George's bed.

George reflected on how much he loved Sunday mornings—the *New York Times*, fresh bagels, and above all, peace—delicious, calm, quiet,

FIGURE 9-5

(left) Sketch illustrating platforms of varying heights and a soffit with new recessed lighting. A twin-size mattress above storage drawers doubles as a couch and bed for the occasional overnight guest. Perimeter illumination comes from incandescent fixtures tucked behind the fascia board that ties into the soffit. Design and drawing by Andrew Pressman. (right) Storage is everywhere: In this view into the bathroom, access doors under the towel rack capture space underneath a platform. Photo by Greg Sharko, © Times Mirror Magazines, Inc.

leisurely. The harsh buzz of the doorbell violently intruded on George's reverie. He stood and reluctantly made his way to the front door.

"George! How the hell are ya? Well, c'mon, ask us in—where's the Gatorade?"

George stared for a second in silence at the sight before him: two of his closest and most dreaded old college buddies—perched on bright red mountain bikes with full packs on their backs.

"Listen, babe, let us bunk here, just for the night and we'll cook you a dinner just like at Kappa Sig, whaddya say, huh?"

George called me on a Monday morning with a plea to help preserve his sanity, his marriage, and his family. He wanted to convert an underused sunroom into a guest room with bath. George felt as though he *always* had guests, but was aware that most of the time, his children used the sunroom as an all-purpose area. The question was whether or not the old space could be transformed into a guest suite. At the same time, it would still need to be able to function as the multipurpose playroom for the kids (aged three to seventeen) when there were no house guests. I assured George that these were indeed achievable goals, and that both his family and sanity were likely to remain intact.

(IV) Cooking with Design

The little Southwest Airlines 737 skidded and bumped its way through twenty thousand feet. As we descended—rather quickly, I might add—the Sandia Mountains loomed large through the windows on the right side of the airplane. My usual flying headache escalated with the rate of descent, and any awareness I might have had of the approach into Albuquerque was quite muted.

When the old Boeing finally came to a stop, I pushed toward the front door as fast as etiquette permitted. I needed air ASAP. The crispness of the fresh air and the vividness of the colors actually began to relieve the pain in my head. I shouldered my carry-on bag, marched down the exit stairs, and made my way through the airport. National Guard F-4 Phantoms streaked across the desert as I picked up my Hertz Escort and pointed the hood toward Santa Fe.

As I drove north on I-25, I reviewed what I knew about the client. Billie Campbell, an artist and Navajo activist, was referred to me by one of my contacts at the Department of the Interior. She was described as "bright, gifted, and perhaps too passionate to be very effective as a politician." Flying in to design her kitchen seemed comically trivial as well as inefficient, but my friend at the Department of the Interior insisted that he would "owe me big." Anyway, I was ready for a change, and this opportunity seemed like a good way to begin a brief vacation.

Everything in Santa Fe, from fast-food places to the exquisite historic buildings, emulated the Spanish-Pueblo style of adobe and wood construction. In contrast to the warmth and apparent age of the city were the cold purple hues of the jagged peaks of the Sangre de Cristo Mountains. I found my hotel, checked in, and began to anticipate the next morning's meeting with Ms. Campbell.

"Located amid the greatest repository of human memory in North America, the Program for Indian Arts would invite close, successful contact between students and visiting artists and mainstream society in a rich and truly Indian framework. We can utilize our culture as a medium for outreach—as a means of channeling and educating the energies of youth on the reservations. We need your help now. Give generously. Thank you."

I clapped vigorously in concert with the rest of the crowd assembled in the small exhibit space of the Institute of American Indian Arts. Billie Campbell was indeed a passionate individual, and, from my glances about the gallery, a compelling painter. Here I stood, a struggling architect, about to design a *damn kitchen*. Suddenly, this vacation was not helping my carefully justified and tenuous professional self-image.

Without figuring out how to reconcile the kitchen with my own need to do something socially meaningful, I introduced myself to Ms. Campbell. She greeted me politely and with appropriate enthusiasm, and suggested we talk over coffee in her home on Canyon Road. The house was a ten-minute drive from the institute. We parked in an elongated oval space dusted with bleached gravel and sand. A six-foot-high garden wall marked the beginning of Campbell's property and created a private courtyard, beyond which sat a modestly scaled but beautifully proportioned home.

Inside, it was instantly apparent that Billie Campbell had not only already selected manufactured kitchen cabinets, but had them delivered as well. Boxes were stacked in the living room and kitchen, and a few seemed to tumble into the adjoining studio. The kitchen itself was a mess, and underneath various appliances, it seemed rather unfinished.

When a client has already made irrevocable decisions, then the architectural task is rather haphazardly narrowed. There is a loss of control over the big picture, and it is more difficult to explore and demonstrate what may be possible. Looking on the positive side, the more difficult the constraints, the greater the need for creative thinking, and the greater the satisfaction if the project turns out at all well.

"You know," Billie said, casually waving at the piles of boxes, "I saw these same cabinets at my boyfriend's shop, and figured I would get a head start."

"Mm-hmm," I replied.

Billie came back with a remark that seemed slightly sarcastic. "So, Ray [our mutual acquaintance] tells me you're the rescuer of all good kitchens gone bad?"

"When you put it that way," I answered, "it sounds as if I belong in a gothic romance novel. But yes, I have recently attacked kitchens, family rooms, and back porches with some success."

Billie Campbell then all but leaped upon my loose comment: "Am I to take it that you're less than thrilled to be here? You know there are a dozen local people, including three Indian architects, I could have approached."

I collected myself and said, "Look, Ms. Campbell, I didn't mean it that way. Like you, however, I see myself as trying to be an activist wherever possible, and your talk back at the institute had an impact. I will admit to feeling a bit guilty about engaging work that someone once described as 'more socialite than socialist.' And I'll bet you'd want your architect to think just that."

Billie Campbell shook her head, silently clapping her hands in mock applause. We were back in business.

After I'd completed taking measurements of the space and compiling an inventory of what Billie purchased, the two of us finally sat down for the promised cup of coffee. Apart from design, this was the aspect of being an architect I consistently found most interesting: sitting with a client and promoting a little self-revelation in order to gain a feeling for what he or she really wants. Once in a great while, this task is startlingly easy. Such was the case with Billie Campbell. A more psychologically minded individual was rare, and her multimedia capacity for self-expression made her all too transparent.

Only several sips into her coffee, and seconds into the answer to my initial probe about the timing of her kitchen project, Billie opened her soul: "You know, it's funny. I tend to work in the kitchen."

I smiled.

"No, really. Not just my writing, but I paint here. For now, I moved all my things into the studio, but the bulk of my work that's not actually done in the desert is created right here. I love this space."

"So all your good works are completed in the kitchen?"

"Exactly. That's it—*completed*. And the one thing I can't get off the ground, much less complete, is my most important work."

"The Program for Indian Arts," I interjected.

Billie went on, "It's been three years since I began the crusade. It just seems stuck. Everyone cheers and is excited and then the Board of Trustees can't agree to approve the funds—money that is already sitting in the reservation treasury—that's the tragedy. So I'm now in the position of a fund-raiser and my audience is white."

"I don't understand," I said. "There's no ambiguity that your program is likely to be of great benefit to your people."

Billie smiled sardonically and said, "Of course not, but that's not the issue. Half the board is composed of very angry young men who will do anything to avoid facilitating intercultural dialogue; their purpose is to preserve and even energize barriers between our societies—they believe that is the only way to achieve a healthy Indian self-esteem."

Before I had a chance to really temper my words, I blurted out, "So if you're stalled with the program, at least you can complete your kitchen!"

To my amazement, Billie did not register disgust. Instead, she seemed to soften. Looking right at me, she said, "Thanks for understanding."

FIGURE 9-6
The built project. New beams reinforce a path through the kitchen to the back door. This path became the major organizing element for the entire space: There is a U-shaped work area on one side, and an alcove for appliances, countertop, and pantry on the other side. The beams add warmth and texture to the raw space, suggesting the intimacy of a lowered ceiling while maintaining a feeling of openness. Design by Andrew Pressman. Photo © Steinkamp/Ballogg.

FIGURE 9-7

A more costly alternative: Demolition of a wall would have allowed additional space to be captured for a work area within the kitchen. The soffits, cabinets, and counter all work together to "step" in three dimensions, defining the proposed new focus for the space. Napkin sketch by Andrew Pressman.

With her usual composure again, but without the edge, Billie spoke: "Dumb as it may sound, completing this little personal project is something I need to do, something I *can* control. And it's a distraction too—a way I can escape and renew a bit. So you see, Mr. Architect, you are not only designing me a respectable kitchen, but you are saving me from spending a lot of money on therapy!"

WHEN CLIENTS THINK THEY'RE ARCHITECTS AND OTHER TALES OF WOE

Roger K. Lewis, FAIA, concludes his contribution to *Curing the Fountainheadache* with a series of brief tales and accompanying "morals" that can be appreciated by architect and client alike. (The biography for Roger Lewis appears in "The Hospitable Tunisians" in Chapter 4.)

When Clients Think They're Architects

It's among an architect's worst nightmares.

The large house was being framed and sheathed when I left for my summer vacation far up the Maine coast. A few days after my departure, the client, a couple with whom I had worked for over a year designing the house, called and informed me that they and the construction contractor had decided to make a small modification, one that they were certain was of no consequence and that I could readily accept. It concerned the fenestration.

To save money, both in material and labor costs, they had agreed in my absence to substitute a pair of windows at each of several locations on the façades where I had shown an ensemble of four windows. Who would notice the difference? The two windows would contain about the same amount of glass and occupy about the same overall area, they reasoned, as the quartet of windows called for in my meticulously studied elevation compositions. It seemed to them to be such a subtle distinction.

And by the way, my client said, the contractor already had done the work—framed the openings and bought and installed the windows. They just thought I should know about it before I returned from Maine. I gagged, expressed my concern, and then resigned myself to another aesthetic compromise. After all those months developing and refining the design, those countless hours spent explaining concepts and compositional details, my clients still didn't get it. And, practical souls that they are, they probably never will. It didn't completely spoil my vacation.

MORAL
Architects should carefully time their vacations so that clients and contractors are not left alone together.

Promises

Another client had paid us for the first couple of months, but now he owed us seventeen thousand dollars for the most recent month when the bulk of the work, a master planning study, had been done. From that point on, I was told every story in the book. The check is in the mail. The money will be in the bank next week. New financing is about to be consummated. New partners are about to sign on. Any day now. Papers await execution. Wait just a few more days.

I waited for months. He was always amiable and apologetic and, incredibly, always sounded sincere and convincing. Finally, after repeated demands, he sent a check, a partial payment, but said not to cash it until he called. He never called. More time passed. The check was worthless. Finally, he agreed to give me a confessed judgment note, still imploring me not to worry and assuring me that payment in full was imminent. When the note came due, he defaulted. I hired an attorney who obtained the judgment and recorded a lien against the property. Nevertheless, all I had was a piece of paper.

After another year or two, I wrote off the seventeen-thousand-dollar judgment as uncollectible and soon forgot about it. Therefore, it was nothing less than astounding when, more than ten years later, I received a call from the collection attorney—I had even forgotten his name—informing me that I soon would receive full payment on the note and judgment. The land had just been sold and, to clear title, my lien had to be satisfied. I would receive the entire principal amount, seventeen thousand dollars, plus years of accrued interest, less legal fees. The check arrived. And it didn't bounce.

MORAL
Sometimes it pays to wait, but, even better, it helps to have a lien against the client's property.

Vapor Lock

The circulating hot water heating system in our new, low-income housing project never worked properly. Several apartments just didn't get enough heat and sometimes got none. For nearly two years, no one could ascertain the cause with certainty—not us, the architects, not the contractor and subcontractor, not one of several independent mechanical engineering consultants called in to evaluate the problem. The mechanical engineer who had designed the system thought it was the pump installation and blamed the subcontractor and operators. The subcontractor insisted that he had constructed the system as designed. And the owner, a municipality, just wanted someone, whoever it might be, to take responsibility for finding and implementing a permanent remedy. The town's position was quite reasonable.

The flaw was finally discovered. There were no relief valves installed at high points in the circulating water line to release entrapped air. Intermittent vapor lock was blocking the flow of hot water. And sure enough, no such air-bleeding valves were called for in the drawings and specifications. It was a design omission by our mechanical engineer. In the meantime, he had moved to another region of the country, was uninsured, and refused to take any financial responsibility for the error. As the architect, I alone was left holding the proverbial bag. The municipal officials knew that I was not personally at fault, but they also knew that I was insured.

The town demanded arbitration under the AIA Owner-Architect contract, and, pursuant to the usual negotiations, my insurance company settled and paid for the repairs. To collect anything from my engineering consultant would have required my filing a separate lawsuit, which was not worth the trouble. In the end, it personally cost me my deductible—five thousand dollars—and a lot of time and aggravation. But the town got its system repaired.

MORAL
Don't assume that mechanical engineers know what they're doing.

ROOM WITHOUT A VIEW

According to industry estimates, over a hundred thousand retail outlets were projected for renovation at the start of the new millennium, at a cost of thirteen billion dollars to upgrade and "modernize" their existing properties. There will likely be significant impacts upon the construction industry and upon consumer behavior in the improved retail settings.

A subset of store owners undertaking major changes in physical appearance for their very survival are the independent booksellers. These owners are a fascinating group: They are entertaining the public with a bottom-line purpose, and they seem uniquely committed to making their stores reflect the cultural and intellectual nature of their product. The designs they commission are intended to be fashionable, yet often express something very personal and unique, and therefore attract more customers. Sheila Wilensky-Lanford, owner of Oz Books in Southwest Harbor, Maine, exemplifies the mind-set: "I love the books, order the books, read the books, and touch the books. I love to connect the books with the people I know."

Competition from chain- and superstores has forced bookstore owners to become partners with their architects, to work together against the common enemy. It is this kind of political context that translates to predisposition toward successful collaboration between architect and client.

The following three stories exemplify the clients' potential for identifying and communicating their own niche and strengths. Armed with this information, the challenge for the architect then becomes translating the goals to dramatic physical designs without spending a lot of money on what are usually leased spaces.

Southwest Harbor, Maine

I decided to take a friend on the scenic drive along coastal U.S. Route 1 from Portland to my new client—Oz Books—located in one of the prettiest rural vacation resort towns in the state of Maine. To break up the three-hour drive, I couldn't resist pulling into the parking lot of the Miss Stroudwater Truck Stop, near Brunswick.

"This is where you're taking me for brunch?" The hint of horror in Sue's tone might have been for real, as she was no doubt expecting one of the more mainstream bed-and-breakfasts. But the scene was so great, so much like I remembered from childhood vacations, I parked.

We entered the diner to an overture of tractor-trailer diesels resonating at idle, amid splotches of neon signage. It was almost Norman Rockwell: The old sagging plank floor on its eighth or ninth coat of brown paint, the booths, and the stools at the counter were classic. I guided Sue, who appeared as if she was trying hard not to breathe, to a booth at the end, away from the crowd. Immediately, freckled, white fat hands delivered mugs of coffee, setting them on the faded-blue Formica counter.

This stop at a local hangout was more than just nostalgic. The owner of Oz Books had insisted I get a sense of "the low-keyed small community feeling." She wanted me to design an expansion to her children's bookstore that was "magical, warm, exciting, and friendly," but more important, *"wasn't too fancy."* And I should be able to do this "for someone like me, who thinks a hundred dollars is a lot of money."

Getting something for nothing is usually part of the design challenge in most of my projects; but to pull it off in a case such as this, the client must have complete faith and trust in the abilities of the architect. Small construction budgets usually mean small design fees, so my cost-effective consultation typically involves a set of "implementation documents" sufficient to build the project. They usually do not include a three-dimensional representation, and even though relatively simple and straightforward, many clients have difficulty reading and understanding

FIGURE 9-8
View upon entering the children's bookstore. The arched reading alcove at the rear, scaled for kids, is an immediate magnet. Design by Andrew Pressman. Photo © Robert Darby.

FIGURE 9-9
The centralized pavilion provides a new focus for the expanded store. Soffits with integral indirect lighting are supported by columns of bookshelves. Design by Andrew Pressman. Photo © Robert Darby.

two-dimensional drawings. This is where faith and effective communication must predominate.

How things get done in the town was another more political issue: who builds what, who coordinates the work, and who makes decisions during construction when the out-of-town architect can't come up for a field visit. The client was instrumental in identifying the various talented resource people. It was my job to orchestrate their involvement—who would be appropriate to contribute in terms of the special design features of this project. For example, all new book display fixtures would be fabricated by a good-quality manufacturer in another state. The pavilion in the center of the store, above the sales desk and main circulation aisle, would be built by a local carpenter. The new flooring, though not in accordance with the original design (I specified a wide strip of wood along the main entry axis, terminating in an arched reading nook), was all carpet, selected and purchased by the owner from a local distributor.

Working in a small town, with a very limited budget, and with the mandate for a bold design were all interesting constraints. And, to my surprise, working within and around these constraints proved feasible and more gratifying than I could ever imagine. A connection with the community, the region, and with the industry that the client represented were together more satisfying than the completed project itself. My feeling was that derived from providing a "service" in contrast to an isolated product.

Valparaiso, Indiana

This bookstore, in the Hoosier State, also involved a renovation and expansion into an adjacent space. The client was distinctive in her sensitivity and political responsiveness to staff needs. She solicited their opinions from the outset, continued to ask for feedback, and made sure I heard what they had to say.

Driving from Chicago on Interstate 90 east during a lake-effect winter snow squall required my full attention to avoid becoming one with the blur of rubber and steel of the trucks that, in concert, appeared to be the size of nearby Gary, Indiana. Daydreaming about design possibilities was out of the question in this circumstance. So for better or worse, I arrived at the store for my first meeting without any preconceptions.

I was greeted by the owner, Susan Schenone, and her husband. They explained how they were able to interest a local business college to conduct surveys of customer attitudes—another unusual and clever strategy to fine-tune their proposed new design—this time from the customers' point of view. Schenone reiterated her comments that first appeared in a recent *Publishers Weekly* article: "The study said that it was awfully tight in here, and that one woman wouldn't even come in if she saw more than a couple of lingering customers." She continued, "We have to return to our original mission—to make the store a comfortable place to browse for books."

Achieving a balance between packing in as many books as possible and allowing pockets of space for leisurely browsing is critically important, fairly obvious, and often overlooked—particularly when there is rapid or ongoing growth. An uninspired layout of display fixtures, gradually added to over the years, may present a maximum number of books but may not generate maximum sales. The point is that the character and quality of the space are just as important as efficiency; these are not mutually exclusive goals.

A concept for the Book Bag was to design a cost-effective intervention—one that was targeted to a particular area within the store to yield the biggest impact. This translated to an indoor pergola, a modest structure extending from the entry to the sales desk. While modulating the overwhelming proportions of the high ceiling and creating a more human scale, it would serve as an entry gallery for displays. Thoughts of Peter Eisenman's spectacular axis of white scaffolding for the Wexner Center at Ohio State jumped into my mind as a precedent, even though neither the scale nor the mission quite matched.

Annual sales for both the Book Bag and Oz Books have increased by 30 percent. The bottom line? Good design, active client participation, rapport with all involved parties, and a little luck make for satisfying architectural service.

Champaign, Illinois

The big, black rubbery nose of the Old English sheepdog was mounted on a smiling, fuzzy snout, which in turn was attached to a great fluffy head. This was connected to a body—a shaggy, tailless mass of good-natured dumbness, an endearing quality that is typical of the breed.

"Isaac! Come here boy!" Steve, my client, raised his voice, commanding the animal.

Isaac loped over, probably thinking how graceful and petite he was. Miscalculating, he put brakes on a bit too late and crashed into my legs, his rear half still wagging in the excitement of greeting a stranger. A massive paw plopped on my knee, asking to be shook. A hand-to-paw exchange with this noble creature was perhaps worth my entire fee for the bookstore project that I was about to undertake: What a showcase of textures, forms, and sweetness.

Sweetness, however, is not how I would describe my relationships with the principal parties involved in developing one of the larger bookstores in the state. The major problem was that my client was not the owner of the store. He was acting as a retail consultant, primarily in working out financial operations, as well as coordinating the entire effort of starting the new enterprise. So I was essentially working through a middleman.

FIGURE 9-10
View of centralized sales desk of the Pages For All Ages bookstore from the main entry. Painted gypsum board and steel stud openings serve to unify the displays and integrate all of the architectural elements. Design and drawing by Andrew Pressman.

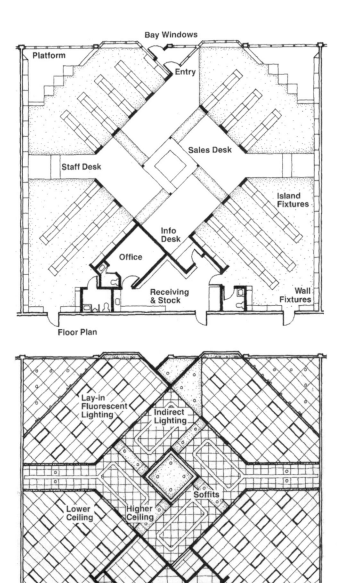

Bay Windows

Platform

Entry

Sales Desk

Staff Desk

Island Fixtures

Info Desk

Office

Receiving & Stock

Wall Fixtures

Floor Plan

Lay-in Fluorescent Lighting

Indirect Lighting

Lower Ceiling

Higher Ceiling

Soffits

Ceiling Plan

FIGURE 9-11

The pinwheel layout of the store (left) and lighting and ceiling design (right) are intended to provide visual excitement and drama. Display quadrants are organized around the sales desk. Design and drawings by Andrew Pressman.

We all first met at the owner's house, where I was to present my preliminary design scheme. Steve, the retail consultant, had provided me with requirements for the store, and I had created a design without a dialogue with the owners. Everyone, however, seemed to like and approve the design, including the always unconditionally supportive Isaac.

The big departure in terms of design was an emphasis on three-dimensional forms, rather than on costly finishes. The forms—built from gypsum board and steel studs—would impart a unique identity and promote exploration through every square inch of the six-thou-sand-square-foot area. The idea was to use common materials in an uncommon way, and break the conventions of the typical right-angled box. The experience of browsing was intended to be dynamic, and change with every repeat visit.

Problems manifested themselves subsequent to completion of final construction documents. The events, unfortunately, were never clear to me: The owners were so upset that they simply refused to talk. It was their apparently irreconcilable differences with Steve that spilled over to my work. I had no control—I was powerless to do anything to help correct any misperceptions. My sense from Steve was that the overar-ching issue was cost, and a contractor who undermined my design and documents. I could neither explain nor defend my position.

This was, by a considerable amount, the most frustrating project I have ever encountered. I felt that the design was noteworthy, and was quite proud of my work. The project was built (I've heard that much of the design was not followed), and the owners would not allow me to photograph it. I could not bring myself to take the three-hour drive to see the aborted work, and to confront the owners. To this day, when I see similar design elements in other buildings, I have momentary flash-backs, and picture my own project in its built reality. At least I maintain a good and ongoing professional relationship with Steve, who has since referred work to me. However, I now contract directly with the owners. You can't even *begin* to be a good politician if there is no personal rela-tionship with your client.

CHAPTER 10

THE CLIENT PERSPECTIVE

". . . There was no way on earth to cut a thirty-one-thousand-dollar house down to a twenty-one-thousand-dollar house any more than there was a way of making marmosets out of a zebra by trimming down and rearranging the zebra."

" '. . . It only costs us the price of an eraser to make our changes now,' [the architect] would say as he obliterated one set of lines to make way for another. 'Get them all out of your system early—they'll cost you real money as soon as the building starts.' "

—Eric Hodgins, *Mr. Blandings Builds His Dream House*
(Academy Chicago Publishers, 1946).

Money not design seems to be the overarching concern for all clients across all building projects. And it should be. However, as Phoenix-based architect Will Bruder has stated, "It's not surprising for architects' designs to be over budget since the architect is always striving to achieve the most that is possible for the client." Therefore, money and design are inextricably connected; architects should indeed push the limits of the budget in the best interests of the client. Frequently, the most innovative designs arise from challenging constraints, including limited construction cost.

In this chapter, there are tales of great client–architect relationships that are (in part) considered great because the architects were cognizant of costs and responded accordingly in their designs.

Surprisingly little attention has been paid to the importance of the client–architect relationship from the point of view of clients. The following material—written by various client types—imparts much about the nature of the dialogue, with some important tips for prospective clients sprinkled throughout.

I intended this book to be as much about clients as it is about the profession of architecture and architects. To the extent that this goal has been accomplished, I wanted to suggest something that is crystallized in this final chapter: Architecture is a team sport. Architects are generally passionate, creative people who want to make beautiful objects and do some good in the world. But, like their clients, architects have a lot at stake, so, left to their own devices, they may lose sight of the big picture. Clients must realize the enormous power they wield over architects—if this power is used wisely, the result is a collaboration that results in a "win" for all involved. If this is not the case, the process and result are the stuff of a major fountainheadache!

SWEET COTTAGE ON A LAKE

Nellie DeBruyn, after completing the house in the story that follows, so enjoyed the process that she built a second house designed by the same architects as the first one. During that time she started taking architectural classes, and is now the general contractor of yet a third house, designed by Ralph Nelson, her studio professor at the University of Minnesota.

It was a beautiful wooded lot, with 130 feet of frontage on a coastal dune lake, which opened intermittently into the Gulf of Mexico. There was a thick understory of saw palmetto and wild rosemary, and longleaf pines fringed the edges of the shore. Standing on the site where I would build that dream beach getaway, a thousand miles away from home, in frigid Minnesota, I was contemplating the first small hurdle: One of the dictates of the neighborhood was that all homes be designed by an architect. How was I going to find an architect?

My first stop was with a Minneapolis architect whose contemporary residential work, usually in the million-dollar range, was frequently featured in local design magazines. I left my interview with him intrigued by his ideas, but puzzled at his insistence that a visit to the site really wasn't necessary, and also convinced that I would be allowed only minimal input into the design. My next visit, to the office of Mulfinger,

Susanka and Mahady, was more promising. I met with the principal, Dale Mulfinger, described the site, and our needs, the constraints of the community design code, and our modest budget. I had a lot of frequent flyer miles, and he had a free weekend. This arbitrary set of facts clinched the deal. I still remember the fax he sent me, one short line . . . "I can already smell the salt breeze."

So on a sultry night in July of 1998, I met Dale's plane at the airport in Fort Walton Beach. It was odd to be meeting a relative stranger under such circumstances. He seemed out of place in the tropical heat, looking professorial in rumpled khakis, carrying a worn leather briefcase, and wearing eccentric wire-rim owl-shaped glasses. On the long drive back to the condominium where we were staying, we made small talk, discussing our strategy for the next few days. It was my first close encounter with an architect, and I was a little put off by his serious demeanor . . . or was his sense of humor just so dry that I was missing it? My limited experience with architecture included having survived the experience of a builder-designed home construction and the ten years of gift subscriptions to magazines such as *Met Home, Elle Décor,* and *Architectural Digest.* Regardless, I thought I was fairly savvy about architecture, and felt surprisingly self-conscious talking about it with someone who had been in practice for over twenty years. It was the beginning of an intense education.

The next day we headed directly for the site, and discussed the parameters of the design codes, which nebulously called for a "seaside cottage aesthetic." The materials dictated were Galvalum roofs, wooden windows and doors, and wood or stucco siding. There were setback and height limitations, and a request to clear as little vegetation as possible. Further, the code stated that, in an attempt to promote architectural integrity, variances would be allowed only at the discretion of the design review board.

Our small budget would be the determining factor for most elements of the program. At around two hundred thousand dollars, even though construction costs in Florida were inexpensive, we would be paring down square footage and keeping interior finishes bare bones. We needed bedrooms for our two sons, and for us, and room for the guests whom we imagined would be knocking at our door. We needed bathrooms, a functional kitchen, room for a large dining table, a living room

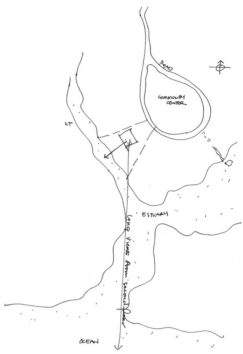

FIGURE 10-1
Sketch of the site plan showing context: access road, community center, lot, views, estuary, and ocean. Courtesy of Dale Mulfinger.

with a wood-burning fireplace, large windows for making the most of lake views, and, of course, a deck. Dale reassured me that we could meet these goals within the budget, but I had serious doubts.

We spent a long morning scouring the coast in search of examples of seaside architecture. Dale needed to investigate county building codes for hurricanes, and check out local materials and building practices. Simultaneously, he was trying to fathom, from my commentary, what my tastes were. We walked through the town of Seaside, stopped and looked at architecture books, and I could sense his probing, and his equal puzzlement.

A second visit to the lot prompted some serious discussion about how to site the house.

My lot was severely pie-shaped, about ten feet across at the entrance. It had been damaged by Hurricane Opal, as evidenced by some huge

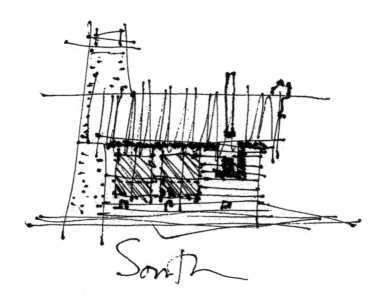

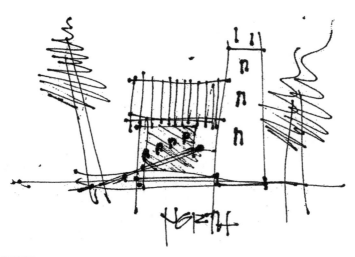

FIGURE 10-2
The very compelling napkin sketches of the initial scheme with tower.
Courtesy of Dale Mulfinger.

downed trees at the shoreline. We climbed up the branches of a fallen sand live oak, straining for a glimpse of the Gulf. One coastal eccentricity, to which we committed on the spot, is the upside-down floor plan—that is, an arrangement where the living area and kitchen are on the second floor, facilitating better views and breezes from the Gulf. We discussed orienting the house toward the south, Gulfward, and tried to predict what future development would potentially obstruct the views. These dialogues were a novelty to me, accustomed to thinking of architecture in terms of floor plans, closet space, and the modern Italian kitchen cabinets and Sub-Zero appliances gracing the pages of *Met Home.*

Our short visit to Florida ended in a bar, where, after sharing a bottle of wine and a couple of scotches, Dale drew some sketches on cocktail napkins of a beautiful-looking cottage, ingeniously placed at an angle to the lake, with a tower attached diagonally, complete with floor plans, and even an electrical layout. I was enchanted.

Back in Minnesota, we arranged for a quick meeting with my husband to present the plans and a sketch model of the napkin schematic, which seemed like a fait accompli. In a puzzling move, Dale brought along an architectural intern, who had also drawn some schematics of a second, completely different house. The intern, John Abbott, seemed very young. He was tall and thin, with strawberry-blond hair, pulled back in a ponytail. He was also distractingly nervous.

The meeting was a disaster. First of all, my husband disliked the scheme with the tower intensely. Further, he engaged us in a long debate about the proper siting for the house. He thought we should opt for the protected view toward the lake. We both liked John's very compact and contemporary cabin, but it seemed unsuited to the site. In another move, my husband upped the ante on the budget to $250,000. Afterward, we debated whether we were supposed to put all our cards on the table, or whether we should treat the relationship with an architect the way we would when bartering with any other subcontractor for the price of work to be performed. We sent two very puzzled and dejected architects back to the drawing board that night.

It shouldn't be surprising that their next passes at design schematics were faxed directly to my husband. He fired back a complimentary note before I had even seen them. I was not nearly as enthused, but didn't

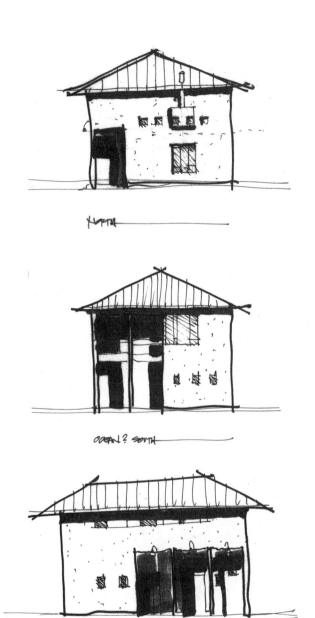

FIGURE 10-3
Schematic elevations for an alternative scheme without the tower.
Courtesy of Dale Mulfinger.

have the nerve to reject another scheme. When the impressionistic lines and shading of the hand-drawn schematics gave way to eighth-inch-scale hard line drawings, I started to express my doubts. The proportions suddenly seemed awkward. Were the pillars skinnier or taller? Was the roof more pitched or the overhang shallower? They explained to me that the schematics were a truer rendition of the eventual project, and, somewhat mollified, I gave the go-ahead to proceed.

After producing the ultimate design solution, Dale phased out his participation in the project and handed over the production of construction drawings to John. Whatever alarm I may have felt at Dale's sudden departure was mitigated by a naive belief that most of the important design work had been completed, and also an assumption that the intern's fees would undoubtedly be less. As John was younger and less experienced, I felt less intimidated expressing my opinions to him. With him at the helm, the project became more of collaboration. While he was working out the intricacies of the floor plan, trying to make the most of every square foot the minimal budget allotted him, and delving into the structural issues of coastal construction, I pored through magazines books, and the Internet, looking for interesting materials, and comparison-shopping.

It was a slow start. For weeks we vacillated over the choice of siding materials for the house, then finally settled on stucco. My builder balked at the use of stucco on wood siding, and, as it turned out, the design covenants dictated concrete block as a surface for stucco. With the building system for the house altered, John needed to retool all the work that had been done. Little did I know how much work was being generated by this change; how the dimensions of block versus wood would affect everything, from the usable dimensions of interior space, the wall depth perceived in the apertures, and the application of insulation and drywall. Many decisions needed to be rehashed. We added several feet to the western wall, easing up some impossible space constraints that were evolving. In an attempt to salvage the budget, we decided to use the slab as our finished floor, and to expose a wall of concrete masonry units (CMU)—also known as concrete block—on one end of the house. These decisions, somewhat unorthodox and contemporary design moves, excited John at a time when the prospect of starting from square one was a little overwhelming. They also confirmed an alignment of our aesthetic agendas.

John was treating the project like more than just a job, which made me more willing to agree to decisions that might push the budget beyond our limits. I eagerly anticipated and prepared for our weekly meetings, during which we debated a variety of design minutiae, sometimes making very few substantive decisions after hours of talk. John began to gently remind me that time was money. I remember reflecting that the weekly meetings were akin to psychotherapy or massage. What could be more narcissistic than having hours of intense discussion focused on you, and the space you are going to live in?

As famously as John and I were collaborating on the house, the budget was an issue of constant stress. It was frustrating how generally clueless John was about the relative cost of materials. He drew beautiful elevations of windows arranged in Mondrian-like compositions, which we submitted to the window manufacturer for preliminary bids. The price was astronomically high. After several conversations with the window rep, John realized that by choosing stock sizes, by reducing the number of operating units, by using units from the manufacturer's "Support Series," we could cut the bid almost in half without compromising the design. John recognized that he was learning on my time. The bills rarely reflected extra hours he spent educating himself.

The primary issues where John and I disagreed on matters of "taste" were relative to the merits of cost versus value. I was happy that he agreed to using stock birch veneer interior doors, and he was correspondingly pleased when, after comparison-shopping, I opted to have all the exterior doors custom-made from mahogany. While we were eliminating expensive trim work and substituting it with gypsum board reveals and returns, somehow the increased labor costs represented by these changes went unnoticed.

Many of these details were incomprehensible to my builder, a man who ran a poultry farm as a sideline, and who had just graduated from building spec homes to building for clients. The construction drawings, though adequately detailed, were sometimes incomprehensible to a man who had never seen contemporary architecture. As construction proceeded, I found myself taking on the role of interpreter for some details that even I didn't fully understand myself. He was making his best effort to perform the sequential tasks suggested by the drawings, but without a holistic understanding of the building, it was difficult. John had a hard time comprehending how his articulate instructions

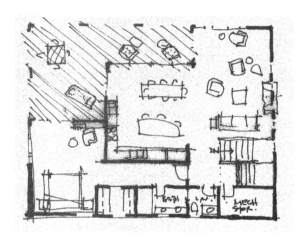

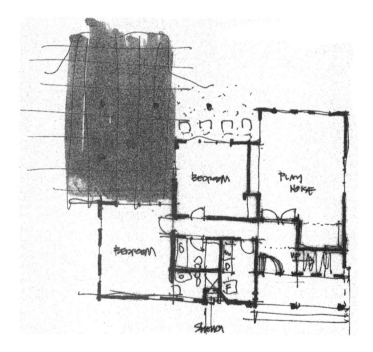

FIGURE 10-4
Floor plans that approximate the built condition. Courtesy of Dale Mulfinger.

could so often be misunderstood. I was caught in the middle, listening to an explanation from the builder as to why a detail was impossible to execute and needed to be changed, then calling John to have him tell me the objections were ridiculous. And yes, once again, it all came back to money.

This trend repeated itself with the subcontractors. My cabinetmaker and John engaged in an endless debate over an inch of tolerance where a drawer needed to clear the handle of the stove. Such debates erupted with regularity, and as a client, it was difficult to know how to proceed. Even when John prevailed in these standoffs, the eventual results were often not as intended. It is entirely possible to believe both that your architect has created a beautiful, functional design and that there may be errors that arise in execution of the parts that create the whole. It is hard to understand how, despite the hours of work represented by the construction drawings, there are still dozens of details that need to be worked out on the site. As construction drags on, the integrity of the design becomes increasingly difficult to defend, especially when subcontractors start chanting the dreaded words, "Change order."

Remarkably, the house was completed about a year after first walking the site with Dale.

The budget, while being stretched, did not escalate to the point of creating hard feelings. It is not perfect. More research could have been done about the climate and the site. I wish we had provided for more windows on the eastern, street side of the house. I long for more morning sun and a connection with the neighborhood. We underestimated the amount of space we needed, and squeezed a little too much out of our square footage. The kitchen and great room are not as functional as they should be. Life at the beach turns out to be more like life at home than we anticipated.

Now, sitting in the second-story great room, I am distracted by the lake, which seems to lap at edges of the house. The composition of the window has the intended effect of framing the views perfectly. It is a sensual pleasure to sit in this room, a contrast in materials, the concrete block wall juxtaposed with a birch ceiling that perfectly echoes the hip roof above. The slope of the roof continues out onto the deck, where heavy rafters support a delicate metal roof. On a rainy afternoon the urge to experience the sound of the rain under this architectural umbrella is irresistible. The powerful connection with the outdoors, which was created here, is like a punctuation mark making me pause throughout the day. This house, as unique as a chain of DNA, is utterly simple, yet I have never seen a house even remotely similar to it. I think this is the reason for architecture.

THE LEAP OF FAITH: WHAT EVERY CLIENT SHOULD KNOW ABOUT RESIDENTIAL ARCHITECTS

S. Claire Conroy is chief editor of *Residential Architect* magazine, the only national professional magazine focusing exclusively on the practice of residential design. For more than fourteen years, she has written about houses and housing for Hanley Wood, LLC, publications. Prior to Hanley Wood, she served for eight years as managing editor and arts editor of a city magazine based in Washington, DC. In 2003, she received the American Business Media's Jesse H. Neal Award for Best Staff-Written Editorials. She is a graduate of Vassar College.

We may be the only species that elevates basic necessities to the ranks of high art. Food and shelter are particular favorites for our powers of invention. We could consume basic food just to stay alive, but we prefer more carefully and imaginatively prepared meals that make us feel we're really savoring life. A great meal is a creative endeavor for the chef and for the diners, too. It's an art that requires an audience to complete the experience. Similarly, we can and we do build basic houses that provide shelter from the elements, but we dream of homes that also satisfy other, less corporeal concerns—something beyond need and closer to desire. We see these homes in magazines and television shows, fueling our appetites for similar transformations in our lives. But how do we make it happen for us?

How do we track down the right architect to make our vision a reality? Should we look for a reliable builder first? And, most important, how much will it all cost? These are questions the glossy home magazines and glitzy TV shows never really answer, leaving the whole process mysterious. These days, we're all pretty sure an architect's involvement means the house will turn out more beautiful than without it. But identifying the appropriate one feels complicated and intimidating. We know where to get that gourmet dinner—we simply read the restaurant reviews in the newspaper and we bolster them with recommendations from friends. Then we just give the restaurant a try. The prices are all listed on the menu, so what the heck? If we make a mistake, we know the limits of the damage. We know it won't break the bank. Not so with commissioning a custom home or a substantial remodel. For most middle-class families, the greatest portion of their assets is tied up in their house. They can't afford to just close their eyes and take a leap of faith.

But a leap of faith is exactly what many architects ask for. They ask for your trust, they tell you to abandon your preconceived notions of what your house should look like, and, in some cases, they require a third of their commission up front. You think you're asking for a product—a well-designed house in this amount of time for this amount of money. Architects want you to think of it as a process—a creative journey you'll take together with everything open to evolution and revolution along the way. This difference in perspective is at the root of most misunderstandings between architects and clients. You want a good house to live in; residential architects want a fulfilling life designing houses. You seek a service; they pursue an art. The best collaborations happen when clients also seek and appreciate the artful in their project, and when architects honor the basic needs and constraints of their clients, while finding a way to answer some of their heartfelt desires, too.

Looking for Mr. Good Architect

Getting that mix just right is the tough part. It's too bad potential clients and architects can't take a test to determine their leanings on the art–service scale. Because aligning those expectations is important to everyone's happiness during the project and after it's completed.

But finding the perfect architect seems like a search for the Holy Grail. Especially during a housing boom. And even more particularly when your project is budget-driven. Most novice clients are grateful just to locate a single architect with a decent word-of-mouth reputation. Continuing the search for the best fit can be overwhelming—and pricey, as labor and material costs skyrocket while you look. Some clients just grab hold of the port in the storm and hope for the best. They hope they can pay what the architect charges and they hope they can afford to build what he designs. And most of all, they worry they won't love the house when it's done.

Architects don't always understand how alien their vocation is to the first-time client. Because the profession is subject to regulations governing price fixing, its organizations are barred from recommending and enforcing standard payment practices. This shrouds consumers' most important questions in obscurity. Will the architect charge for a preliminary meeting? If we hire him, will he charge by the hour, for a percentage of construction costs, a fixed price? Which way is the fairest? And how do you compare firms if they each charge differently? If they're all charging a percentage of construction, what makes one worth 15 percent and another 20 percent? And when they charge a percentage of hard costs, where's their incentive to watch your pennies in both the design and construction? Then there's the scariest question of all: What will the bank think the house is worth when it finally gets built?

It's really no wonder many people throw up their hands in frustration and buy an existing house or a new house built by a builder. The costs are reasonably clear-cut, and you can see what you're getting. You can walk through the existing house; or you can tour the builder's model. The builder will even let you make some modifications and upgrades. And he'll tell you exactly what they'll cost. By comparison, the process of working with an architect is rife in ambiguities and fuzzy math, and the product you'll end up with is equally uncertain.

So, many potential clients never make it to the first step of dialing an architect's office. Instead they take the path of least resistance, the well-trodden road with as few surprises as possible. In the case of the existing house, they also get the benefit of almost instant gratification. This is a powerful lure. Not only does it remove the frightening unknowns of the architect's "process," it halts the blizzard of what-ifs that can stop decision making cold. The average custom home project takes at least two years from design through construction. Whose life is static for that amount of time? What if your company gets sold and you're suddenly out of a job? Will you need to take unpaid leave to care for elderly parents? What if your spouse, who's always grumbling about her job, decides to go back to school? What if you've spent a year and forty thousand dollars in design fees, and then find your circumstances have changed so substantially you can't build your house? Chances are you're out the money and out of luck. You spent your research and development funds, and you have no product to bring to market.

Decisions, Decisions

Even if budget and future circumstances are not concerns, there's another catalyst for catatonia among home buyers. We in the United States are blessed and cursed with a nearly limitless selection of products for the house. If an existing house represents a take-what-you-get scenario, the custom house is a choose-anything-you-want situation. For some people it's not only daunting, it's potentially crippling. Everyone wants some level of choice in the important decisions in life, but how many people can discern the differences and advantages among fifty cabinet pulls?

Production home builders are very smart about this. They know just how many options to provide their customers to make them feel empowered but not staggered. And those choices are often intimately linked to price—a high-line choice, a moderate choice, and a budget spec. This makes decisions even easier.

It's a well-kept secret among architects and other custom home professionals that not all relationships can withstand making so many decisions together. Every choice has two very important and divisive factors: what it will look like and what it will cost. What two people, even those in a long-term intimate relationship, think exactly alike in matters of money and taste? Fundamental differences in managing money are at the root of many relationship failures. In building a custom home, the decisions, the expenses, the stresses, and the fears escalate as the project winds on. Some couples don't make it through construction, breaking up and selling the house as soon as it's done.

There's a subtle reason why the new generation of prefab houses is capturing the imagination of the American public. Although they're still in the prototype phase, their ultimate promise is high design without the headaches of custom building. Like the customizable BMW or Mini, you start with a well-thought-out, beautiful base car and you select the options that suit your taste and budget. Your choices are limited, your costs are clearer, the timetable is faster, and you still end up with an architect-designed house. An architect-designed house on your lot without suffering through "the process"—that sounds like bliss to some people. They get the beautiful product without the dreaded process.

Whose House Is It Anyway?

Ah, but if you divorce the product from the process, you lose what's truly custom about a custom home. You're back to buying off the rack, a suit that's tailored to someone else's generic measurements. There is nothing transforming in that experience; there is nothing of you in that house except your furniture. The term "custom" has been misappropriated by so many businesses that it's now simply a marketing term. It means you can select a couple of options—someone else's choice of options—and add them to the standard product. You may spend less money in the short run, but you'll also have less emotional investment in the long term. There really aren't any shortcuts to designing and building something of enduring value.

Ikea is a good case study. The Sweden-based store fills an important niche in the U.S. home furnishings market. It provides us with solid, decently made case goods at "impossibly low prices." The furniture designs are moderately stylish, simple and bland enough not to offend the masses. The company solves a real problem (i.e., I need a dining table immediately, and I can't wait for the perfect, beautiful one) with expediency. The trouble is, no matter how much time and money you saved buying that table, it was a poor long-term investment. This won't be the table your family hands down through generations. It won't improve and appreciate with age. It has no history or stories to tell.

Much of today's housing is like furniture from Ikea: generic, decently made, expedient. Its character and charm are not likely to improve with age. When it no longer solves the problem, the owners will discard it for something different. How do you design a house worth keeping? If you think about that table again, the answers are obvious. Something worth keeping is functional, is beautifully made from lovely materials, and has strong personal associations. Details, specificity, flexibility, craftsmanship, and basic good taste—these are the characteristics of houses that delight and endure. They look better with age; they grow more loved over time. They add value to their owners and their communities.

You can choose basic shelter, or you can spend the extra time and effort for something more meaningful to you and your family. It's no accident that most custom home clients have owned several homes in the past. They know how they use a house—what works for them and what doesn't. Invariably, the houses disappoint or hinder them in some critical ways. They have lots of ideas about how they want to live and how they want a house to serve them. And they know there's no such house on the market, because it's their house they want and not someone else's.

Own the Process

Although you feel you need this house and you need it now, it's imperative you take the time to do it right. You can take control of the "process" and make it work for you. Interview half a dozen architects—at least. Find them through magazines, Web sites, the home section of your newspaper, job-site signs, and that all-important word-of-mouth recommendation from people you know and trust.

Don't be afraid to ask them how much they charge for a consultation, schematic drawings, design development, construction administration. Tell them—honestly—your real budget and your expectations. Make a list of needs, wants, and pie-in-the-sky desires. When you meet them and talk to them, make sure, above all, that they listen to you. Tour some of their houses and talk with the owners. Do they have any regrets? Were drawings delivered in a timely fashion? Did the house come in near budget? Speak also with several of the builders. Were the architect's drawings clear, accurate, and buildable? Did he answer questions quickly?

Then listen to your gut. Do you like this person? Does he set off alarm bells? And, most important, do you delight in his work? You're hiring him for a service, but you must also respect and admire the artist in him. Together you will design and build something beautiful. This is your work of art, too. It's your journey of self-expression. The house you build will represent who you are and what you find important, and it will announce these to the world.

Each custom home is a prototype. As such, it takes more time to design, more time to build, and firsthand attention to appraise. The best architects will rethink even the most obvious elements, to make them more beautiful, useful, and significant to you. They want your magazine clippings, your lists, and your musings—not as gospel to follow, but as clues to who you are and how you think. That's the leap of faith they want you to make. And if you've done your part to find an architect whose work you really love, he'll connect the dots in ways that will amaze and inspire you.

The essential secret about architects is they'll seldom turn down a job that allows the artist in them to emerge—no matter how tight the budget. Take the leap with them and you'll get not only that good house to shelter you, but also one that adds richness and meaning to your life. It will tell wonderful stories of who you are and the journey you and your architect took together to bring you home.

SPEAKING "CLIENT"

Mary Fitch, AICP, is the executive director of the Washington chapter of the American Institute of Architects and the publisher of *ArchitectureDC* magazine. Prior to joining AIA/DC she was in practice for ten years as a city planner and urban designer. A native of California, she is married to Ron O'Rourke, son of an architect, who spent his formative years in an Eichler town house in San Francisco. Mary believes that being surrounded by great modern architecture while they were growing up influenced their decision to hire an architect.

My house is a very modern renovation of a Washington town house. It includes interesting geometry, unexpected materials, and abundant light. It is the recipient of about twelve local, regional, and national design awards. But that wasn't what it looked like when we found it.

The house was the eyesore of the block. Left open to the weather for about eight years, it was calling out to some bright mind to renovate. It wasn't supposed to be us; having worked around the design field (I was a city planner at the time), I knew the pitfalls and horror stories and wanted no part if it.

My husband, on the other hand, had wanted to do a project like this since he was about ten years old. The son of an architect, it was part of his DNA. I told him I'd be happy to let him do this and just call me when we needed to move. Of course it didn't turn out that way. We chose Bob Gurney as our architect because, while it's a little embarrassing to admit, my heart raced when I looked at his work. My one contribution to the early stages of the project (besides the chorus of no) was to select the architect based on one single project. While I always advise others to go with their gut, I do recommend a lot more research. In our case, though, it worked. Like everything else in this project it seemed meant to be. It

FIGURE 10-6
"Why are we doing this?!" was the refrain underscored during preparations for the new construction to transform "the eyesore of the block." © Daniel L. Hamilton, courtesy of Mary Fitch.

all fell into place; it was almost like the house was waiting for all of us to play our part.

My husband had written an eight-page analysis of what we wanted in the house. To tell a Washington architect that you want a pull-out-the-stops modern house in the 1990s was like giving him a winning lotto ticket. We quickly realized that ours was going to be a signature project for Bob, one where he got let off his leash to explore the Washington town house in a way that had never been done.

The project was initially supposed to take four months to design. It took a year. From the beginning it was a team approach. Each one of us had an equal vote. Each one of us also had veto power if it was something that just didn't work. You had to feel really strongly about it, though, to overrule the other two. Four months turned into a year because there was a lot of back and forth. We must have built thirty different models of the kitchen island, for example. However, because

FIGURE 10-7
View of the kitchen. © Hoachlander Davis Photography, courtesy of Mary Fitch.

we took the time up front there is really nothing in the house that I would have done differently.

We met once a week, usually on a weeknight at our old apartment. Meetings always started after nine P.M. so that Bob could have dinner with his young children. Following the meetings my husband invariably would stay up until the wee hours pondering the proposals and providing alternatives. His great strength was encouraging, and sometimes forcing, Bob to resolve all the lines in the house. If a curve presented itself, we needed to know what it related to, how it helped to carry the design of the house. It couldn't just happen because it was pretty. This was absolutely critical, because the odd shape of our house, eighteen feet wide at the front and thirteen feet wide at the back, meant balance was critical. Because we wanted warm-modern, instead of cold and stark, we have a rich palette of materials that also had to be carefully balanced or it would have been chaos.

As often as Ron held Bob's feet to the fire, however, there were moments of discovery and surprise that are the very reason one hires an architect. The day he presented the fireplace, which is a signature feature of the living room, we were struck dumb with amazement. All we could say was, "How did you know that is exactly what we wanted?" In the same way, a simple color shift in the floor pulls the entire house together: It's a simple twist that I have come to appreciate more and more.

My relationship with Bob deepened when we ran into contractor problems, and two-thirds of the way through construction I had to shoulder much of the burden. Although I was completely terrified, Bob was on site with me every day. It was as much his dream as it was ours and he completely committed to getting it done. One important lesson is that you want your architect to love the project as much as you do; it makes all the difference.

Midway through the project, a friend of mine who ran the local chapter of the American Institute of Architects decided to leave her job and suggested I might want to give it a try. Who would be the next executive director was a subject of great speculation at some of our weekly design meetings with Bob, although we never let on that I was the candidate. In fact I worried at one point that this might complicate matters between us. When I finally got the job I thought Bob was going to keel over he was so pleased. As much as I tease him now that he changed my life, I think in reality he did. I believe that having this very

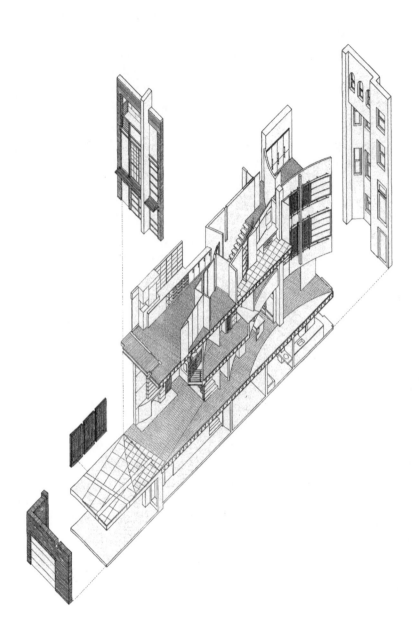

FIGURE 10-8
Axonometric drawing illustrating the Washington, DC, town house. Design and drawing by Robert M. Gurney, FAIA, Architect.

FIGURE 10-9
The living room and second floor balcony as seen from the outdoor patio. © Hoachlander Davis Photography, courtesy of Mary Fitch.

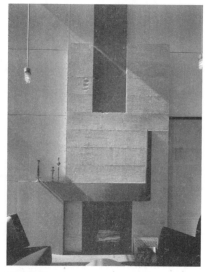

FIGURE 10-10
The fireplace is the focal point of the living room. © Paul Warchol Photography, courtesy of Mary Fitch.

positive, collaborative partnership has really made me better at helping others when they need design services. I've been there; I speak "client."

Finding an Architect 101

1. Be prepared. Put together a list of what you are looking for in your new home or renovation. Do a wish list and include everything, whether you think you can afford it or not. It's more important that your architect see what you really want rather than what you will settle for. Include an image file: Go through all your favorite shelter magazines and find things that you like.

2. Do your research. Visit your local American Institute of Architects chapter or visit Web sites such as www.aia.org where you can find architects in your neighborhood. Talk to friends and find projects you like and knock on the door and ask who the architect was. All house-proud owners will be happy to tell you who designed their house.

3. Talk to at least three architects. Even if you fall madly in love with the first one (metaphorically speaking, of course), talk to at least two more. This will, at the very least, make you feel more certain in your choice and more than likely give you some additional ideas.

4. Talk about money. One of the most important features of the architect–client relationship is trust. One of the fastest ways to determine if you are communicating is to talk about money. Does this conversation go well or do you feel somewhat uncomfortable? Pay attention to those feelings. This person is going to be around you every day for months— make sure you can communicate well.

5. Be patient. If you want something fast, buy a tract house! Great art takes time. The more time you take up front, the more the house will be right for you. This is actually the hardest thing to remember when you are in the thick of the project, but it is well worth it in the end. Trust me. I've been there!

CLIENTS BEHIND THE BUILDINGS: A CONVERSATION WITH ANDREW WOODEN

Andrew Wooden is head of the Bosque School in Albuquerque, New Mexico. He received his BA in English in his home state at the University of Maine and an MA in religion from the Yale Divinity School. He began his career in education in 1977 at Brewster Academy teaching English, house advising in the dormitory, and coaching basketball and sailing. He joined Choate Rosemary Hall in 1984 and directed the admissions and financial aid department and worked on capital projects. Under Andrew's leadership, the Bosque School has completed the first phase of the capital campaign to build a permanent campus, and the second phase to grow an endowment, establish the Ford Library, and build the Findlay Arts Center. Having completed his research fellowship at Yale University in August 2003, he returned to campus to commence planning for Bosque's next stage.

Bosque School's challenge was to design an independent school campus for grades six through twelve on twenty-three acres of environmentally sensitive undeveloped land. The architectural challenges were both many and complex. To our north is land that holds a Native American archeological site. To the east is a hundred-acre mature cottonwood forest that connects us to the Rio Grande. To the southwest is the La Luz Community, Antoine Predock's first commissioned development. To the due west is some of Albuquerque's worst urban sprawl. In short, we needed an architect who could lead us through campus master planning and design being sensitive to our desire to be unobtrusive to the natural setting, aesthetically sensitive to our nearest neighbors, and still produce a campus whose front door is a commercial corridor. The campus had to blend into a variety of mutually exclusive surroundings and still have integrity. Among the competing priorities we determined that our commitment to the Bosque environment trumped the others. Because of Bosque School's commitment to environmental education and because of the contiguous hundred-acre wood we wanted most for the campus to have a seamless relationship to the Bosque to the east.

Because we were a new school without a reputation we had to be practical. Could we design a campus with academic buildings that would attract the city's top applicants? Schools and colleges learned long ago that is naive to assume that "if you build it they will come." We knew that the architecture would either help or hinder admissions and fundraising. We needed a design that would be traditional enough to speak to "academic tradition" yet progressive enough to inspire imaginative students and teachers.

We also believe that architecture affects learning. We wanted classrooms, corridors, meeting spaces, pathways, and outdoor areas designed to inspire young people to learn and to interact with the larger community with civility. As a new school we were free to rethink school design—to take a fresh look at school architecture. We wanted to design space where students and teachers wanted to work together.

The school, as the client, posed other hurdles for the architect. We needed to build at a very low square-foot cost. We also believed that we had a great deal of educational experience and we wanted our voice heard. We had done our homework and we had a sense—right or wrong—for what worked and didn't work in school settings. We also knew that we were speaking out of both sides of our mouths. We wanted an architect who was creative, imaginative, and free to break with tradition and to dream big, but we as the client had strong opinions and limitations. We laughed often as we said to our architect, "We don't know what we want, but we know what we don't want." In short, the project had to please a variety of constituencies—teachers, students, parents, city officials, and potential donors. We needed a campus that would be aesthetically pleasing, creative and inspiring, sensitive to the environment and its neighbors. Because we trust that the school will exist in perpetuity, we hoped that the design would last centuries.

The Best and Worst of Engaging an Architect

At the end of a long and exhaustive search, we engaged Ed Mazria, an architect with huge talent and healthy self-confidence. The best of engaging a good architect is watching wonderful ideas take shape. It was a joy every week to see a new idea, a new lovely shape, a creative solution to a vexing problem; the architect was giving us something we could never have done ourselves. Although our project was highly cost-sensitive, when architecture is delightful the fees seem negligible. In fact, for the services we received, we felt as though architects are woefully underpaid for both their talent and training. It was inspiring to hear Ed Mazria describe his ideas and to see his drawings. We felt as though we were in a creative process together. He not only came forth with great ideas, but he also listened to our hopes and fears and found creative solutions based on our client needs. For example, we said we needed to keep construction costs as a minimum but wanted the buildings to be interesting. He came back and said, "Daylight is both playful and free—let's use a lot of it. We can use inexpensive materials, but vary texture, color, size, and shape. The classrooms, offices, and meeting spaces can have dramatically different sizes and shapes to reduce redundancy." Our architect listened to our problems and solved them.

The worst part of the relationship was negotiating materials with regard to cost. He would suggest an interesting, cutting-edge light fixture; we would suggest something less interesting at half the cost. He would suggest beautiful detailed steel trusses; we would suggest unattractive wood beams at half the price. He would suggest expensive storefronts and complicated angles. We would counter with stucco and right angles to save money. In these negotiations there was healthy tension and we navigated reasonably well. As in all negotiations, when we tried to listen and understand what was most important to whom, we both came away with increased pride and value. In the end, when we were open and honest with each other, made priorities clear, and gave concessions, we reached resolution. On the occasion when we would try to "sneak one by" each other the fallout was unpleasant. Neither architect nor client enjoys surprises.

Our Relationship

Our relationship was excellent from the start because of mutual respect and our admiration for Ed's talent, creativity, humor, taste, and skill. In the middle of the project the relationship became stressed by financial pressures concerning construction costs and by timetable. The only other frustration is that we often had draconian time deadlines, and "we don't have time to redo this" was often an unwelcome answer to our request for revision. Because our architect didn't give up listening to us and trying to compromise we came through the process whole. The relationship returned to excellent as we neared completion. To his credit, Ed never lost interest in the project even after completion. We have him speak regularly at the school about the architectural intent. We brag about him; he brags about us—and it works. He continues to be a resource for us. We have used a different architect subsequently for two additional buildings, but that was based on a particular set of circumstances. He understood the decision, and we have remained close and we would be proud to use him again and again for subsequent buildings. Because Mazria created the vision for the school in the beginning, this campus will always be his; because our campus has grown to forty-four acres, there will be buildings in the future where we may turn to other architects based on the particular design needs.

A sense of humor can help through the ups and downs of a long project. At one point, we had what we called a "Mazria Meter" drawn on my white board. It gauged the degree to which we believed Ed Mazria was "client-friendly." It looked like a speedometer and we would adjust the needle from zero to ten depending upon how well we thought he was listening to us. In retrospect, it gauged both our frustration and elation. When Ed would come into the office and see the needle buried at negative two, we would laugh and say, "Let's take a break and figure out how to get back on track." In our case it was the client who was more likely to stress the relationship, and then the architect had the next move. He usually responded with humor and flexibility and would save the day. Occasionally, we could push too far, and it was fair for the architect to bite back.

Challenge for Excellence

We chose our architect for his reputation for striving for excellence. We were more worried that we would need him to make his design more mundane and less excellent based on our limited finances. Where he did challenge us was with regard to programming. He was right to have us spend more time discerning what all our goals were for each building. He knew that excellence was not simply in beauty of design, but more important, in how the space would be used. Just because we thought we knew all we needed for programming didn't mean that we did. He forced us to keep digging deeper concerning all the potential uses for the campus and he was right to challenge us to think longer term. We gave him quite a bit of scope on aesthetics; we hired him because we like his work and trust his eye, so we were glad that we didn't micromanage him, and we felt he pushed himself for excellence.

In our search we defined excellence as both beauty and function. We eliminated many submittals of equal prominence from consideration because we feared that we would get aesthetics, but could not control the functional objectives of the project. A classroom can be breathtaking, but cold—or worse, have serious acoustic problems. Paths on campuses can be beautiful, but if they are not the closest distance

FIGURE 10-11
The Bosque School, view of the arts building. Photo courtesy of Mazria, Odems, Dzurec, Architect, Santa Fe, New Mexico.

FIGURE 10—12
The Bosque School, west elevation of a classroom building. Photo courtesy of Mazria, Odems, Dzurec, Architect, Santa Fe, New Mexico.

between two points they won't work. I believe that the client and architect have to be explicit about these concerns before the architect is selected. We benefited in the search process by both looking at the architects' portfolios and, even more important, talking to previous clients. Perhaps a lesson learned is: Know each architect's strengths and weaknesses before offering the job.

People Skills

Our architect has plenty of ego and self-confidence, but we knew that before we hired him and that was one of his strengths. We enjoyed working with an architect who was larger than life. It was okay with me that when I would suggest something I thought aesthetically pleasing, he would respond, "G-R-O-S-S," taking the time to spell out each letter.

What I appreciated most was his willingness to listen, to take each and every call, to return calls promptly, to track down and check out each suggestion. We would suggest a building that we liked in Dallas or Boston and we would all hop on a flight. In looking at others' work he was never defensive; he was always open to new ideas. Some of our best times were in rental cars, airports, and site visits that allowed us to spend time both getting to know each other and lots of time to think, imagine, and talk.

There existed a wonderful balance between the strengths and weaknesses of our respective skill sets. He was skilled at letting me know when one of my ideas would not work architecturally; I tried to let him know subtly that eleven-year-olds and public water elements don't mix. It was because of his interpersonal skills that he could listen and filter— his skills also allowed him to win us over when he had a good idea that was risky.

Lessons Learned

Here is a summary of the lessons described above:

- If you are in a small city, do not broadly invite Request for Proposals (RFPs) and then interview a long list. It only creates hard feelings and wastes architects' valuable time. If you can narrow your list before RFPs and do client checking before the interview process, your post-selection period will be less stressful and hurtful.

- Understand your total project budget and talk about it in the interview process. Few clients can handle big surprises later. One of the best things about our architect was that he promised to build to a square-foot cost and achieved it.

- Do not expect an architect to change his aesthetic style for yours. We were lucky that our styles were compatible; the architect you choose will come with her or his unique style.

- Do not do a complicated project on a tight time schedule. For the programming to be done well, to visit buildings of interest, to be sure that materials are available, plan for extra time. It is frustrating to hear "We are out of time" when you want to make a change. Also, get it right the first time. Contractors make their money on change orders. The fewer the change orders, the more likely the project will come in on budget.

- If you make the right decision in architect selection, you can afford to kick back and let the creative process take its course.

Critique

There was one aspect of the project that we as clients woefully underestimated. In retrospect, it is too much of a challenge to design a large campus and its several buildings at the same time with an accelerated schedule. Unintentionally and unconsciously, we worked so hard getting the campus vision and master plan figured out, some of the individual buildings got less attention. For example, we spent so much time trying to figure out where the library should go we didn't have enough time to think fully through how the library would be used. In a perfect world there would be one group working specifically on each distinct building while another worked on the large site plan.

It is easy to look back at small things: Did we push hard enough when we negotiated items like square footage in a variety of different spaces? Should we have increased the budget in a variety of highly visible spaces that would have improved the overall quality of the project? Did we cut too many costs in too many areas that will come back to haunt us in plant replacement long term? The answers are probably yes and no, but it is rewarding to remember that the architect was open to all these questions of balance and, most important, we have never second-guessed the key design elements. And we have the architect's talent and diplomacy to thank. Diplomacy is time consuming but worth it. I also feel very good about civility. We were never "brutally honest" because honest is brutal enough. Often, it seemed that classic negotiation tactics worked best. There were design elements that the architect felt so strongly about I knew not to fight, but there were elements that I felt so strongly about that he would often give in. We always showed mutual respect.

Final Comments

The more a client knows about architecture and the design process, the better. A client should know the architect's work and why it works. A client should have a broad understanding of the kind of architect that is desired before the selection process. For example, we had one architect in mind for one site where the neighborhood design criteria were traditional and strict. When we moved from that first site to the second where we were free to have more freedom in design, and allowed a more modern approach, we sought an entirely different architect.

Clients also need to be honest with the architect—and vice versa—concerning decision making. If a client expects to call all the shots, that should be made known to the architect up front. And likewise, if the architect expects to have complete control of the concept with little receptivity to "starting over," that too should be understood. There are too many examples of clients charging their architects of being faithful to their portfolio rather than their client. I believe if clients did their homework there would be less of that friction. There are equally discouraging claims that clients forced bad design choices that hurt the project. Much of this is avoidable with the proper research and a well-chosen team.

The Architect's Description

The architect for the Bosque School, Ed Mazria, describes the project below.

As architects we are aware of the importance of the educational setting to the overall well-being of children. Many school buildings are housed under a single roof with one entrance and endless corridors; they are difficult for children to understand and navigate, are difficult to use, provide little natural light, isolate students and teachers from the natural environment, and are expensive to maintain. Bosque School, with its environmental focus and innovative approach to education, allowed us to take a fresh look at school design.

The school's environmental education focus is reflected in both site planning and building designs. The buildings are located along the edge of the Bosque to encourage student interaction with their environment. We incorporated water harvesting strategies, wetlands, and indoor and outdoor classrooms that orient to the Bosque, to foster an awareness of the school's riverside setting. Materials and colors were selected so that the campus would blend into the shadows of the Bosque when viewed from surrounding neighborhoods. We daylit, passive solar-heated and -cooled all the buildings to reduce energy and resource consumption and lower school operating expenses.

To address the school's goal for more interactive learning, we designed the campus as a group of small buildings, closely arranged in a composition to form a plaza, paths, courtyards and outdoor classrooms. The protected outdoor places provide opportunities for informal meetings between students and faculty, as well as accommodating formal school functions and classes. Each building contains classrooms of different shapes and volumes that students can identify with. We clustered the classrooms around common indoor and outdoor spaces and galleries to encourage casual student interaction and socialization. In addition, the building's materials and systems were deliberately exposed to function as teaching/learning tools.

FROM A CLIENT'S POINT OF VIEW

The following was contributed by David R. Dibner, FAIA, whose diverse experience during more than fifty years of architectural practice has enabled him to develop understandings about the crucial role of the client in the design of the built environment. Mr. Dibner has been involved in the development of a wide range of building types for private and governmental clients. As an adjunct professor, he taught architecture to graduate-level nonarchitecture students on the premise that they will be the future clients: board members, corporate executives, decision makers, and teachers— and with more knowledge about what makes good architecture could help create a better built environment in the future. He is now a volunteer in the Architecture in the Schools program, helping elementary and middle school students become more aware of their built environment. As he puts it, "It's great—like planting seeds of understanding in these young minds."

Mr. Dibner was also a *client* hiring architects for major projects, while in charge of design and construction for the General Services Administration. In this role he experienced the other side and learned much about the challenges that the client faces when dealing with various architects.

He is the author of several books on client–architect relationships including *You and Your Architect*, written for the American Institute of Architects to assist clients in their dealing with architects. His latest book, *Dreams and Schemes: Stories of People and Architecture*, contains more than seventy true stories of his experiences as architect and client. Condensed versions of several of these stories have been included below.[5]

---

5. © David R. Dibner.

A Building Is as Good as Its Client

This title comes from Ada Louise Huxtable, the Pulitzer Prize–winning architecture critic, who recognized the essential role of the client in the creation of a building project. The following describes the role of the client in the building process and how he/she ("you" in this essay) can best contribute to the process of creating better architecture.

I am convinced that while there are as many different clients as there are projects, certain truisms apply to all architect–client relationships. I would like to share some of my experiences and insights that I learned as both architect and client—with the hope that it may help you and your architect to create a better relationship and therefore a better project.

I have always subscribed to the age-old definition of good architecture as being a balance of *commodity* (usefulness), *substance* (well built), and *delight* (well designed). To achieve this goal it is essential that both the architect and client exercise their individual roles in a cooperative and thoughtful manner.

Start with the Basics

First, let's establish the fact that in any building project *the architect needs you, the client, in order to practice his/her art.* You bring to the project the qualities that make the building uniquely yours:

- Your dreams, wishes, and functional requirements.

- The property on which the building will be erected.

- The financing to pay for its planning, design, and construction.

    But *why do you need an architect?* Mainly because:

- The architect is the professional best trained to guide you through the project.

- State laws require the seal of an architect on any new building or major alterations to existing buildings.

- The architect contributes the necessary experience, expertise, and aesthetic sensitivity to the process of creating a project that will respond to your needs, be soundly constructed, meet your budget, and look good.

Let us examine the project development process to find ways to produce better architect–client relationships and thereby better buildings. The discussion will be illustrated with insights and examples from some of my personal experiences as both architect and client.

Choosing the Right Architect

Probably the most important first step that you as the client will take is to make sure that you choose the right architect for your project. As in most every endeavor, the best way to start is to get recommendations from those whose judgment you trust. If they have had a satisfactory experience with an architectural firm on a similar project to yours, meet with them and personally inspect their project. Most important, ask a lot of questions about how well the project succeeded in meeting their needs, their budget, and their time schedule. Talk to the owners about the communication during the various stages of the project. How well did the architect listen to their ideas and suggestions? Did they feel that the flow of information and ideas was interactive and involved two-way communication? Were they open to the architect's ideas and suggestions? Were they able to maintain their position on the aspects most important to them, or did you feel that they were "forced" to accept the architect's ideas? Did the design and construction process flow as smoothly as they imagined it should? What problems were encountered? How did the final project compare with what they had envisioned at the outset?

If there wasn't the necessary communication, here is a story of what can happen.

The Award Winner

During my senior year of architectural school I was invited to visit a married friend in New England. He and his wife had just moved into a brand-new house and they were eager for me to see it. The designer of the house was a well-known architect whose contemporary residential projects appeared regularly in architectural magazines. He was also my friend's brother-in-law.

On my approach to the house, I was very impressed with its siting and exterior design. The house was beautiful. It seemed to fit perfectly into the rolling hillside. The vertical cedar siding contrasted strikingly with the fieldstone walls that were handsomely proportioned. There was lots of glass and long low overhangs. I remember thinking that this was the kind of house that I would like to design when I got out of school and started my own practice.

Because my friend was at work, his wife showed me around the house. Upon entering the ground floor, I immediately felt the continuity of space throughout the design. A massive see-through fieldstone fireplace dominated the two-story-high living room. The kitchen was well designed and separated from the dining room by a counter that contained all sorts of neat storage and utility functions. The whole feeling was one of openness.

I sensed her pride as she pointed out the various design features. This, I felt was what architecture was all about. Clients taking delight in their architect-designed home.

We went up the open stairway to the cantilevered balcony overlooking the living room. It was dramatic. The flow of space was almost tangible. We continued on into the master bedroom, and it was spacious with many built-in cabinets and roomy "his and her" bathrooms, dressing rooms, and walk-in closets. A very impressive house.

We then went into their child's bedroom, and suddenly I sensed a distinct change in her mood—from pride to apology. Her voice became noticeably more strained as she talked about the space. And I understood why. Where everything we had seen before had been large and open, it was now small and constricted. And worse yet, there seemed to be no satisfactory way to place the furniture. One wall was all taken up with built-in cabinets. Another wall consisted entirely of sliding glass doors leading to an outside deck. The opposite wall had the entrance door to the room. This left only one wall for furniture placement, but that was restricted by the need for a passage to get to the sliding glass doors. As a result, each room had only a bed, protruding into the room at an angle, with no space for any other furniture. It was extremely tight. And there were two more rooms exactly like this one!

"This was our only mistake," she said with strong emotion in her voice. "John [the architect] insisted that the children's bedrooms be just sleeping cubicles and there be a large common interior play space. We told John that we wanted larger bedrooms, at least to have a small table and a chair and to be able to place the bed against the wall. But he wouldn't listen. He insisted that this way was better. We argued a long time about it, but John was very insistent."

"But it's *your* house and you have to live in it. Why didn't you just *tell* him that's what you wanted?"

"I told my husband to *demand* the larger rooms, but he wasn't strong enough. John would not give in. He kept telling us to trust him; that this was the best arrangement; and that we would get used to it. Well, we haven't, and I guess we never will." There were tears in her eyes.

I'll now skip to the end of this story:

- The house won a design award from the local chapter of the AIA.

- The house design was published in several architectural magazines.

- The couple had to move the children's beds into the large interior common playroom, thereby gaining space but losing privacy and light.

- My friend and his wife were divorced within a few years of their moving into the house.

- The house was put on the market and took a long time to sell at a greatly reduced price. The main objection was the small size of the children's bedrooms.

This experience early in my architectural career left me with strong lasting impressions about the importance of balance between the architect's design suggestions and the client's lifestyle requirements. How strongly should the architect promote his/her ideas when the client must live with the consequences?

Basically, whose house is it anyway?

The Interview

It is always important to interview several architects before selecting the one to do your work. Depending on the size and complexity of your project, it is best to interview three to five architects. Include at the interview your spouse, older children, and possibly a friend whose judgment you trust, because they may bring other insights into the process. The interviews not only provide you with a chance to gauge the "chemistry" you feel with the architect, but also, especially if you are a first-timer in a building project, give you a broader view of the profession with which you may be dealing for a considerable time. You can learn a lot by listening to several architects' presentations.

This is the time to ask questions. You want to know about their previous work in projects similar to yours. If interested in the firm, request the names and contact information of their clients on these previous projects and visit them to find out how well the design and construction process proceeded and how satisfied the client was with the completed project. Ask a lot of questions, similar to those described previously.

You also want to know about the background and experience of the *specific* firm members who will actually work on your project. It is important that you meet them. Ask for assurances that they will be the people who will continue throughout the project. Too often as a client, I was promised that certain firm principals would lead the work, only to have them replaced with others at critical times in my project. To help avoid this problem, include in your agreement with the architect the specific names of firm members who will do your work. Substitutions may be made only with your prior approval.

During the interview, the architect will most likely show you projects they have completed. Do not look for projects identical to yours, but rather judge the materials they present based on your feelings about the architects and the architecture. Other points to cover during your interviews with architects are:

- How busy are they? Do they have the personnel and capacity to take on your project?

- How familiar are they with your project type and the location and special conditions of your site?

- Do they do their own engineering work? Especially if the project is large or complex, you should also talk to the engineers who will be doing your work.

- What do they expect of you?

At this time, don't expect the architect to suggest detailed design solutions to your project, but rather ask them to describe the *process* of how they would approach your project. In fact, getting design solutions at the interview stage may be a negative, since at that time, they have very little knowledge of the actual site conditions, your requirements, and your ideas. Welcome their questions because it is just as important that they learn about you as you do of them. This is the time to tell the architect of your general hopes and dreams, but it is not the time to tell them about your design solutions, because you in turn have not heard their ideas about the design of the project. Think of it as the beginning of a close relationship that must be maintained throughout the project.

Here is a true story of a potential client who was so fixated on his own requirements and design solutions that he almost left no room for the contributions of the architect.

The Site Plan

The invitation came by telephone. A developer had heard of my firm and wanted to see me in his office. I knew nothing about him except that he identified himself to my secretary as a planning consultant doing work for a large corporation. His office was in a glitzy suite in a high-rise office building in the center of New York City.

My immediate observation of him was that he was relatively young, fast-talking, self-assured, and quick in his movements. He was also stylishly dressed in what turned out to be the first double-knit business suit I had ever seen.

Anticipating that he would want to see examples of my firm's past projects, I brought with me some brochures and photos of large corporate and university campus projects. It turned out to be a waste of effort. When I offered to show him my work, his response was that he had no time to see it. He said that he had heard good things about my firm, and added, "I go by my gut feelings, so let's get to work!"

He laid out a topographical plan of a large, apparently undeveloped site. It appeared to be on a hillside, with steep slopes and dramatically changing contours. On this site drawing, someone (I later learned it was him) had laid out a set of long multistory apartment buildings. These long blocks appeared to sit on the site without any regard to the existing topography. In some instances there was a sixty-foot difference between the grade at one end of the long building and the other end. Proposed roads were also shown on the drawing, again seemingly without any relationship to the existing slopes. The road grades would have been precipitous and unusable. It seemed to be a terribly amateurish layout.

In showing me the plan, he indicated proudly that he had "his people" lay it out at his direction. He certainly didn't lack for ego, I thought. I asked him what he expected from me. And the conversation went something like this:

"I'd like you to draw this up, just like this. I want this layout. Just change it into architectural plans, and put on your seal, so that I can get the project moving."

I replied, "There are some things about the layout that don't seem to work. We would like the chance to study it and suggest changes so that the buildings fit the site better." I pointed out several major problems with the grades.

"No. I don't want any design changes. I just want you to draw it up and make it look good for the authorities to approve."

"I'm sorry then. I can't accommodate you. We are architects and are in a position to help you with the site planning and design. What you seem to want is a drafting service. You can probably find many of them in the phone book." I got up to leave.

"Are you telling me that you don't want the job?"

"That's right. We would not do just the drafting that you want. And I may as well tell you why. Do you realize that most of these buildings would be almost impossible to build as drawn? Do you know that you would never be able to get a car up a steep road like this? Have you considered the cost of filling in this ravine? As professionals, we could not draw up this design without major changes!"

I thanked him and left his office.

As I rode back to the office, I was disgusted. How could someone like that call himself a planner?

A few hours later, the client called me in my office to tell me that I was the first person that ever turned down a job from him. However, after reflection he realized that what I had told him about the problems with his plan were true. He wanted us to revise the site plan.

The project was eventually built and was successful. We also found out that we could work well together, as long as he did the *economic* planning and we did the *physical* planning. In fact, this approach worked out so well that we completed quite a number of projects together.

What Is Expected of the Client?

Having selected your architect, the next step is to sign an agreement, which will include the scope of the architect's services and fee. It is best to use a standard form of agreement such as the one published by the American Institute of Architects, which has been tested and proven through many years. As the client your main responsibilities include providing the functional requirements for the project; the money for the building permits, construction costs, and architect's fee; and a survey of the property.

Generally, the project proceeds as follows. At the beginning there is a lot of discussion in which you and the architect will establish a written list of the project's requirements. This is a most important stage, since it sets the direction for the entire project. This is the time for you to let the architect know what you consider your important requirements. State your needs clearly and firmly. This not the time to be timid about your opinions. However, this is also the time for you to listen to the architect's suggestions and opinions.

These discussions set up *rapport* and a system of communication that must last throughout the project. It is probably the most important ingredient in the relationship and will determine to a great degree how successful the project will be for both parties. Throughout the course of the project's design, it is important that both parties listen to each other and not be hesitant to express their opinions and feelings.

This talking stage then converts into a drawing phase in which the discussions are translated into sketches and drawings. Insist that there be periodic meetings so that you can understand why the design is progressing in a certain direction. If you don't understand something, insist on an explanation. Remember that in the early stages of design, changes will usually result in inexpensive erasures on paper, compared to later, when changes can mean extensive and costly work to resolve issues. This phase is when architect and client together strive for a balance of the major elements of the project: functional requirements, cost, buildability, and aesthetics.

Following is an example of the type of discussions during the design development that can lead to a successful project outcome.

We Don't Eat in the Kitchen

One of my earliest projects was to design a fairly large house on a magnificent site overlooking a lake in New Jersey. Remembering what my professor had taught me about communication being an essential ingredient to producing responsive architecture, I really worked hard to find out all about the family's lifestyle. I tried to spend as much time with the family members as I could in order to get to know them well and understand their personal requirements. The hours of discussion were well spent, because when it came time for them to sign off on the concept drawings, we were almost in total agreement on all aspects of the design. The only major question that remained was when Susan, the wife, said, "David you show a dining space in the kitchen. Please take it out and put in a storage area. We don't eat in the kitchen. We only eat in the dining room."

"No, Susan, you don't understand," I said. "This isn't really a *dining* space, but just a place in the kitchen to have an informal meal. For instance, when your child comes home from school for lunch. You know, a place for a quick meal or a snack."

"No," she replied, "we wouldn't use that space. We don't eat in the kitchen."

To this day I clearly remember my feelings as I went back to my office. It was obviously *my* failure to communicate. Everyone, I was sure, needs a space like that. She just hadn't understood the logic. And so I made the few other minor revisions that they had requested, but left the dining space in the kitchen, and went back to meet with my clients. They were very happy with the entire design, but Susan, again spotting the dining area in the kitchen, said, "David, you forgot to take the dining space out of the kitchen."

Here we go again, I thought. I've got to explain this better.

"Susan, I don't think I made myself clear the other evening and I'm sorry." I then repeated and elaborated upon all the arguments of how everyone needs an area in the kitchen for informal dining in addition to a formal dining room. I even devised the approach of calling it an "eating space" instead of a "dining space" to emphasize the difference between formal and informal dining areas. I ended up with the statement, ". . . and so, you too, should really have an eating space in the kitchen."

Susan and her husband listened carefully and patiently, and at the conclusion of my explanation, she stated that they understood everything that I was saying, but they would prefer a storage area because "we do not eat in the kitchen."

I went back to my office, again feeling frustrated by my inability to communicate. But the project had to go out to bid, so I completed the drawings without the eating space in the kitchen. However, I designed a storage unit in that area that could be removed easily at a later date, to provide a dining space. I was sure I was doing the right thing because they would eventually come to realize they *needed* this dining area. And anyway, if they ever sold the house, the buyer would want the eating space. I was sure my client would thank me for my sound professional judgment.

The construction of the house proceeded on schedule and on budget and it was indeed the best thing I had designed to that date. The clients were very happy with how it turned out and they moved in.

After the house had been occupied for one year, my wife and I received an invitation to dine with my clients and celebrate the house's first birthday. The house and its occupants all looked great. They seemed even more in love with their home. I felt great. This is the "spiritual remuneration" that is unique to architecture—happy clients in a well-designed building.

We had a wonderful meal in the dining room. I knew that they entertained a lot, and they told stories about how well the house worked for their living style.

I waited until after-dinner drinks were served and we were all feeling mellow. I reasoned that this was the best time to ask the question.

"Tell me, Susan, really, don't you miss having an eating space in the kitchen?"

Susan laughed. "No, David, I told you. We don't eat in the kitchen."

And so I was again reminded that an architect has no right to dictate lifestyle to a client. This was *their* house, designed to suit *their* needs. While my obligation is to suggest alternative solutions to their requirements, my prime responsibility remains to respond those needs with the best design I can. At the same time, I feel I did contribute to the future resale and renovation of the house by making the storage area removable. This learning experience, which thankfully occurred early in my practice, taught me a very important lesson about my function as an architect—and also how important it is for clients to firmly express their needs.

It is also important that you be fully open with your architect and not have any hidden agenda that can affect the outcome of the project. Here is an example.

Mirror, Mirror on the Wall

I had a client who owned a motel on a beautiful site in upper New York State. His business was so good that he wanted to extend his one-story motel by adding more rooms. He also wanted an enclosed six-foot-wide space between the end of the original building and the extension. He told me that he would use this space for the storage of linens, and it was noted on the drawings as a "Linen Room." However, he insisted that the entrance to this room be in the rear of the building, even though the best circulation pattern would have dictated that the door be in front, so that the maids would not have to walk around to the back. Despite our discussions, he insisted that it be designed and built in accordance with his instructions.

While I did not have the responsibility to oversee the construction, I happened to stop at the site while it was being built. The new extension was enclosed and the interior partitions were framed in. While inspecting the new linen room, I noticed that one-foot-by-two-foot openings had been built into the each of the two side walls. These openings had not been included in the drawings I had prepared. They allowed a view into the two adjacent motel rooms. When I questioned the contractor about these changes, he stated that the openings had been built at the owner's request. When I asked the owner for the reason for these openings, he said that they were for recessed wall cabinets.

I had no firm reason to doubt him, although the openings were rather small for the stated use. However, this experience really left an impression on me. Since that time, when in a hotel or motel, I have always checked to make sure that the mirror on the wall was truly a mirror on a *solid* wall!

What Can You Expect from Your Architect?

Your architect should bring to your project the necessary experience and capabilities to design your project to your satisfaction and produce a complete set of drawings and specifications that will clearly show the contractor how to build your building. Along with you, the architect will develop a program of requirements specific to your needs. He/she will contribute ideas that may differ from yours, but which you should consider, because they often result from experiences on similar projects. The final acceptance of the program is, obviously, up to you.

During the development of the design, the architect will continue to contribute ideas and alternative solutions to your requirements. Make sure that the sketches and drawings are fully explained as to their impact on your functional requirements, cost, and time schedule, so that you are able to make decisions. At each stage of the development, the architect should completely review the documents and explain anything that is not understood. The best projects are those in which there are no surprises, because you and the architect have had continuous communication.

After the completion of the construction documents, the architect will assist you in the bidding process and help you to select the contractor to build your project. During the construction phase the architect will visit the construction site periodically to see whether the construction documents are being followed, and to approve the contractors' requests for payment. At the completion of the project, the architect will examine the construction and will make a checklist of items of work still required to complete the project.

Conclusions

The best design results from a client–architect relationship based on respect, trust, and open and free communication. Each party has much to contribute to the final goal of outstanding architecture. Respect for the views of each must be established at the outset of the project and maintained through the life of the project. A building that does not fit the needs of its occupants is a failed building as much as one that is not aesthetically pleasing, poorly constructed, or too costly. For both architect and client there is no greater joy than a successfully completed project.

INDEX

ABC Chicago project, 162–165
ABC New York project, 170–173
Acoustical rework project,
   84–87
African American architects. *See*
   Racial issues
Ando, Tadao, 17
Aphorisms, architectural,
   178–184
"Archiphobia!," 31–34
Authority, 10
Bakalars, Thomas
   biography, 173
   mistaken-identity project,
   173–177
Bangladesh/Pakistan
   projects/political struggle,
   93–95
Barn conversion project, 90–91
Barney, Carol Ross
   biography, 133–134
   gender-based marketing
   success, 135–136
   going independent, 134
   USPS design, 136–139

Black architects today, 128–129.
   See also Racial issues
Bookstore renovations,
   201–208
   Champaign, Illinois, 205–208
   overview, 201–202
   Southwest Harbor, Maine,
   202–204
   Valparaiso, Indiana, 204–205
Brooklyn brownstone project,
   121–129
   black contractor requirement,
   125–126
   communication problem,
   126–128
   design process, 123–125
   inspiration for, 121–123
Brown, Carter, 57
Budget fears, 32–33
Builders. *See* Contractors
Bumanis, Al, 49
Bunshaft, Gordon, 50
Cantor, Marvin J., 96–99
Caudill, Bill, 141, 146
Caywood, Jim, 48–49

Choosing/finding architects, 34,
210–211, 221–222, 231–232,
234–235, 239, 243, 245–247
Client perspective, 209–253
architect-as-client, 242–253
architect relationship, 211,
214–219, 223–226, 227–231,
235–238, 239–240, 244–245,
247–253
budget issues, 209, 211–212,
217, 219
contractor issues, 217–219
custom home advantages,
224–225
of David Dibner, 242–253
decision quagmire, 223
expectations for architect, 253
finding/choosing architects,
210–211, 221–222, 231–232,
234–235, 239, 243, 245–247
institutional client, 232–241
interviewing architects,
245–247
lake cottage project, 210–220
of Mary Fitch, 226–232
of Nellie DeBruyn, 210–220
overview, 209–210
owning design process, 225–226
planning/design, 211–217,
223–229, 232–234, 247–252
Residential Architect editor on,
220–226
what clients must provide,
242–243, 249–250

what every client should know,
220–226
Clients as "architects,"
198–199
Clients as patients, 147–151
Closet conflict project, 2–10
Cohen, Ed, 49
Collaboration, xxi
Bill Lam approach, 78–82
compromise vs., 59, 71–72, 73
Florida second-home project,
71–77
husband/wife project, 66–71
ideal, 78–82
with specialty consultants,
83–88
St. Matthew's project, 60–66
team design and, 79–82
Committees. *See* Design by
committee (institutional
architecture)
Communication, 140–158
architects as great communicators, 151–153
Bill Lam perspective, 78–79
breakdown, examples, 126–128,
141–147
clear explanations, 78–79
CRSS Architects perspective,
141–147
deterring residential clients, 34
essences of, 141
Jeremiah Eck perspective,
147–151

Kirby Lockard perspective, 140,
    151–153
listening to clients, 78–79
overview, 140
poor, legal suits and, 153–155
treating clients as patients,
    147–151
visualization and, 145–147
Condominium flooring project,
    83–84
Conroy, S. Claire
    biography, 220
    what every residential client
        should know, 220–226
Contractors
    African American, Spike Lee
        project and, 125–126
    as allies, 10, 15
    conflicts with, 19–22
    diplomacy with, 21–22
    making changes, 199
    objecting to architects,
        33–34
Corporate politics, 159–177. *See
    also* Profit and social
    responsibility
    name-clout project, 173–177
    power structure and,
        159–161
CRSS Architects, Inc.
    communication perspective,
        141–147
    company overview, 141
Decision quagmire, 223

Design by committee
    (institutional architecture),
    103–119
    Cathy J. Simon on, 114–119
    client on, 232–241
    Kent Larson on, 105–109
    Norman Rosenfeld on, 110–113
    Roger K. Lewis on, 103–105
    school district projects,
        114–119
Dibner, David R.
    biography, 241
    client perspective of, 242–253
Dickinson, Duo
    architectural aphorisms,
        178–184
    biography, 178–179
    on choosing architects, 34
    on design process, 32, 33
Dixon, John, 35
Do-it-yourself challenges,
    189–192
East German chancery project,
    96–99
Eck, Jeremiah
    biography, 147–148
    treating clients as patients,
        147–151
Educating clients
    Bill Lam approach, 78–82
    lectures/field trips for, 80–81
    in public projects, 57–58
Emotional/ethical connections,
    89–95

Emotional/ethical connections
(*continued*)
Bangladesh/Pakistan
projects/political struggle,
93–95
Indiana dunes pornographic
house, 92
Michigan barn conversion, 91
Wisconsin barn conversion,
90–91
Entrance project, 185–188
Ethnicity. *See* Racial issues
Expectations, managing, 188
Fellows, Rushia, 128
Finding/choosing architects, 34,
210–211, 221–222, 231–232,
234–235, 239, 243, 245–247
Fitch, Mary
biography, 226
on speaking "client," 226–232
Florida second-home project,
71–77
Foreign affairs. *See* International
projects
Gender/minority-based
marketing, 135–136
German Democratic Republic
chancery project, 96–99
Graham, Jackson, 53
Greenstreet, Bob, 140
biography, 153
legal suits/poor communica-
tion, 153–155
Gropius, Walter, 59

Guest room project, 192–194
Guggenheim project, 35–46
Gwathmey, Charles
credentials, 36
Guggenheim project interview,
37–46
Harris, Ernie, 32
Harris, Joe, 184
Hartman, George, 54–58
High school design projects,
114–119
Homebuilder proposals, 4–5
Hospital projects, 110–113
HVAC noise case, 87
Indiana dunes pornographic
house, 92
Institutional architecture. *See*
Design by committee
(institutional architecture)
International projects
auto manufacturer/communi-
cation case, 141–147
Bangladesh/Pakistan
projects/political struggle,
93–95
disappearing country/lost
project, 96–99
Tunisian hospitality, 99–102
Jahn, Helmut, 59
James, Jim Florida home project,
71–77
Kitchen-therapy project,
194–198
Knight, Ken, 49

Kohn, Gene
 ABC Chicago project, 162–165
 ABC New York project,
  170–173
 on bringing religion to client,
  161–162
 on community/client relationship, 170–173
 demanding client project,
  167–170
 Logan Square Philadelphia
  project, 165–167
 on patience/faith, 162–165
 Proctor & Gamble project,
  167–170
 on unifying profit/urban redevelopment, 165–167
Lake cottage project, 210–220
Lam, Bill, 59, 78–82
Larson, Kent
 biography, 105–106
 design by committee perspective, 106–109
Lee, Spike, 121–128, 129
Legal action
 design problems and,
  200–201
 liens, 200
 poor communication leading
  to, 153–155
 reconciling problems with,
  155–158
Lewis, Roger K.
 biography, 99–100

 on clients thinking they're
  architects, 198–199
 on corporate power structure,
  159–161
 design by committee perspective, 103–105
 on legal action, 155–158
 on Tunisian hospitality,
  99–102
Lockard, Kirby
 on architects as communicators, 140, 151–153
 biography, 151
Logan Square Philadelphia
  project, 165–167
McAfee, Charles F.
 biography, 130
 interracial collaboration amidst
  prejudice, 130–133
McCabe-Miele, Gigi, 2
Michigan barn conversion
  project, 91
Mistaken-identity project,
  173–177
Moore, Charles, 59–66
Nelson, Ralph, 210
O'Neill, Bob, 49
Over-funded project, 173–177
Payment woes, 199–200
Penn Plaza project, 54–58
Political savvy. See also
  Collaboration
 Bill Lam approach, 78–82
 contractor relations and, 21–22

Political savvy *(continued)*
  education/compromise and,
    78–82
  Guggenheim project and, 36–46
  international politics, ethics
    and, 93–95
  obnoxious personalities, oppor-
    tunity and, 30–31
  Penn Plaza project and, 56–57
Politics of small projects, 184–197
  do-it-yourself challenges,
    189–192
  entrance identity, 185–188
  guest room necessity, 192–194
  importance of, 184–185
  managing expectations, 188
  Native American kitchen
    therapy, 194–198
Pornographic house, 92
Proctor & Gamble project,
    167–170
Profit and social responsibility,
    161–173
  ABC Chicago project, 162–165
  ABC New York project,
    170–173
  bringing religion to client,
    161–162
  client demanding, 167–170
  community/client relationship,
    170–173
  Logan Square Philadelphia
    project, 165–167
  patience/faith and, 162–165

Proctor & Gamble project,
    167–170
  unifying profit/urban redevel-
    opment, 165–167
Provey, Joseph R., 31
Public projects
  board reviews/criticisms,
    39–46, 49–53, 54–57
  education role in, 57–58
  Guggenheim renovation, 35–46
  Penn Plaza, 54–58
  Washington Metro, 46–53, 81,
    82
Racial issues, 120–133
  black architect on mission,
    120–129
  black architects today, 128–129
  interracial collaboration amidst
    prejudice, 130–133
Rannells, John, 47–48
Residential clients, 1–34. *See also*
    Small projects
  acceptance, then changes, 7–8
  "Archiphobia!" of, 31–34
  asserting authority with, 10
  bad communication deterring,
    34
  budget fears, 32–33
  closet conflict project, 2–10
  construction stress and, 22–24
  contractor as ally and, 10, 15
  dealing directly with, 25
  "episodic technophilia" from,
    19

homebuilder proposals and,
4–5
leaky-roof-excuse project,
10–17
Maine intermediary project,
24–31
participation by, 2, 10
personal closeness with, 6
post-mortem evaluations, 9–10,
16–17
project trial by jury, 11–15
reasons for hiring architects, 34
reluctance to hire architects,
31–34
resale fears of, 33
spousal discord, 5, 6, 9–10
what every client should know,
220–226
young architects and, 1–2
Retail renovations. *See* Bookstore
renovations
Richardson, Heidi, 33, 34
Rosenfeld, Norman
biography, 110
on institutions/clients/service,
110–113
School district projects, 114–119
Siebein, Gary W., 83–88
Simon, Cathy J.
biography, 114
institutional projects perspective, 114–119
Small projects
architectural aphorisms,
178–184

bookstore renovations, 201–208
clients thinking they're architects, 198–199
design flaw responsibility and,
200–201
do-it-yourself challenges,
189–192
entrance project, 185–188
guest room necessity, 192–194
kitchen-therapy project,
194–198
legal liability on, 200–201
payment woes, 199–200
politics of, 184–197
Social responsibility. *See* Profit
and social responsibility
Speaking "client," 226–232
Specialty consultants, 83–88
acoustical rework project,
84–87
condominium flooring project,
83–84
HVAC noise case, 87
using from the start, 87–88
Stageberg, James, 66–71
Stephens, Suzanne, 1–2
St. Matthew's collaboration,
60–66
Team design, 79–80
Tigerman, Stanley, 89–96
Toth, Susan Allen, 66–71
Travis, Jack
biography, 120–121
black architect on mission,
120–129

Travis, Jack *(continued)*
    Brooklyn brownstone project,
        121–129
    Spike Lee relationship, 121–128,
        129
Tunisian hospitality, 99–102
Two/Ten Foundation project,
    173–177
Vacuum cleaner analogy, 87
Vapor lock case, 200–201
Washington Metro project,
    46–53, 81, 82
    architects/engineers as separate
        and equal, 47
    architects/engineers cooper-
        ating, 48–50

BART system and, 47, 53
coming together, 50–53
Commission of Fine Arts and,
    49–53
final design contracts, 53
general architectural
    consultant, 47–50
Jackson Graham memo-
    randum, 51–52, 53
Weese, Harry, 49–50, 53
Wisconsin barn conversion
    project, 90–91
Wooden, Andrew
    biography, 232
    institutional client perspective,
        232–241